TEACHING INFORMATIONAL TEXT IN K–3 CLASSROOMS

BEST PRACTICES IN ACTION

Linda B. Gambrell and Lesley Mandel Morrow,
Series Editors

Connecting research findings to daily classroom practice is a key component of successful teaching—and any teacher can accomplish it, with the right tools. The Best Practices in Action series focuses on what elementary and middle grade teachers need to do "on Monday morning" to plan and implement high-quality literacy instruction and assess student learning. Books in the series are practical, accessible, and firmly grounded in research. Each title provides ready-to-use lesson ideas, engaging classroom vignettes, links to the Common Core State Standards, discussion questions and engagement activities ideal for professional learning communities, and reproducible materials that purchasers can download and print.

Teaching Informational Text in K–3 Classrooms

Best Practices to Help Children Read, Write, and Learn from Nonfiction

Mariam Jean Dreher
Sharon Benge Kletzien

Series Editors' Note by
Linda B. Gambrell and Lesley Mandel Morrow

THE GUILFORD PRESS
New York   London

© 2015 The Guilford Press
A Division of Guilford Publications, Inc.
370 Seventh Avenue, Suite 1200, New York, NY 10001
www.guilford.com

Printed in the United States of America

This book is printed on acid-free paper.

Last digit is print number: 9 8 7 6 5 4 3 2 1

Library of Congress Cataloging-in-Publication Data

Dreher, Mariam Jean.
    Teaching informational text in K–3 classrooms : best practices to help children read, write,
and learn from nonfiction / by Mariam Jean Dreher and Sharon Benge Kletzien.
        pages cm.— (Best practices in action)
    Includes bibliographical references and index.
    ISBN 978-1-4625-2226-2 (paperback : acid-free paper) — ISBN 978-1-4625-2227-9 (cloth :
acid-free paper)
    1. Language arts (Primary) 2. Exposition (Rhetoric)—Study and teaching (Primary)
3. Creative nonfiction—Authorship. I. Kletzien, Sharon Benge. II. Kletzien, Sharon Benge.
Informational text in K–3 classrooms. III. Title.
    LB1528.K57 2015
    372.6—dc23
                                                                                    2015014156

About the Authors

Mariam Jean Dreher, PhD, is Professor in the Department of Teaching and Learning, Policy and Leadership at the University of Maryland, College Park. Previously she was an elementary classroom teacher and Title I specialist. Her research interests include ways to integrate informational text into literacy instruction to enhance students' comprehension, vocabulary, and motivation. Dr. Dreher has published numerous articles and books, including *Engaging Young Readers*, and has served on many editorial advisory boards, receiving the Outstanding Reviewer Award from the *Journal of Literacy Research*. She is a consultant to National Geographic Children's Books on a series of information books for young children. Dr. Dreher is also a recipient of a Fulbright Senior Specialist Grant and was recently awarded an honorary doctorate from the University of Oulu, Finland.

Sharon Benge Kletzien, PhD, is Professor Emerita at West Chester University of Pennsylvania, where she was Chair of the Literacy Department, taught reading courses, and supervised the Reading Center. Previously she served as a reading specialist in elementary, middle, and high schools. Her research focuses on the areas of comprehension, using information books for instruction, and supporting students who struggle with reading. Dr. Kletzien has published many articles and book chapters, as well as an earlier book about informational text, coauthored with Mariam Jean Dreher. She also serves on the editorial boards of several major literacy journals and is a recipient of the Outstanding Student Research Award from the American Educational Research Association, Division C, and the Program of Excellence Award from the National Council for the Social Studies.

Series Editors' Note

For the first book in the new series Best Practices in Action, Mariam Jean Dreher and Sharon Benge Kletzien focus on research-based methods to help young children read, write, and learn from informational text. The timing is right for this book. As educators, we are more aware than ever of the significant role that informational text plays in children's literacy development and academic achievement.

Informational text differs in organization and structure from fiction and poetry. Dreher and Kletzien identify these differences and provide strategies and techniques firmly grounded in research to support students in successfully navigating a variety of informational texts.

During the past two decades, a converging body of research has yielded remarkable insights about the nature and importance of teaching students how to read informational text in K–3 classrooms. In the not-so-distant past, primary-grade reading instruction was overwhelmingly conducted with narrative text. Nell Duke's (2000) now classic study revealed the paucity of informational text in first-grade classrooms and marked an important shift in our thinking about the importance of balancing narrative and informational reading materials. More recently, the Common Core State Standards (National Governors Association Center for Best Practices & Council of Chief State School Officers, 2010) called for reading a variety of texts for a variety of purposes, with particular emphasis on developing students' abilities to comprehend informational text. In this volume, Dreher and Kletzien provide important guidance for answering that call.

Books in the Best Practices in Action series focus on what teachers need to do "on Monday morning" to plan, implement, and assess high-quality literacy instruction. We are delighted that Dreher and Kletzien have written such a timely and informative book on the crucial topic of helping young children develop a solid foundation in reading, writing, and learning from informational text.

LINDA B. GAMBRELL, PhD
LESLEY MANDEL MORROW, PhD

References

Duke, N. K. (2000). 3.6 minutes a day: The scarcity of informational texts in first grade. *Reading Research Quarterly, 35*(2), 202–224.
National Governors Association Center for Best Practices & Council of Chief State School Officers. (2010). *Common Core State Standards for English language arts and literacy in history/social studies, science, and technical subjects.* Washington, DC: Author.

Preface

Teaching Informational Text in K–3 Classrooms represents an integrated approach to best teaching practices based on current and recent research. Although researchers and practitioners have been calling for the use of more informational text in the early grades for well over a decade, teachers continue to explore and develop more effective and motivating ways to help children read, write, and learn from informational text. We hope this book will provide a resource for teachers to use as they work with informational text in their classrooms.

This book could not have been written without the cooperation and expertise of countless primary teachers whose classrooms we visited. These classrooms were in urban, suburban, and rural districts and represented inclusive classrooms as well as resource rooms and reading specialists' classes. The students and teachers described in the numerous examples included throughout the book are composites with pseudonyms, except where teachers' full names are used with their permission. We are grateful that students and teachers welcomed us into their classrooms and freely shared their experiences with us.

At the end of each chapter are questions that can provide a springboard for discussion in professional learning communities. Like all good questions, these are not designed with a right or wrong answer in mind but as a way to promote discussion about some of the important issues in each chapter. We have also included in the end-of-chapter appendices ideas about specific activities or lessons that teachers can use in their classrooms immediately. There are many other activities described in the chapters, but these end-of-chapter suggestions offer a way to get started.

In Chapter 1, we explain the importance of using informational text in K–3 classrooms. The Common Core State Standards, as well as other state standards and professional organizations, call for children in the primary grades to become proficient with informational text. Using informational text in classes results in greater student achievement and greater motivation. Evidence from the National Assessment of Educational Progress shows that students who read more than one type of text generally read better than their counterparts who read only one type. Additionally, some children are "information readers" who can learn to read only when given the opportunity to read information books. Information books are often the book of choice among younger readers, so using informational text is both motivating and a key to reading development.

Chapter 2 explains how a teacher can develop a classroom library with a full range of informational text. It explores the different types of informational text and suggests how a teacher could go about finding the appropriate library resources. Our goal in this chapter is to provide support as teachers work to make sure that their students have adequate informational texts to support their growing literacy.

In Chapter 3, we identify ways to choose information books for the classroom. Good-quality books should have accurate content, an appealing design and format, an engaging writing style, appropriate text complexity, and good organization. We suggest sources for identifying quality books and provide some ideas about choosing e-books and websites. We also include a guide that teachers can use to think about potential problems that certain books might present and how they might use these problems to further engage students.

Chapter 4 provides ideas for making informational text an integral part of read-aloud time in the classroom. We supply ideas for pairing fiction and information books, suggest using read-alouds to expand content-area instruction, explain how read-alouds support all readers in the classroom, and summarize ways to conduct interactive read-alouds.

Chapter 5 addresses how to help children develop comprehension through informational text. We identify likely strategies to be used with these texts and show how individual teachers have integrated these strategies into their lessons. Classroom discussion and the quickly changing field of digital text reading are dealt with in this chapter. We also describe close reading of informational text and feature an example of a teacher conducting a lesson in close reading.

In Chapter 6, we explore the many opportunities teachers have to help children develop academic vocabulary through informational text. Developing vocabulary is particularly important for English language learners and children who begin school knowing fewer words than their peers. We offer ideas that teachers can use to provide rich and varied language experiences, suggest techniques for teaching individual words, and identify ways to teach word-learning strategies that children will be able to use when they are reading independently. Research suggests that teachers who promote word consciousness in their classrooms are effective in increasing their students' vocabularies.

Chapter 7 focuses on using information books and Internet resources for research. Even in the primary grades, children are expected to be able to find information, synthesize information from multiple sources, and organize their findings. In this chapter, we give suggestions for helping children learn about information book features and Internet resources. We offer examples of how teachers have helped children take notes and organize the information they find.

Writing informational text is the focus of Chapter 8, which describes various kinds of informational writing and suggests ways that teachers can use informational texts as models for children's writing. We provide ideas about how to use technology for composing and sharing children's writing. We also offer examples of how teachers have incorporated multimodal writing into their classrooms, capitalizing on its great potential.

Chapter 9, the final chapter, encourages teachers to move forward by incorporating more informational text in their classrooms, while also continuing to use fiction for the important role that it plays in developing children's literacy. In this chapter, we suggest ways that teachers can keep track of how they include more informational text in their teaching.

As you read this book and try out some of our recommendations, we hope that you will share your comments and your experiences with us. We learn from collaboration with others, and we are eager to hear how you are incorporating informational text in your classrooms. Please send your comments to us at *mjdreher@umd.edu* and *sbkletzien@msn.com*.

Acknowledgments

We gratefully acknowledge the teachers and students of the many primary classrooms we visited and worked in while writing this book. We express our special appreciation to the following teachers and their classes: Jen Boyk, Sandra Greim Connor, Sharon Craig, Adria Creswell, Kristine Gannon, Kim Gery, Kate Hartenstine, Becky Hatherill, Kelly Loomis, Renee Miller, Kathy Simpson, Jenn Smith, Susan Smith, Lindsay Stout, Jess Verwys, and Cathy Yost.

Contents

CHAPTER 1

Supporting Motivation and Achievement with Informational Text

Today's primary-grade teachers need to know how to engage their students with informational text. As we will explain, current curricular expectations in the United States demand that they do so. Thus, instead of featuring only stories that have predominated in young children's reading instruction, teachers need to integrate a wide range of both print and electronic informational text into their classrooms.

Some teachers may view this undertaking as a chore to be carried out because they are required to do so. But even if current curricular expectations were to disappear, we would argue that primary-grade teachers should integrate informational text into their instruction anyway, because informational text offers exciting opportunities for motivating children to achieve. As we show in this chapter, increasing evidence documents that young children benefit when teachers include informational text in reading instruction, and therefore knowledge acquisition through reading should be an integral part of learning to read from an early age. There are several reasons that this is true:

- Recent advances in technology place additional literacy demands on all readers.
- Most of what children read in school, except during reading instruction, and most of what they will need to read as adults, is informational text.
- Standards call for even young children to be capable readers of information.
- Standardized tests measuring young children's literacy achievement typically include informational text.
- Reading informational text can pay off in higher reading achievement.

- Informational text has motivational potential.
- Children *like* informational text.
- For some children, informational text provides a way into literacy that stories cannot.

In this chapter, we elaborate on these reasons and explain why it is crucial for teachers to use informational text with children in K–3 classrooms. In doing so, we draw on research and our own extensive experience, which includes a combined 27 years of teaching preschool through 12th grade. As teacher educators and researchers, we have an additional 53 years of working alongside teachers and children in classrooms exploring the use of informational text. We also have supervised university reading centers in which teachers and children have been actively engaged with both informational text and stories. Our experiences have led us to value the educational possibilities of informational text for teaching reading as well as for extending content-area knowledge.

We are not suggesting, however, that teachers add to an already full curriculum or that they discontinue using stories with young children. Rather, we propose that they examine their reading selections and replace some of the stories that they use with informational text. Much of their reading instruction, including word recognition, vocabulary, and comprehension, can be accomplished through informational text just as well as through stories. A balanced mix of informational text and stories would provide a good introduction to the variety of genres that children will be expected to read and enjoy.

What Is Informational Text?

When we refer to informational text, we include a wide range of nonfiction material, just as we did in our earlier work (Kletzien & Dreher, 2004). Our use of this term matches the way the Common Core State Standards (CCSS) use it. Specifically, the CCSS define informational text as "Literary Nonfiction and Historical, Scientific, and Technical Text," which "includes biographies and autobiographies; books about history, social studies, science, and the arts; technical texts, including directions, forms, and information displayed in graphs, charts, or maps; and digital sources on a range of topics" (National Governors Association Center for Best Practices & Council of Chief State School Officers [NGA & CCSSO], 2010a, p. 31).

Although the term *informational text* seems clear, the distinctions among the various types of informational texts make a difference in children's classroom experience. In Chapter 2, we describe in detail the various kinds of informational text written for young children and explain why teachers need to carefully consider the types of informational text they use.

Stories and Informational Text in K–3 Classrooms

Despite long-standing efforts to highlight the importance of using informational text (Hiebert & Fisher, 1990; Pappas, 1991), ample evidence exists that most of what teachers use to teach reading and writing in the early grades involves stories. For example, when Duke (2000) studied first-grade classrooms, she found few information books in the classroom libraries, little informational text displayed in the classroom, and almost no instruction involving informational text. Indeed, Duke found that teachers spent an average of only 3.6 minutes a day using informational text.

Although Duke's research took place some 15 years ago, more recent research indicates that stories are still predominant in many classrooms. Jeong, Gaffney, and Choi (2010) found results similar to Duke's in second-, third-, and fourth-grade classrooms, with second-grade teachers averaging 1 minute of instructional time daily on informational text. In addition, research on read-alouds in primary grades indicates that most teachers chose to read few information books (Yopp & Yopp, 2006). Moreover, while Moss (2008) found an increase in the amount of informational text in recent basal readers as compared to basals in the past (e.g., Flood & Lapp, 1986; Moss & Newton, 2002), she concluded that there is still a need for more informational text in basal readers to match the expectations that we describe next.

Expectations about Children's Reading and Writing

Even though most literacy instruction involves stories, expectations for children to be able to read, write, and learn from informational text are increasing as society has more access to a greater amount of information. To be able to find, understand, evaluate, and synthesize information across a variety of sources requires more sophisticated reading and writing strategies for informational text than has been required in the past (Dreher, 2002; Karchmer, Mallette, & Leu, 2002; Kletzien & DeRenzi, 2001). In order to develop these strategies, it is important that teachers provide children experience with informational text early in their developing literacy.

Today's K–3 children are expected to be able to read and understand informational text. These expectations are very clear in the CCSS (NGA & CCSSO, 2010a) that are now being implemented across the United States. As we write, 43 states, the District of Columbia, and four territories have adopted the CCSS (*www.corestandards.org/standards-in-your-state*). These standards aim to help all children finish high school ready for college and careers, and because workplace reading is overwhelmingly informational (Smith, Mikulecky, Kibby, Dreher, & Dole, 2000; White, Chen, & Forsyth, 2010), balanced attention to informational text in school makes sense from the start. Some years ago, Venezky (1982) noted that literacy instruction in schools involves a steady diet of fiction and literary interpretation, resulting in a "chasm between adult literacy needs and school literacy instruction" (p. 112). As we have noted, this chasm has persisted. Hence, although literature remains important, the CCSS call for "students to be proficient in reading complex informational text independently in a variety of content areas" (NGA & CCSSO, 2010a, p. 4).

For K–5 students, the CCSS lay out Reading Standards for Informational Text (downloadable at *www.corestandards.org/the-standards*; see pp. 13–14). These standards are organized into four categories—key ideas and details, craft and structure, integration of knowledge and ideas, range of reading and text complexity—and specify what students should be able to do grade by grade. By the end of third grade, students are expected to have developed the ability to "read and comprehend informational text, including history/social studies, science, and technical text, at the high end of the grade 2–3 text complexity band independently and proficiently" (p. 14). Consequently, much attention must be directed to informational text in primary-grade classrooms to enable students to reach that level of performance.

It is important to note that the emphasis on informational text in the CCSS follows in the footsteps of earlier efforts to give children the opportunity to experience informational text from the beginning. For example, in their influential report, the Committee on the Prevention of Reading Difficulties in Young Children (Snow, Burns, & Griffin, 1998) concluded that a successful learner in kindergarten "demonstrates familiarity with a number of types or genres of text (e.g., storybooks, expository texts, poems, newspapers, and everyday print)" (p. 80) and that a successful learner in first grade "reads and comprehends both fiction and nonfiction that is appropriately designed for grade level" (p. 81), with the same expectation repeated for second and third grades. The committee also noted that a successful second grader "interprets information from diagrams, charts, and graphs"; "reads nonfiction materials for answers to specific questions or for specific purposes"; "connects and compares information across nonfiction selections"; [and] "given organizational help, writes informative well-structured reports" (p. 82). By third grade, a successful student "summarizes major points from fiction and nonfiction texts"; "asks how, why, and what-if questions in interpreting nonfiction texts"; "in interpreting nonfiction, distinguishes cause and effect, fact and opinion, main idea and supporting details"; [and] "combines information from multiple sources in writing reports" (p. 83).

Similarly, the CCSS initiative builds on the work of national educational organizations and the states. In their joint position statement about developmentally appropriate practices for young children, The International Reading Association (IRA) and the National Association for the Education of Young Children (NAEYC) argued that children in kindergarten should "enjoy being read to and themselves retell simple narrative stories or informational text" (1998, p. 200) and that, by the time children are in the third grade, they should be able to "recognize and discuss elements of different text structures" (1998, p. 201). Additionally, well before the CCSS initiative, many U.S. states had established standards specifying that children should feel comfortable dealing with nonfiction by the time they are in the third grade (e.g., Pennsylvania Department of Education, 2003; Virginia Department of Education, 2003) and had included substantial informational texts on state assessments (e.g., Wisconsin Department of Public Instruction, 2003).

The CCSS emphasis on informational text also matches trends in reading assessment. Estimates some years ago already indicated that 50–85% of the reading passages in standardized tests were informational (Calkins, Montgomery, Santman, & Falk, 1998). Moreover, since 2009 the National Assessment of Educational Progress (NAEP) has used informational text for 50% of the passages on its fourth-grade reading assessment (American Institutes for Research, 2005). The NAEP, known as the Nation's Report Card, uses even higher percentages of informational text for older students (55% in 8th grade and 70% in 12th grade). The CCSS aim is to match the NAEP's percentages in the amount of informational text students encounter in instruction.

Assessments developed as part of the CCSS effort were field-tested in the spring of 2014 and were implemented in the spring of 2015, with third graders as the youngest students to be assessed. As with the NAEP, these assessments require students to do well with informational text. Two groups prepared the assessments—the Partnership for Assessment of Readiness for College and Careers (PARCC) and the Smarter Balanced Assessment Consortium—and both groups have released sample items (see *www.parcconline.org/samples/item-task-prototypes* and *www. smarterbalanced.org/sample-items-and-performance-tasks*). The specifications for these assessments, as well as the sample items, make clear that students will not only need to read and comprehend informational text but will also need to engage in performance tasks in which they must deal with multiple diverse texts.

Finally, for any teachers who are not already convinced, we note that the United States is not alone in stressing the importance of young children learning to understand informational text. Informational text has long been an important part of literacy instruction in other countries, including the United Kingdom (Littlefair, 1991; Mallett, 1999; Wray & Lewis, 1998) and Ireland (Shiel, 2001/2002). In Canada, British Columbia's reading standards also require that young children become proficient with nonfiction (British Columbia Department of Education, 2002). Although these are just examples, they help illustrate worldwide awareness of the importance of informational text for young children. The importance of informational text is also reflected in an international assessment of fourth graders across 49 countries—the Progress in International Reading Literacy Study (PIRLS). As with the NAEP in the United States, the PIRLS assessment is evenly split between reading for literary experience and reading to acquire and use information (Mullis, Martin, Foy, & Drucker, 2012).

Improving Reading Achievement by Using Informational Text

Providing a balance of genres for children to read helps improve their reading ability. Considerable research supports this claim. For example, in a special study, the NAEP interviewed fourth graders about their reading habits and examined those responses in relation to reading achievement. Students were asked about whether they read stories, magazines, and information books. The results showed that those who reported reading all three types had higher reading achievement than those who read only one or two (Campbell, Kapinus, & Beatty, 1995).

Although the NAEP study was correlational, intervention studies have documented the benefit to achievement of expanding primary grade children's range of reading experiences to include reading and learning about informational text. For example, Guthrie et al. (2004) found that integrating science text into reading instruction enhanced third graders' reading comprehension and was also highly motivating. O'Hara and Dreher (2008) found similar results with struggling third-grade readers. Williams, Stafford, Lauer, Hall, and Pollini (2009) improved second graders' comprehension by teaching them compare–contrast text structure in science texts, while Halvorsen et al. (2012) facilitated comprehension of second graders of low socioeconomic status (SES) using social studies content. Moreover, in later chapters we will describe additional work with young readers that illustrates the benefits of increased instructional focus on informational text.

Children who have had experience with informational text in the earlier years will be better able to read and understand these texts as they progress through school. Indeed, there are reading skills and strategies that are appropriate for informational text (and not for stories) that need to be taught. Rather than wait until the intermediate grades, when children are expected to be able to read informational text and learn from it, teachers need to introduce these skills and strategies while children are learning to read.

Beginning Reading Instruction and the Information Reader

Some children, who might be referred to as "information readers," have difficulty learning to read using stories. For these children, informational texts can form the basis for teaching them to read and make the difference between success and failure in their learning to read.

Information readers find informational text much more compelling than stories. Hynes (2000) described a student who thought of himself as a nonreader because he liked to "read for facts" rather than for stories. But when reading and writing facts became an accepted part of classroom instruction, the student's attitude changed, and his self-concept as a reader and writer grew.

Similarly, Caswell and Duke (1998) described two children who struggled with reading and writing until their teachers recognized that they were much more successful with informational text than with stories. Once the children began working with informational text, they were able to progress much more quickly.

We also have seen children with whom we have worked come alive with interest when given the opportunity to read and write informational text. For these children, stories are not as compelling. The chance to read and write about a subject of great interest gives them the motivation to develop literacy skills. This has proven true even for children who have been identified as struggling readers and writers.

Informational text has motivating potential for children who are curious about their world. Curiosity is a powerful motivator for reading (Baker & Wigfield, 1999), and children who are interested in a particular topic are motivated to read about it in informational texts (Dreher, 2003). In addition, Alexander (1997) has argued that knowledge seeking through informational text is motivating because it contributes to readers' sense of self as well as giving them an opportunity to learn about the world around them. They can become "experts" in areas of interest, giving them confidence in their ability to read as well as in their ability to learn and share their knowledge. For example, our experiences working with Jeremy, a struggling reader, showed that when he was given the chance to read and write about trucks his interest and motivation soared. He read and studied the pictures in several books and created a brochure describing his plans for a truck sales and leasing company. When he presented this brochure to the other children in his class, his excitement and sense of accomplishment were evident. As the other students asked questions, Jeremy's confidence in himself and in his ability to read and write was strengthened.

Sometimes children who are struggling with reading and writing find informational text more appealing because the content seems more mature. Second or third graders who are reading on a primer level may feel more comfortable reading a book about insects on their level than reading a storybook at that level. There are many accurate, colorful information books written at lower levels that may appeal to these young readers.

Reading Preferences and Informational Text

In classroom visits and informal discussions, we have heard teachers comment that children do not like information books—that they are boring and too hard to read. Some teachers are concerned that information books are "anti-fun" (Warren & Fitzgerald, 1997, p. 356). Others think like Correia (2011), who "was convinced that kindergartners preferred fiction" (p. 101). In contrast, we have encountered many instances of a preference for information books, like the kindergartner who complained that she did not like reading at school because everything was stories. As she said, "I don't just want to read, I want to *learn* something."

In fact, there is research evidence that young children presented with both options are just as likely to choose information books as they are storybooks

(Cervetti, Bravo, Hiebert, Pearson, & Jaynes, 2009; Kletzien & DeRenzi, 2001; Kletzien & Szabo, 1998; Mohr, 2006). In a study of children's preferences in the United Kingdom, Coles and Hall (2002) found that outside of school both boys and girls read books but also read magazines and newspapers, most of which are informational. Pappas (1993; Pappas & Barry, 1997) established that children enjoy information books and learn from them, and ongoing research continues to prove her point (e.g., Maloch & Horsey, 2013; Varelas & Pappas, 2006).

Therefore, children *do* like informational text, often choosing it over stories. Summarizing their research on first graders' book selections in science, Donovan and Smolkin (2001) captured the situation well: "Not only do they freely choose science texts, but . . . [c]learly enjoying themselves, . . . children share their own experiences, knowledge, and feelings ('yucky spiders!') during these inter-actions with texts from the world of facts" (p. 435). As Dreher (2003) pointed out, a powerful way for teachers to motivate children to read is to provide them with diverse materials, making information books an important part of balanced reading.

Summary

Primary-grade literacy instruction should include the use of informational text for both reading and writing. State standards, standardized tests, and national organizations recognize the importance of young children being able to read and understand information. In addition, children enjoy information books, often finding them more motivating than storybooks. For some children, informational text provides an entry to literacy that stories do not.

The emphasis on using stories for instruction persists, however, in spite of the many voices that have been raised urging teachers to use more informational text in their classrooms. One reason that teachers may be reluctant to use more information books in their classrooms is that they are less confident in their ability to design appropriate lessons. In the remaining chapters of this book, we suggest ways that teachers can develop their classroom libraries, choose good quality informational texts, and incorporate informational text into their literacy and content area instruction.

Throughout this book, we provide suggestions for using informational text with all children in the primary grades. The teaching and learning techniques that we recommend work with struggling readers and writers as well as with average or advanced readers and writers. Examples throughout are drawn from diverse classrooms that include children reading above and below grade level, children who have learning disabilities, children who are gifted in literacy, and children who are English language learners. Examples reflect urban and suburban districts and inclusion classrooms as well as self-contained special education classrooms.

QUESTIONS AND REFLECTIONS FOR PROFESSIONAL LEARNING COMMUNITIES

1. This chapter notes, "One reason that teachers may be reluctant to use more information books in their classrooms is that they are less confident in their ability to design appropriate lessons." Discuss this point with the teachers in your professional learning community, sharing your thoughts on this issue. Some teachers are likely to be more confident when using informational text than others. Discuss how you might support one another in raising the confidence of the entire group as its members seek to make informational text an integral part of class instruction.

2. Review the section on "Expectations about Children's Reading and Writing." Carefully consider just what students are supposed to be able to do by the time they leave the primary grades. As a group, consider where your students are in terms of the sophisticated skills they need to develop. What kinds of initiatives might your group undertake to increase the likelihood that students at your school will reach the appropriate level?

3. You may have heard the view that children first learn to read and then read to learn, starting at about the fourth grade. In this chapter, we disagree: "Rather than wait until the intermediate grades, when children are expected to be able to read informational text and learn from it, teachers need to introduce these skills and strategies while children are learning to read." Consider the evidence that we have presented, and come to a consensus on your professional learning community's view on this issue.

CLASSROOM ENGAGEMENT ACTIVITIES

1. Look around your classroom and reflect on your instruction. Do you see the pattern researchers have found in many primary-grade classrooms of a lack of informational text in classroom libraries, little informational text displayed in the classroom, and almost no instruction involving informational text? If so, are there changes you could make? If not, how far have you progressed in making changes, and what else could you try?

2. Consider Jeremy, the struggling reader, who blossomed when he was given the chance to read and write about trucks, and the kindergartner who proclaimed, "I don't just want to read, I want to *learn* something." Are there struggling or unmotivated students in your class who might be "information readers" like these students? What actions might you undertake to find out?

3. Review the assessments required at your school. What kinds of text must children read or listen to in order to do well? In particular, determine whether these assessments include informational text, and, if so, reflect on whether your instruction provides opportunities for students to learn to handle similar informational text.

CHAPTER 2

Developing Classroom Libraries with a Full Range of Informational Text

Both national assessments and international evaluations have shown that well-stocked classroom, school, and public libraries contribute to reading achievement (Elley, 1992; Krashen, Lee, & McQuillan, 2012; Mullis et al., 2012). Furthermore, in its position statement titled *Providing Books and Other Print Materials for Classroom and School Libraries*, the IRA argued that libraries are important because "children who have access to books are more likely to read for enjoyment, and thus increase their reading skills and their desire to read to learn" (1999, n.p.).

In this chapter, we focus on the classroom library because it offers the most easily accessible library for most children and hence has the potential to have a tremendous impact on their reading motivation and achievement. As Smolkin, Donovan, and Lomax (2000) put it, "Simplistic as this may sound, what is not present in classroom libraries does not get selected, thought about, or discussed" (p. 518).

Having books readily available appears to increase children's likelihood of reading them (Lindsay, 2010: Neuman, 1999; Neuman & Celano, 2001; Worthy, Moorman, & Turner, 1999). And frequent reading is a strong predictor of reading achievement (Anderson, Wilson, & Fielding, 1988; Taylor, Frye, & Maruyama, 1990), even after factors such as level of parent education are controlled (Guthrie, Coddington, & Wigfield, 2009).

Although the class library is important for all children, it is particularly important for children who are at risk for developing reading difficulties. Many of these children come from low-income homes where few books are available to them (Neuman & Celano, 2012a; Smith, Constantino, & Krashen, 1997). Also, the public and school libraries in low-income neighborhoods are not well stocked in comparison to those in middle- and upper-middle-class neighborhoods (Chandler, 2015; Neuman & Celano, 2012b; Smith et al., 1997). Moreover, school libraries across the United States have been hit with budget cuts that have reduced staffing and resources (American Library Association, n.d.). This means that the class library may well be the main source of reading material for many children.

Yet children are often in classrooms with no libraries or with small collections that are not adequate to make a difference. In a study at the elementary level, Fractor, Woodruff, Martinez, and Teale (1993) found that 72% of kindergarten classrooms had libraries, but the percentage having class libraries fell dramatically as children moved through the grades. The figures for first, second, and third grades were 55%, 52%, and 38%, respectively. Unfortunately, even when primary-grade classrooms had a library, over 90% were rated as basic, with a very small number of books.

Another difficulty with class libraries is that, whether large or small, they tend to contain mostly storybooks rather than information books. Studies that have inventoried primary-grade classroom libraries indicate that they consist largely of fiction (Baker et al., 2011; Dreher & Dromsky, 2000; Duke, 2000; Jeong et al., 2010; Ness, 2011). Yet children benefit from an opportunity to read and receive instruction about both fiction and nonfiction (Dreher, 2000; Guthrie & Humenick, 2004).

The immediate access afforded by classroom libraries is crucial to helping children become skilled and motivated readers. But even when classrooms have libraries, they are often very basic and overwhelmingly consist of fiction. What can teachers do about this problem? Teachers who do not have a class library need to start one. Those who do have a library can most likely improve it. The advice in this chapter will help in either case.

A well-designed class library needs to have plenty of books and other materials. In this chapter, we focus first on books, discussing the types, numbers, and levels of books that are needed. Then we discuss other resources—magazines, newspapers, e-books, and the Internet—that enhance children's opportunity to experience diverse types of reading. Finally, we discuss the design of classroom libraries and offer tips for obtaining resources and managing the library. In Chapter 3, we expand our discussion by showing how to select books and other materials with an emphasis on quality.

A 50/50 Balance of Fiction and Informational Text

There is wide agreement that children need to be exposed to diverse literacy genres. The Committee on the Prevention of Reading Difficulties in Young Children

(Snow et al., 1998), for example, concluded that primary-grade children must have the opportunity to interact with both fiction and nonfiction. Similarly, the IRA's position is that "genres should include picture storybooks, novels, biography, fiction and nonfiction material, magazines, poetry, and a multitude of other types to suit the interests and range of reading abilities of all children" (1999, n.p.). More recently, the CCSS have echoed these ideas in that, although literature remains important, the standards call for "a special emphasis on informational text" (NGA & CCSSO, 2010a, p. 4).

Despite such calls for diverse reading materials, however, fiction continues to be predominant in many classrooms (e.g., Jeong et al., 2010; Ness, 2011). So, a prime concern for teachers is to change the situation. The class library is an important place to start. We suggest that teachers aim for class libraries with a 50/50 balance of fiction and informational text. We base this suggestion on the argument that if children are to become equally proficient with both fiction and informational text, they need a balanced opportunity to experience these texts (Dreher, 2000; Kletzien & Dreher, 2004). Drawing on similar reasoning, the CCSS also target 50% literary and 50% informational text (NGA & CCSSO, 2010a).

Aiming for a 50/50 balance of fiction and informational text is more complicated than it seems, largely because both fiction and informational text encompass many different genres. Fiction can include folktales, fables, myths, fantasy, modern fiction, and historical fiction. And good libraries should offer children the chance to read all of these genres. Similarly, if children are to fully experience informational text, class libraries need to include a wide range of informational text. Consequently, we next discuss important distinctions to be considered when selecting informational text for the class library.

Informational Text Can Be Narrative, Expository, or Mixed

The term *informational text* is widely used, but its usage differs (see Maloch & Bomer, 2013). Some use the term to indicate a specific type of nonfiction (e.g., Duke, 2000). However, we and others use *informational text* and *nonfiction* as equivalent terms. Our use of the term *informational text* is similar to that of the CCSS, which refer to informational text as including "biographies and autobiographies; books about history, social studies, science, and the arts; technical texts, including directions, forms, and information displayed in graphs, charts, or maps; and digital sources on a range of topics" (NGA & CCSSO, 2010a, p. 31). Thus, informational text can include a wide range of material. Within the umbrella term informational text, we have found it useful to distinguish among narrative-informational text, expository text, and mixed text, as in Table 2.1. By considering informational text in these broad categories, teachers can help ensure that their class libraries include a full range of informational text.

TABLE 2.1. Types of Informational Text

Type of book	Characteristics	Examples
Expository	• Purpose is to convey accurate information. • Written with timeless verbs, generic nouns. • Often uses typical expository structures: cause–effect, compare–contrast, sequence, description, generalization–example. • Includes essays, descriptions, explanations, reports, procedural text, chronological accounts.	• *A Farm through Time* (Wilkes, 2001) • *Time for a Bath* (Jenkins & Page, 2011) • *How Did That Get in My Lunchbox?* (Butterworth, 2011)
Narrative-informational	• Purpose is to convey accurate information. • Usually uses past tense verbs and specific nouns. • Often written with story elements including characters, setting, problem, resolution. • May use one "character" as representative of a group and tell a story to give information. • Includes biography and fictionalized biography.	• *The Taxing Case of the Cows* (Van Rynbach & Shea, 2010) • *Hip-Pocket Papa* (Markle, 2010) • *Summer Birds: The Butterflies of Maria Merian* (Engle, 2010)
Mixed	• Includes elements of narrative and expository text or elements of expository text and poetry.	• Magic School Bus original series • *The Chiru of High Tibet* (Martin, 2010)
Poetry	• Purpose is to convey accurate information, but text is written in poetry.	• *Swirl by Swirl* (Sidman, 2011) • *Our Big Home: An Earth Poem* (Glaser, 2002)

Narrative-Informational Text

Much nonfiction for young children is in story or narrative format. The purpose of authors who write narrative-informational text is to convey factual information; but they use a story format because they believe a story will make the information more appealing or easy to approach. These books contain story elements including characters, goals, and resolutions. *Hip-Pocket Papa* (Markle, 2010) and *Charlie Needs a Cloak* (dePaola, 1973) are examples of narrative-information books. These books convey factual information via a story. *Hip-Pocket Papa* provides information about the life cycle of hip-pocket frogs as it tells the story of one male frog as he feeds and guards the eggs his mate lays from the time they hatch until they are ready to leave his pockets and live on their own. As in this excerpt, the story of a particular frog is used to represent the characteristics of a group:

> A male hip-pocket frog ducks beneath a button-sized mushroom cap. It's a tiny space, but since he's no bigger than a thumbnail, he fits with room to spare. Settling there, he croaks in a creaky voice: Eh! Eh! Eh! Eh! Eh! Eh! (n.p.)

Similarly, *Charlie Needs a Cloak* follows a shepherd through the steps of making his own cloak. This excerpt gives the flavor of the story:

> He really needed a new cloak. So, in the spring, Charlie sheared his sheep. He washed the wool, and carded the wool to straighten it out. Then Charlie spun the wool into yarn. (n.p.)

Many biographies and autobiographies for young children are written in narrative form. This approach is illustrated by *Pablo Neruda: Poet of the People* (Brown, 2011):

> Once there was a little boy named Neftalí who loved wild things wildly and quiet things quietly.
>
> From the moment he could talk, he surrounded himself with words that whirled and swirled, just like the river that ran near his home in Chile. (n.p.)

Expository Text

Expository books do not include story elements such as characters, goals, and resolutions. Instead, they might be characterized as reports using expository text structures such as cause and effect, comparison and contrast, sequence, description, and problem and solution. They explain things about the natural and social world such as animals, places, and cultural groups. Examples include the National Geographic Readers such as *Deadly Predators* (Stewart, 2013), the Pull Ahead Books such as *Exercising* (Nelson, 2006), the Picture the Past series such *as Life on a Viking Ship* (Shuter, 2005), and many of the Let's-Read-and-Find-Out Science books such as *Light Is All Around Us* (Pfeffer, 2014).

The writing in expository texts differs considerably from narrative-information books, as this excerpt from *Manatees* (Marsh, 2014) illustrates:

> Manatees are mammals that live in the water. They are sometimes called "sea cows." Why? Manatees are gentle and they move slowly, like cows. They also graze on sea grass, just like cows eat grass. (p. 7)

In this excerpt, manatees in general are being discussed rather than an individual manatee, as would be done in a story. Note also the use of the present verb tense (timeless verb) to convey the sense that the characteristics being discussed apply in general, not just to a specific manatee.

But even though expository books are not stories, that doesn't mean they can't be appealing. *Time for a Bath* (Jenkins & Page, 2011), for example, draws children in with this opening:

> Do you like taking baths? Enjoyable or not, baths are important because they keep us clean. Many animals also take baths to keep themselves clean. But some animals

bathe for other reasons. They may be trying to cool off, warm up, or get rid of para-
sites. Some take dust baths or wallow in the mud. . . . Strangest of all is the ant bath,
something you probably don't want to try yourself. (n.p.)

Time for a Bath continues with wonderful illustrations of animals such as emus,
vultures, and tigers, each accompanied by a paragraph on their fascinating bath-
ing habits.

Mixed Text: Combining Narrative and Expository Writing

Many information books combine narrative and expository writing. Although a
number of terms have been used to describe these books, such as *dual-purpose,
fuzzy, blended*, and *hybrid*, we use the term *mixed text*.

An example of mixed text is Joanna Cole's original Magic School Bus series.
In *The Magic School Bus: Inside the Human Body* (Cole, 1990), for instance,
readers follow the story of an imaginary teacher and her class as they take a trip.
But surrounding the story are facts in boxes, charts, student reports, and illus-
trations containing lists and labels. (A later book series based on episodes of the
Magic School Bus TV series differs from the original books. The television-based
titles, such as *The Magic School Bus Wet All Over: A Book about the Water Cycle*
[Relf, 1996], feature narrative–information books. In addition, a new series has
recently been introduced called *The Magic School Bus Presents*, described as "A
Nonfiction Companion to the Original Magic School Bus." These books, such as
The Magic School Bus Presents: Our Solar System [Jackson, 2014], fall into the
expository category.)

Another example of a mixed text is *The Chiru of High Tibet* (Martin, 2010).
This book uses free verse poetry to tell the true story of chiru, endangered antelope-
like creatures, and how a scientist and others worked to save them. In addition to
the main text in free verse, the book presents fact boxes.

Some Cautions on Narrative-Informational Text and Mixed Text

We recommended earlier that one-half of the class library be information books.
Now we add to that recommendation by suggesting that narrative-informational
or mixed texts make up no more than one-third of those information books. Following this recommendation would mean that most of the information books in
the class library would feature expository writing. As we explained, we believe this
is a good idea because young children typically get more exposure to narratives.
Clearly, if children's exposure to informational text is mostly narrative material,
they will not have the opportunity to experience expository text. As the CCSS
put it, "Students today are asked to read very little expository text . . . [but] . . .

students need sustained exposure to expository text to develop important reading strategies" (NGA & CCSSO, 2010b, p. 3).

There are other reasons to look for high-quality expository writing. We see some particular problems that are more likely to occur with narrative-informational or mixed text than with expository text. One potential problem is that *the story often takes precedence* over the factual information. With mixed text such as many of the Magic School Bus books, some children may simply read the story and ignore the factual portion. In fact, Donovan and Smolkin (2004) found that many *teachers* did just that. Narrative-informational text can also result in a focus on the story even when children are directed to focus on the factual information. In Jetton's (1994) research, second graders listened *to Dear Mr. Blueberry* (James, 1991), a story that included science concepts about whales. Half of the children were told they would be listening to a story about a girl who likes whales, while the other children were instructed to listen to a book that tells interesting things about the life of whales. Regardless of the purpose given, the children in both groups focused on story ideas rather than on factual information.

Similarly, narrative-informational and mixed text books can cause children confusion in *differentiating fact from fiction.* In a book like *I Am a Leaf* (Marzollo, 1998, n.p.), children may be misled by the anthropomorphism as they read: "Hi! I'm a leaf. I live on the maple tree. See the lady bug? She's crawling on me. It tickles!" Many authors use similar approaches. For example, in *Kids Meet the Bugs* (Abramson, 2013), each bug addresses readers, as in "Hey, it's me, a flea! I make your dog scratch and your cat freak out. People don't like me much either" (p. 38), while in *Guinea Pig* (Rayner, 2008) children encounter text with points like "Feed me! I love to eat. It is my favorite way to pass the time!" (p. 14) and photos with speech bubbles such as "I will do anything for a bite of banana!" (p. 21). In other cases, the text of the book may not be anthropomorphic, but the accompanying illustrations may be misleading. Gill (2009) noted a number of examples, such as in *Extreme Animals* (Davies, 2006), where "the text says that some birds sleep huddled together to keep warm, but the illustration is an anthropomorphic depiction of birds sleeping in a row of beds" (Gill, 2009, p. 263).

The younger the children, the more difficulty they may have telling fact from fiction. This problem is illustrated by the work of Brabham, Boyd, and Edgington (2000). Second, third, and fourth graders engaged in read-alouds of two narrative-information books, *Everglades* (George, 1995), in which a Native American storyteller gives children historical and scientific information as he takes them on a canoe trip in the Everglades, and *Call Me Ahnighito* (Conrad, 1995), in which an anthropomorphic meteorite named Ahnighito tells his story. There was some confusion at all grade levels, but the second graders had much more difficulty sorting out the facts from the fictional elements, and they were more likely to attribute anthropomorphic characteristics to the meteorite.

Differentiating fact from fiction is often problematic even when no anthropomorphism is involved. Many children's information books are heavily fictionalized—so much so that they may lead to misconceptions. For example, when we examined dozens of books recommended for young children by the National Council for the Social Studies and the National Science Teachers Association, we found numerous instances of such things as purported dialogue with no evidence that such conversations ever occurred or fictionalized information on thoughts or feelings.

To help avoid such problems, teachers should pick narrative-information books with care (see Chapter 3 for criteria to use in choosing books). Some authors of narrative-information books do a better job of avoiding potential problems, for example avoiding anthropomorphism, than others. In addition, some authors take care to let readers know what is actually known and what is conjecture (see Chapter 3 for a more detailed discussion). In *Bard of Avon: The Story of William Shakespeare* (Stanley & Vennema, 1992), for instance, the authors include such comments as: "No one knows when he left [Stratford for London]" (n.p.) and "Perhaps he allowed his five-year-old son, William, to sit in front with him for the special performance. If so, it was the first play he ever saw" (n.p.). Other authors include notes detailing what is fact versus conjecture. In *Betsy Ross* (Wallner, 1994) readers are told:

> We know many facts about Betsy Ross's life, but there are also many conflicting stories. Some historians suggest that she won contests for her needlework. Others say she did not. . . . There is no absolute proof that Betsy Ross sewed the first American flag. The story . . . was passed down by Betsy's relatives and friends. (n.p.)

Similarly, unlike many biographies that invent dialogue, the picture book *Abraham Lincoln* (Cohn & Schmidt, 2002) includes only utterances for which we have historical evidence: "Leading a nation at war was the hardest task of all his life. People died, too many to count. President Lincoln grieved for each one. 'Sometimes I think I'm the tiredest man in the world'" (n.p.).

Years ago, children's literature experts Sutherland, Monson, and Arbuthnot (1981) argued:

> Information can and should be written in a straightforward fashion; young readers need no palliative with books on science or geography or nature study. No "Mother Nature knew it was springtime" is admissible in children's nonfiction books, nor does a squirrel need to be referred to as "Little Nutsy." Children don't like to be talked down to. They can take information straight, although they can be bored stiff if the writing is too dry or too heavy. (p. 445)

Sutherland and her colleagues' position is still timely. Indeed, their view was echoed by a second-grade boy who looked over a narrative-information book and commented, "Oh, I know what this is. It's one of those fact books trying to pretend it's a story." If a book is that obvious, then it is probably not a successful one.

Fortunately, there are lots of excellent information books for young children—including expository text—that are wonderfully appealing. This means that teachers can indeed find good expository books for their libraries. We provide many examples throughout this book.

Choosing Good-Quality Books

By now it must be clear that narrative-informational text, expository text, and mixed text offer children quite different experiences with nonfiction. However, the type of writing is not the only consideration. In selecting these books, quality is a concern. For all three information book categories, there is much to consider, ranging from accuracy to style to search features such as a table of contents, index, and headings. We will focus on choosing quality information books in Chapter 3.

Taking Stock of the Classroom Library

To be sure that children have the opportunity to experience the full range of reading experience, it is important to inventory the classroom library. By taking stock of what's in the class library, teachers can target what they need to do to achieve a better balance of fiction and nonfiction.

Inventorying the Types of Books

Two examples show how inventories can help teachers set goals for improving their libraries. Table 2.2 presents the inventory of a third-grade class library. The teacher had a large number of books, but they were mostly fiction, with information books making up only 22% of her class library. Moreover, more than half of those information books were narrative-informational. Thus, expository books made up only 9% of her collection. When the teacher examined the results of her inventory, she decided she would need to target information books, in particular books that feature exposition.

Next, Table 2.3 lists by category the inventory of a second-grade class library with a similar pattern. Information books accounted for a much smaller percentage of the collection than fiction (17% vs. 80%, respectively). But because this second-grade class library had many fewer books than the third-grade class library, the underrepresentation of information books was even more problematic in that students had much less opportunity to experience information books.

TABLE 2.2. A Beginning-of-the-School Year Snapshot of Books in a Grade 3 Classroom Library

Type of book	Reading level						Total
	1st and below	Low 2nd	High 2nd	Low 3rd	High 3rd	4th and above	
Fiction (narrative)	85	206	169	73	29	20	582 (74%)
Informational book							
Expository	3	22	17	13	12	4	71 (9%)
Narrative-informational	8	36	31	11	6	3	95 (12%)
Mixed	0	2	1	0	2	0	5 (1%)
Other (e.g., poetry, jokes, music)	4	11	9	7	0	0	31 (4%)
Total	100 (13%)	277 (35%)	227 (29%)	104 (13%)	49 (6%)	27 (3%)	784 (100%)

TABLE 2.3. A Beginning-of-the-School Year Snapshot of Books in a Grade 2 Classroom Library

Type of book	Reading level						Total
	1st and below	Low 2nd	High 2nd	Low 3rd	High 3rd	4th and above	
Fiction (narrative)	6	63	29	14	5	2	119 (80%)
Informational book							
Expository	0	3	2	1	2	3	11 (7%)
Narrative-informational	2	2	6	2	1	0	13 (9%)
Mixed	0	0	1	0	0	0	1 (1%)
Other (poetry, riddles)	0	1	3	0	1	0	5 (3%)
Total	8 (5%)	69 (46%)	41 (28%)	17 (11%)	9 (6%)	5 (3%)	149 (100%)

These two examples match research findings that classroom libraries often contain mostly fiction titles. Thus, many teachers will find that carefully categorizing their library inventory will lead them to seek out more information books for their classrooms. As they do so, we believe teachers should emphasize expository rather than narrative-informational or mixed texts because expository material is what young children have less exposure to and because of the cautions we have raised about narrative-informational and mixed books. As we suggested earlier, narrative-informational or mixed texts should make up no more than one-third of the information books in the class library. That way, most of the information books will offer children experience with expository writing.

Range of Reading Levels

It is also important to consider the reading level of the books in the classroom library in relation to the reading abilities of the children who are using it. Mismatches between children's reading abilities and the books in a classroom library are not uncommon. Martinez, Roser, Worthy, Strecker, and Gough (1997) found that the percentage of easy books in second-grade class libraries did not match the demand for those books. For example, in one classroom, the easy books made up only 24% of the class library, but those books made up over 60% of what the children chose to read during the school year.

Tables 2.2 and 2.3 show the breakdown of each class library according to reading level. Both classrooms are in Title I schools with a very high percentage of minority students from low-SES families. Both classes include some highly capable readers, but also many struggling readers. Thus, in the third-grade classroom, it makes sense that many books are at reading levels lower than the third grade. In the second-grade classroom, 74% of the books are at the second-grade level. Given the students' reading levels in that class, the teacher may need to increase the percentage of lower-level books. Further, it is clear that both libraries could use more information books at each reading level.

Providing an Adequate Number of Books

How many books should a classroom library have? Based on a review of research, Fractor et al. (1993) concluded that a "basic" class library should include at least one book per child, a "good" library at least four books per child, and an "excellent one" at least eight books per child. In its position statement, the IRA (1999) came to a similar conclusion, explaining that "given that there are approximately 180 days in the school year, a child should be able to select within the classroom a new book to read each day. This averages to about seven books per student in each classroom library" (n.p.). These figures should include multiple copies of some titles so that children can sometimes read a book at the same time as a classmate.

The 784-book library in Table 2.2 served 25 children, so it had over 30 books per child, while the 149-book library in Table 2.3 served 21 students, thus averaging 7 books per child. Both libraries would thus meet the IRA's recommended number of books. In terms of the number of books, the first library would rate as "excellent," according to Fractor et al., while the second would be rated "good."

However, numbers alone don't tell the whole story. If the books are dated, dull, worn-out, unappealing, or at the wrong levels of difficulty, they are unlikely to be read. Thus, books in the library need to be evaluated, as we discuss in Chapter 3. And, as the IRA (1999) has recommended, "One new book per student should be added to every classroom library . . . each year to allow for the addition of important new titles and the elimination of books that are no longer timely" (n.p.). In addition, effective class libraries need to be well designed, as we discuss later in this chapter.

Extending the Classroom Library

Beyond providing printed books, classroom libraries may benefit from related resources to promote children's engagement with print. These resources include listening stations with earphones; flannel boards, puppet theaters, and related props; magazines; newspapers; e-books; and Internet resources. Here we focus on two categories of print resources that offer young children lots of opportunity to interact with nonfiction: (1) newspapers and magazines and (2) e-books and Internet resources.

Children's Newspapers and Magazines

Children's newspapers are perfect additions to a class library. Newspapers such as *Time for Kids* and *Scholastic News* not only offer the chance to read informational text but also provide up-to-the-minute information on current events in a way that children can understand. Similarly, magazines designed for young children also add to the class library's appeal. Children's magazines that feature informational text, such as *National Geographic Kids, Click*, and *Kids Discover*, help extend children's knowledge of the world. Like information books, newspapers and magazines appeal to children's curiosity, and curiosity is strongly related to reading activity (Baker & Wigfield, 1999). Appendix 2.1 lists several magazines and newspapers that feature informational text. Almost all of these magazines and newspapers have websites that teachers and children can visit for extension activities.

E-Books and Internet Resources

Books presented on digital devices can be highly appealing in classroom libraries. As Schugar, Smith, and Schugar (2013) have asserted, "E-books have the potential to change the way our students read and consume text because of their interactivity and convenience" (p. 615). However, they also noted that "interactive features might also channel students' attention away from the actual reading of the text" (p. 620). As we elaborate in Chapter 5, e-books need to be carefully chosen so that students are not distracted by interactive features that undermine their comprehension of the text.

In addition to e-books, there are numerous worthwhile resources available online for young children. Therefore, it is desirable to include computers and Internet access in the class library. Doing so will expand children's opportunity to interact with informational text because the content available on Internet sites, including sites for younger children, has been found to be mostly informational text (Kamil & Lane, 1998). Teachers should be aware, however, that even on sites intended for younger students the reading level is typically higher than conventional expository books at the indicated grade levels (Kamil & Lane, 1998).

Providing computer and Internet access in the class library is also particularly important for children in high-poverty areas. As Celano and Neuman (2010) have pointed out, "Low-income children often lack home computers and struggle to get the computer time they need to achieve the skills necessary to be competitive" (p. 68).

Teachers should consult their school's policy on Internet use. Often, with the youngest children, an adult is required to monitor Internet usage. However, even if an adult is present, it is a good idea to bookmark appropriate sites to help limit accidental access to inappropriate ones. Bookmarks also help make children's use of the computer more efficient. We discuss how to choose good websites in Chapter 3 and refer to numerous examples throughout the book.

It is also important that children receive instruction on how to search for and evaluate the information they find on websites. As we explain in Chapter 5, although children may appear to be capable users of digital resources, evidence indicates that they have much to learn (Dodge, Husain, & Duke, 2011). We offer many suggestions for effective instruction, particularly in Chapters 7 and 8.

Getting Resources for a Classroom Library

At this point, it must be evident that creating an excellent classroom library involves some expense. All too often teachers finance their classroom libraries out of their personal income. To help remedy this situation, professional organizations have called for increased spending on books for the school and class libraries (e.g., IRA, 1999). Unfortunately, as noted earlier, library budgets continue to suffer (American Library Association, n.d.). Continuing advocacy for library funding is needed. In the meantime, here are a few ideas for expanding the classroom library.

Evaluate Existing Budgets

Budgets are always tight. But if class libraries are valued, then funds can sometimes be reallocated from other sources. Teachers may find it helpful to demonstrate the usefulness and value of class libraries. For example, a kindergarten teacher in an urban school conducted an action research study on the effects of establishing a classroom lending library on her students and their parents (Britt & Baker, 1997). The children took turns staffing the library themselves and took great pride in doing so, with parents often coming to school to observe on the days their children were in charge. The project was very successful in promoting parent involvement and home–school communication. The principal was so impressed with the results that she reallocated funds from the school budget so that each classroom could start its own lending library.

Rotate Books and E-Books from the School and Public Libraries

One good way to expand class libraries is to check out books from the school library or public library. This helps bring ever changing titles into the class collection. If the school library is undersupplied, then it may be particularly important to draw on the public library. Many public libraries offer special teacher cards, with extended loan periods and a printout of the titles to help in keeping track of the books.

Some school and public libraries also have e-books available. For example, Montgomery County Public Libraries in Maryland has begun lending out backpacks called "Go Kits" aimed at exciting children about science and math (*http://montgomerycountymd.libguides.com/ace-babies/littleexplorers*). These Go Kits contain a mini-iPad (in a rubber case) with educational apps, two informational science books, and a STEM (science, technology, engineering, math) toy. Funded by the Friends of the Library, this effort has not yet spread to all library branches and is focused on 3- to 6-year-olds, but does provide an example of the types of programs that teachers and parents can take advantage of.

Look for Grants, Donations, and Discounts

Local newspapers, businesses, civic groups, and professional organizations often make small grants to schools for worthy projects. Schools can request funds for trade books to support literacy. Teachers can propose a project that helps obtain funds for expanding the class library. Such programs may help fund a well-conceived project to involve children with books. Teachers might also consider using DonorsChoose.org (at *www.donorschoose.org*), a free website where U.S. public school teachers can propose a project, including ones that involve book purchases. Anyone who likes the project is invited to contribute to it.

Another way to supplement the class library is to maintain a wish list of books and magazine subscriptions. That way, if parents want to give teachers presents for holidays or teacher appreciation day, they can select items from the wish list. At some schools, parents are able to donate a book from the wish list for their child's birthday. In addition, the wish list can guide donations from the parent–teacher association or other organizations that want to help the school.

Discounts and sales are also helpful. Many bookstores offer substantial discounts to teachers on the purchases. Additionally, warehouse and Internet sales can greatly reduce prices. For example, in the Washington, DC, area, both the National Geographic Society and Scholastic sponsor regular warehouse sales featuring deep discounts. Book sales and special offers are often available through online suppliers. Often teachers can sign up for email alerts regarding specials.

Include Student-Produced Books

Books written by the children in a classroom are important additions to the class library. Young children enjoy creating both single-author and group-authored books, and they enjoy reading and rereading their own and one another's books. When second graders each contributed pages to an information book as part of an inquiry unit, the book was among the most popular in the class library (Korkeamäki, Tiainen, & Dreher, 1998).

In one first-grade class, the children write class books all year long and then add these books to the class library. These books are so well loved that the children are eager to own one. At the end of the year, the class holds a lottery for these student-produced books: each book is assigned a number, the children then pick a number out of a hat, and get to take home the book with that number.

Creating an Appealing Classroom Library Environment

The physical environment of the classroom library makes a difference in its appeal to children. Morrow (1991) summarized her own and others' research showing that much more than the number of books influences a library's effectiveness. Features like size, accessibility, arrangement of furniture, open-face shelving, organization, variety of genres, ease of checking books in and out, and regular influx of new books are all important. Indeed, Morrow noted that redesigning the classroom library can result in library corners moving from unpopular choices during free time to highly appealing centers that increase the amount of reading children do.

Thus, research makes it is clear that well-stocked, well-designed libraries should be the goal in every classroom. To achieve this goal, teachers can begin by evaluating their libraries. Fractor et al. (1993) proposed a sliding scale for rating class libraries as "basic," "good," or "excellent." Setting up a basic class library would be a first step in the right direction for teachers without one. However, like Fractor et al., we hope that teachers will not merely settle for a basic library but rather will use it as a stepping stone toward an excellent library. As we just noted, the number of books involved is only one factor. At the primary-grade level, Fractor et al. proposed these characteristics for a basic library:

- Contains at least one book per child.
- Is quiet and well lighted.
- Has seating or carpeting.
- Is large enough to accommodate a minimum of three children (p. 479).

A good library has all of the features of a basic library, plus:

- Has at least four books per child.
- Can accommodate at least four children.
- Is partitioned from the rest of the room in some manner.
- Has an open-faced presentation of books (p. 479).

An excellent library has all of the above characteristics, plus:

- Contains at least eight books per child.
- Has some method of organizing the books.
- Has a flannel board or other props that promote reenactments or rereadings of books.
- Has a name.
- Is large enough for at least five children to use the area at one time (p. 479).

We recommend that all teachers aim to create an excellent classroom library. Appendix 2.2 presents a checklist teachers can use to evaluate progress toward library excellence. This checklist represents the points contributed by Fractor et al. (1993) and Morrow (1991) as well as our own suggestions.

Managing Your Class Library

To make a library work, good management is important. This means that teachers need to set up a system to keep everything in order. There should be a simple method for checking books out and returning them, a plan for organizing the books, and a place to put books that need to be repaired. Teachers do not have to manage their libraries by themselves. Primary-grade children not only can help out but also enjoy doing so. A special benefit of involving children in managing the library is that it adds to their feeling of ownership.

Library-related roles can be included in class jobs. Even children in kindergarten can operate a simple checkout and return system (Britt & Baker, 1997). Children can also be in charge of identifying books that need repair and placing them in the book first-aid corner. Finally, children can help keep the books in order. For example, teachers may code books with colored stickers that match the place in the library where they belong, allowing children to easily help sort and arrange books.

Ensuring Sufficient Time to Read

A second-grade teacher and her class received some new books to thank them for helping with a project. As these books were presented, the class was told that they were for the classroom library. A student spontaneously expressed her frustration, complaining that "we never use our library!" Sadly, data collected from numerous countries, including the United States, document "more availability than actual use of classroom libraries" (Mullis et al., 2012, p. 238).

This situation helps to illustrate an important point: A well-designed library can be a major contributor to helping children become eager and competent readers. But this is true only if children have time to use it. Access to books involves not only having the books available but also having time to read them. In fact, experts have argued that giving students time to read something of their own choosing every day should be a *top priority* in today's classrooms (Allington & Gabriel, 2012). Evidence indicates that giving children time to read and a choice of what to read facilitates both engagement and achievement (Baker, Dreher, & Guthrie, 2000; Krashen, 2011).

In addition to allowing children sufficient time to read, teachers can take many other actions to make classroom libraries successful. Taking action is important because, although the physical environment is part of best practices (Morrow & Tracy, 2014), "Without the support of teachers who introduce the materials and feature books in daily routines, the physical factors alone will not succeed" (Morrow, 1991, p. 687). In the chapters that follow, we provide many ideas to help introduce and feature information books. In the next chapter, we discuss how to choose quality books for classroom use, while the rest of the book offers instructional suggestions aimed at enhancing children's learning from informational text.

QUESTIONS AND REFLECTIONS FOR PROFESSIONAL LEARNING COMMUNITIES

1. Ask teachers in your professional learning community to bring in a few examples of information books. As a group, sort these books into narrative-informational, expository, or mixed text. Then examine narrative-informational and mixed texts to see if these books contain issues to consider (as described in the section "Some Cautions on Narrative-Informational Text and Mixed Text").

2. This chapter notes that children living in poverty often lack access to books and computers at home as well as have less well-stocked school and public libraries. Consider how you and your colleagues can maximize children's access to these resources in your classrooms and across your school community. What actions could you take? What changes could you make in your classroom environment and instructional routines?

3. Think about the student who complained that "we never use our library!" Brainstorm ways to ensure sufficient time to read in your classroom. Develop a plan to support one another in this effort.

CLASSROOM ENGAGEMENT ACTIVITIES

1. Examine your classroom library to identify the types of books you have. First, sort your collection into fiction and information books. Is there a good balance between fiction and information books? Next, categorize the information books according to the types specified in Table 2.1. Is there a substantial percentage of books using expository text?

2. Consider the design of your classroom library. Use the Checklist for a Well-Designed K–3 Classroom Library in Appendix 2.2 to evaluate its appeal.

3. Review the ideas in this chapter's section on "Getting Resources for a Classroom Library." Choose an idea that would work for you, and make a plan to implement it.

Magazines and Newspapers (Organized by Publisher) That Feature Informational Text for K–3 Students

Almost all of these magazines have digital versions, website resources, and/or apps.

COBBLESTONE & CRICKET
www.cobblestonepub.com

Appleseeds

Aimed at children in grades 3–5, each issue focuses on a social studies theme.

Ask

For grades 2–5, *Ask* stands for Arts and Sciences for Kids. Each issue focuses on a theme. This magazine also has a Spanish version.

Click

For grades K–2, *Click* features science and exploration.

Iguana

For grades 2–7, this Spanish-language magazine features science and exploration.

KIDS DISCOVER
www.kidsdiscover.com

Kids Discover

Aimed at ages 6 and up, this magazine features history, nature, science, and geography. Each issue focuses on one topic.

NATIONAL GEOGRAPHIC FOR KIDS
www.nationalgeographic.com/magazines/lp/kids-sem

NG Kids Magazine

For ages 6–14, this magazine is richly illustrated with photos as well as information on animals, explorers, sports, technology, and diverse sites throughout the world.

(continued)

NG Little Kids Magazine

Similar to its sister magazine, this version serves ages 3–6.

NATIONAL WILDLIFE FEDERATION
www.nwf.org/kids

Ranger Rick

Issues focus on nature, with animal photos, information, and stories for ages 7–12.

Ranger Rick Jr.

With the same focus as *Ranger Rick*, this version is for ages 4–7.

OWL KIDS
www.owlkids.com

chickaDEE

This discovery magazine for 6- to 9-year-olds includes hands-on science.

Chirp

For 3- to 6-year-olds, *Chirp* features hands-on science, puzzles, games, and information on topics such as animals.

OWL

Owl engages 9- to 13-year-olds in hands-on science.

SCHOLASTIC MAGAZINES
http://classroommagazines.scholastic.com

Let's Find Out

This edition of *Scholastic News* features nonfiction aimed at kindergarteners, with science and social studies news.

Scholastic News

Scholastic News is a weekly nonfiction magazine focusing on timely science and social studies themes. It comes in versions for grades 1, 2, and 3.

(continued)

Science Spin

This real-world science newsletter comes in editions aimed at K–1, 2, and 3–6. It is a supplement that can be purchased with *Let's Find Out* and *Scholastic News*.

SuperScience

For grades 3–6, this title offers eight issues year covering life, the earth, and physical science topics.

SPORTS ILLUSTRATED
www.sikids.com

Sports Illustrated for Kids

The target audience of this magazine is ages 8–15; so, it is most appropriate for the oldest primary-grade children.

TIME
www.timeforkids.com

TIME for Kids

TIME for Kids has different editions aimed at different grade levels: K–1, 2, 3–4.

WILDLIFE EDUCATION LTD.
www.zoobooks.com

Zoobooks

Aimed at ages 6–12, each issue contains facts and photos about a specific animal or group of animals.

Zootles

Similar to *Zoobooks, Zootles* is aimed at ages 3–6.

 APPENDIX 2.2

Checklist for a Well-Designed K–3 Classroom Library

Characteristic	Yes	Making progress	No
Range of nonfiction, with lots of expository text			
Range of fiction			
50/50 balance of nonfiction/fiction			
Variety of reading levels			
At least eight books per child			
New books added regularly			
Multiple copies of some titles			
Face-out presentation of many books			
Simple method for checking materials in and out			
Quiet and well-lit			
Seating and/or carpeting			
Partitioned on at least two sides			
Books organized in a logical way			
Flannel board/props/writing materials			
Large enough for at least five children at a time			
Assortment of magazines			
Books on tape/DVD/computer with headsets			
Internet access			

Note. These items reflect the recommendations of Fractor et al. (1993) and Morrow (1991) as well as our own suggestions.

CHAPTER 3

Choosing Information Books
and Websites for the Classroom

A wealth of good information books is available to the primary-grade classroom teacher. Publishers now, more than ever before, are producing colorful, attractive, interesting information books designed for primary-age children. However, among these books, some are more effective in engaging children, and it is up to the teacher to choose appropriate ones for the classroom. Likewise, much information is available online, but figuring out which sites are most useful for the classroom is challenging. Teachers should consider accuracy, design, writing style, complexity, and organization when making these choices.

Accurate Content

Perhaps the most important feature of an information book is its accurate content. By its very nature, an information book is written to inform, enlighten, and engage; if the information it contains is inaccurate, the book fails in its primary goal.

Although "accurate content" is a straightforward concept, in reality it is much harder to define. As children's author Russell Freedman (1992) has noted, "Something can be perfectly accurate but untrue" (p. 4). Authors have the responsibility not only to gather facts but to present these in a balanced, responsible way so that truth is not compromised.

Each time an author writes a book, especially for primary readers, he or she must decide what to include and what to omit. These decisions form the basis for the essential truth of an information book. Authors (and illustrators) should strive to present information that will satisfy a child's curiosity about a topic while including all known (or theorized) information that is appropriate for the child's developing level of understanding.

Children learn from reading and looking at information books (Bradley & Donovan, 2010; Neuman & Dwyer, 2011; Pappas, 1993; Rice, 2002; Saul & Dieckman, 2005; Smolkin & Donovan, 2001); therefore, it is crucial that the information presented to them be accurate. Authors and illustrators must be very careful not to mislead through their text or pictures. For example, children reading *Eight Spinning Planets* (James, 2010) can mistakenly believe, based on the illustrations, that Jupiter has an orange spot and purple rings and that Saturn is green. As Dyson (2010) pointed out, "The planets are indeed colorful, but not these colors!" (n.p.). In a different study from the one reported in Chapter 2 using *Dear Mr. Blueberry* (James, 1991), some children who were read the book (which features letters between a young girl and a teacher about a whale) actually came away from it with misconceptions. Instead of remembering the accurate information supplied by Mr. Blueberry, they remembered the misconceptions held by the girl that were depicted in the illustrations (Mayer, 1995). Similarly, as Rice (2002) has noted, children reading the otherwise excellent book *The Reason for a Flower* (Heller, 1983) can learn incorrectly from the text that mushrooms are plants.

As mentioned in Chapter 2, authors should be careful to indicate the differences between what is known and what is merely believed or suspected to be true. When an author is discussing a theory that has not yet been proven, he or she should indicate this through the use of such words as *might* or *perhaps* or *scientists believe*. In *The Ultimate Dinopedia* (Lessem, 2010), the author is careful to make sure that the reader is aware of the lack of certainty about these dinosaurs:

> But *Dracorex* and another fancy-horned little plant eater named *Stygimoloch* might not be different kinds of dinosaurs at all. Paleontologists have recently suggested that they are just young *Pachycephalosaurus* and that as they grew, their headgear would have changed like antlers on a deer. (p. 143)

Authors' Credentials

In determining whether content is accurate, it is useful to consider the credentials of authors and the references they use. Often this information can be found on the book jacket, at the end of the book, or on the verso of the title page. If the author is not a specialist on a topic, subject experts are often listed as having assisted the author or having reviewed the manuscript. Sometimes an author will list print sources as well. For example, in *Meadowlands: A Wetlands Survival Story* (Yezerski, 2011), the book jacket indicates that the author has "lived on the edge of the Meadowlands for twelve years." Still, that might not give him the scientific and historical knowledge he would have needed to write and illustrate this book. So on the verso of the title page, he specifically thanks "Hugh Carola from Hackensack Riverkeeper and . . . the New Jersey Meadowlands Commission for their review and assistance." He also includes at the end of the text a bibliography of sources about the Meadowlands. These references help convey that the information in the book is accurate.

Special care is needed in examining multicultural books. Generally, those individuals who are part of a particular cultural group—*insiders*—can speak with more authority than those outside the cultural group—*outsiders*. It is possible, however, for an outsider to have enough familiarity with a culture to portray it accurately. Rachel Crandell, author of *Hands of the Rain Forest: The Emberá People of Panama* (2009), explained at the beginning of the book that she was asked by the tribe's chief "to record their stories because they have no written history" (n.p.). She then explained that she had returned to their villages numerous times and had even become godmother to an Emberá child. So, even though she was an outsider, she has enough firsthand experience in these villages to be able to describe accurately the people's daily activities.

Sometimes, if the author does not appear to be an insider, consultants may be listed to assure that the information is accurate. For example, in *The Hopi* (Lassieur, 2002), the Hopi Literacy Project and the Bureau of Applied Research in Anthropology at the University of Arizona are listed as consultants. In any book representing minority cultures, care should always be taken that stereotypes are not used, either in the text or illustrations.

Currentness of the Information

An additional component of accurate content is how current the information is. It is important that the most up-to-date information be included in books about science, but it is equally as germane for books reflecting newly independent nations or discussing minority cultures. In many instances, outdated information books may not include all that is known about a subject or may contain information that has been proven false or may include stereotypes indicative of the earlier time when they were written. It is always important, therefore, to check the copyright date of the book.

Even the copyright date doesn't guarantee that the information is up to date. For example, in *Breakfast Around the World* (Perez, 2000), the map of Germany shows only West Germany—yet East and West Germany reunited in 1990! Additionally, sometimes the copyright date in the book represents the publishing date used by the current publisher, not the date when the book was written. For example, *Spiders* (Cullen, 1996), which has a copyright date of 1996, was first published in Australia in 1986.

Using Books with Inaccuracies

As Rice (2002) noted about children's science books, "Errors of omission, incomplete statements, value statements, outdated information, and lack of detail create problems just as overtly erroneous information does" (p. 563). Rice also pointed out that teachers can continue to use books that contain inaccuracies as long as they are aware of them. In fact, pointing out errors or using books that have conflicting information can encourage children to become critical readers, questioning the accuracy of what they read. A first grader in Kate Hartenstine's class spent a great deal of time and energy looking at sources about gorillas because he found conflicting information in one of them. Specifically, one source suggested that gorillas eat meat, whereas several others indicated that they were herbivores. After examining books, teacher-chosen websites, and recommended websites from the books, the first grader along with his teacher decided that searching out an expert might provide the answer. They framed the question and submitted it to the "Ask the Expert" column on the Philadelphia Zoo site. After several days, they received an answer listing what gorillas usually eat and referencing a report that animal DNA had been found in the feces of some gorillas. The expert explained that this might have been caused by something other than the gorillas actually eating animals. The email continued: "Even though other great apes like chimpanzees and bonobos have been observed hunting and stalking other animals, there is no positive proof that gorillas are doing the same. Looks like more studies need to be done before there is a conclusive answer" (Donna McGill, Philadelphia Zoo, personal communication, May 28, 2013). The student added the information about the foods gorillas eat to his report, but said that he wasn't going to include meat because "they need to do more research."

It is important for teachers to carefully examine books that they are planning to use with their classes—identifying potential problems, misunderstandings, and misconceptions—and to develop ways to help children use books effectively in spite of any shortcomings. One second-grade teacher reported, "I can make any book work!" (Dreher & Voelker, 2004). To make a book work in the classroom, however, a teacher must be able to spot the possible problems and design compensatory lessons. This might be as simple as pointing out to the children that, even though the pictures show the beetles as all about the same size in the illustrations in Jenkins's *The Beetle Book* (2012), their relative sizes can be judged by looking at the small silhouette pictures at the bottom of the pages.

Appealing Design and Format

No matter how accurate books are, if they aren't appealing to children, they are not likely to be read. Many recently published informational books are richly designed and visually attractive. Nonetheless, there are particular aspects of design that add to a book's value. The design of the book needs to reinforce its contents.

Illustrations and text should be placed appropriately on pages. Books for primary readers, especially, should have text and illustrations placed in such a way that children are not confused about which part to read first if the sequence is important. Although some information books have text that does not read from left to right and is presented in circles or in other formats, older readers can usually understand these variations, and the unusual formatting actually adds to the interest of the book. However, beginning readers who are reading independently need to have text that reads from left to right and from the top to the bottom of the page. Teachers can show beginning readers how to read books with alternative designs through read-alouds (see Chapter 4).

Illustrations in information books may include photographs, diagrams, maps, drawings, charts, or figures. Illustrations can represent and clarify information in the text and can further extend the information in the text. For example, in *Alligators and Crocodiles* (Gibbons, 2010), illustrations are used to specify what isn't spelled out in the text. The text states:

Alligators and crocodiles are good swimmers and spend most of their time in the water. They use their powerful, swishing tails to move forward. They are able to steer using their tails and back legs. By tucking in all four legs they are able to swim faster. (p. 14)

and the caption for the illustration explains how fast they can swim:

They can swim up to 6 miles (9.6 kilometers) an hour.

In some books, the illustrations do not support the text as well as they might. Children studying these texts may have difficulty understanding either the text or the illustration. The text in the book *Eight Spinning Planets* (James, 2010), for example, explains that Uranus looks like "one big blur," and yet the illustration appears to show that it has blue dots prominently visible. Similarly, the book *Body Numbers* (Loove, 1998) contains text that explains that the human heart has four chambers; however, the illustration provided does not label the chambers, which makes it impossible for children or teachers to figure out exactly what a chamber is, based on the text and illustration.

Captions should be placed close to illustrations and provide clear explanations. If the illustrations are maps or graphs, they should be clearly labeled. In *Bugs Are Insects* (Rockwell, 2001) the illustrations lose effectiveness because the identifying information for each one is simply listed on the last page of the book. Teachers and children who are trying to identify the many animals represented in the book must constantly turn to the back of the book to consult the list.

Illustrations should be appropriate to the contents of the book. For example, the pen-and-ink architectural drawings used to illustrate the somewhat challenging book *Built to Last* (Macaulay, 2010) perfectly fit with the architectural content of the book. Likewise, the colorful drawings by Bonnie Christensen to illustrate *Django* (2009) complement the lively text and Django's music. After Django is injured and in the hospital, colors in the drawings become muted and the language more subdued.

Many information books use photographs to clarify or expand the text. When photographs are used, it may be important to know their origin in order to assess their accuracy. In *Extreme Oceans* (Simon, 2013), for example, all photo credits, such as "Hidden Ocean 2005 Expedition: NOAA Office of Ocean Exploration," are listed at the end of the book.

For many books, it is important that the illustrations indicate relative size. For example, the relative sizes of the beetles that are described on the pages of *The Beetle Book* (Jenkins, 2012) are represented by silhouettes at the bottom of the page. This technique enables readers to visualize the actual sizes of the beetles even though the larger illustrations might lead one to believe that they are all roughly the same size. *The Ultimate Dinopedia* (Lessem, 2010) uses small illustrations throughout to indicate the animals' size relative to humans. These illustrations enable children to compare new information about the animals to known information about humans.

It is also important for books to indicate when photographs have been enlarged so that children can understand the difference between a close-up or magnified view and a more normal view. In the book *Nic Bishop Lizards* (Bishop, 2010), for example, the author has indicated on almost every page the relationship between the size of the actual lizard and the photograph by noting in the caption "shown at 2 times actual size" or "shown at 4 times actual size."

Engaging Writing Style

The best information books use lively, engaging language, with the author's voice clearly evident. At the same time, appropriate terminology is important. Part of the content of a good information book is the introduction of the language of the topic. For example, in *Gorillas* (Gibbons, 2011a), the terms *primates, digits, silverback, troop, poacher,* and *equator* are introduced. Similarly, such appropriate terms as *predator, mucus,* and *gland* are included in *Can You Tell a Frog from a Toad?* (Silverman, 2012). As Pappas (1993) documented, kindergarten children are quite capable of learning new correct terminology through repeated readings of information books. They should have the opportunity to do so.

Authors who write with enthusiasm for their subjects invite children to share in their wonder. Frequent use of the second-person "you" in books often serves to draw children into the text. Informal, conversational language can encourage young readers to feel a personal connection with the text. For example, Martin Jenkins wrote in his 2011 book *Can We Save the Tiger?*:

> Ugly things can be endangered, too. Perhaps I'm being unfair, but I don't think any people would call vultures exactly beautiful. (p. 26)

Use of comparisons, language with cadence and rhythm, and active verbs can make the text engaging. In *Swirl by Swirl* (Sidman, 2011), the author used poetic language to describe the place of spirals in nature:

> A spiral is a snuggling shape.
> It fits neatly in small places
> Coiled tight, warm and safe, it waits . . .
> . . . for a chance to expand. (pp. 1–4)

Text Complexity

Another important feature related to style is text complexity. The CCSS encourage teachers to increase the complexity of the texts that their students are reading as they progress through the grade levels. In considering text complexity, Wixson and Valencia (2014) pointed out that "complexity is not an inherent property of the text. Rather it is a function of the interaction among reader, text, and task factors within a particular situation" (p. 431). The CCSS identify three elements used to determine text complexity (see Figure 3.1).

Complexity depends on quantitative measures such as the length of sentences, the length of words, and word frequency in a text. These quantitative aspects are easily measured by computer programs, and most publishers will indicate what the levels are.

Complexity also depends on more qualitative measures such as structure, language clarity, knowledge demands, and purpose. These elements are more easily analyzed by teachers with specific children in mind. Is the structure of the information straightforward? Are there connecting words that indicate the relationships among the sentences, or are children expected to make inferences for causal connections? For example, in the *Meadowlands* (Yezerski, 2011), the author has stated:

> But even after being dug out, filled in, run over, and dumped on, the wetlands still showed signs of life. The Hackensack River still flowed south. The tide still rose north from the Atlantic Ocean. The river and tide still met in the Meadowlands twice a day, as they had for 10,000 years. Because they did, the ecosystem had a chance to recover. (n.p.)

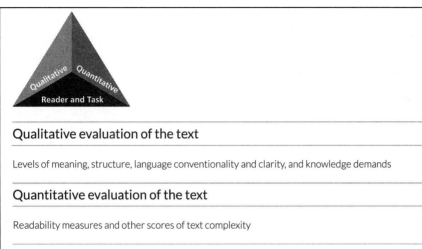

Qualitative evaluation of the text

Levels of meaning, structure, language conventionality and clarity, and knowledge demands

Quantitative evaluation of the text

Readability measures and other scores of text complexity

Matching reader to text and task

Reader variables (such as motivation, knowledge, and experiences) and task variables (such as purpose and the complexity generated by the task assigned and the questions posed)

FIGURE 3.1. Three elements used to determine text complexity in the CCSS. Retrieved from *www.corestandards.org*. Copyright 2010 by the National Governors Association Center for Best Practices and the Council of Chief State School Officers. All rights reserved.

Having the connecting word *because* makes it clear to the reader that the reason the Meadowlands were able to regain their ecological balance was the meeting of the river and the tide.

Language needs to be clear and straightforward. As previously mentioned, authors should use appropriate terminology for the subject so that children can learn the vocabulary associated with the topic. These words, however, can be explained in the text in a child-friendly way. For example, in *It's Snowing* (Gibbons, 2011b), the author has explained *whiteout* in a way that children can understand:

> A whiteout occurs when there is a heavy snowfall with strong winds. It is very hard to see. (p. 21)

Texts should also be analyzed by the extent of prior knowledge necessary for comprehension. Does the text support beginning knowledge, or are the demands so great that prior knowledge or experience is necessary? If prior knowledge is needed, do the students in the class have this knowledge?

Informational texts that have a clear purpose are usually easier to read than those which seem to be a random collection of facts without an underlying purpose and structure. The purpose, for example, of *Can We Save the Tiger?* (Jenkins,

2011) is very clear, as the author addresses the extinction of various animal species and urges children to think about how we can protect and save threatened species.

The third component that the CCSS suggest for analyzing text complexity is the reader and the task. Wixson and Valencia (2014) recommended that "reader and task factors be among the first considerations in measuring text complexity because they are likely to be the most important factors in determining the comprehension of complex text in a specific instructional context" (p. 431). Teachers can note whether their students have the knowledge base needed to understand the text. This will vary according to children's prior experience. Children who live near the sea or wetlands will be much better prepared to read *Meadowlands* (Yezerski, 2011) than children who have never been to the ocean. Children who have great interest in a subject will be much better prepared to read a more advanced text than those who are not motivated by the subject.

Related to this concept is the purpose for using the text. Are the readers using the text to locate information? To learn the basics of a subject? To study for an assessment? To gather important facts for a report? Knowing the purpose for a book can help a teacher decide which ones to choose for the classroom.

All of these elements—quantitative, qualitative, and reader and task—should be taken into consideration when figuring out the complexity of a text. Teachers and librarians play a key role in this determination because they know their students, the tasks, and the desired outcomes.

Good Organization

Choosing information books that are well organized is important because children need to experience typical expository patterns and information book features. Expository patterns such as cause–effect, compare–contrast, sequence, question–answer, description, and generalization–example (Meyer, Brandt, & Bluth, 1980) are characteristic of expository information books. For example, *How Did That Get in My Lunchbox?* (Butterworth, 2011) is written with question–answer and sequence patterns. *Can You Tell a Frog from a Toad?* (Silverman, 2012) follows a compare–contrast pattern. For children to learn to use these patterns to guide their comprehension (see Chapter 5) or use them in their own writing (see Chapter 8), they must have experience with them. Therefore, it is important that teachers choose books with clear organizational patterns. Often headings and subheadings provide clues to the text's organization.

Jen Boyk makes a special effort to teach her first graders to pay attention to headings and subheadings. When she engages the students in interactive read-alouds, she discusses these section markers with the students. When they have books that do not have headings, she and the students figure out what headings might be appropriate. They all agree that books are easier to understand if the author gives them these signposts.

The best information books do not just contain collections of facts but rather present concepts and generalizations about their subject matter. Young readers should come away with a general understanding of the subject as well as specific factual information. In fact, the best books are those that are organized thematically, with specific factual details supporting the themes.

Just a Second (Jenkins, 2011) provides a good example of a thematically organized book with supporting factual details. The entire book describes time, how it is measured, and the relationship between time and events. The unit of time and how people began using this measure is always presented at the bottom of the left-hand page—for example:

> The day is based on the rising and setting of the sun—the time it takes Earth to make one rotation on its axis. The day is the original unit of timekeeping in every human culture. (n.p.)

These explanations are followed by illustrations and examples of specific events that occur within that time frame. On the page with the explanation of the day, there are pictures of a giant anteater, an egg, kelp, a mayfly larva, and a group of people. Text next to each of the illustrations states:

> In one day . . . a giant anteater can lap up 30,000 termites. Chickens around the world lay two billion eggs. Kelp, a kind of seaweed, can grow 18 inches (46 centimeters). A mayfly larva hatches, lives its entire life, and dies. The world's population increases by about 215,000 people (382,000 are born and 167,000 die).

On the following pages, Jenkins explains other events taking place during one day. Children who read this book will understand the general explanations of the time units as well as be given specific examples of events that occur during these time periods.

The Beetle Book (Jenkins, 2012) is organized with generalizations and examples. At the top of the left page of each two-page spread, the author has made a general statement about beetles, such as:

> Clever disguises. Some beetles discourage predators by imitating bees or wasps—insects with painful stings. Others fool ants or termites into caring for them and giving them food. There is even a beetle that disguises itself as a pile of bird poop. (p. 24)

Shown on the two-page spread are illustrations of the eyed click beetle, the ant beetle, the golden spider beetle, the ironclad beetle, and the wasp beetle, with captions explaining how each of these beetles illustrates the disguises the author has described.

Unlike stories, much informational text does not have to be read from beginning to end, and children need to learn this important concept. Children should have information books available that exemplify features that can be used to find information quickly that will satisfy their curiosity. Books such as *Saving Animals from Oil Spills* (Person, 2012), with a table of contents, a glossary, an index, a bibliography, websites, and a list of other books to read, can help children explore these book features. In Chapter 7, we discuss specific ways in which teachers can help children learn to use these features.

Some information books, however, do need to be read from beginning to end. Books explaining topics that are sequential, such as the life cycle of butterflies or the water cycle, need to be read in order. Other books may need to be read from beginning to end because of the repetition and rhyming of the language or because they tell a story, like *The Taxing Case of the Cows* (Van Rynbach & Shea, 2010). Children need to experience all of these different organizational patterns.

Sources for Quality Information Books

Fortunately, numerous sources are available through print journals and online to help teachers identify good-quality information books (see Appendix 3.1 for a list of useful websites). For example, Children's Choices and Teachers' Choices annual lists of popular story and information books are published by the International Literacy Association (formerly the International Reading Association) in *The Reading Teacher* in October and November and are available as separate booklets from the ILA. These can be ordered on the ILA website (*www.reading.org*) and are available online on the Children's Book Council website (*www.cbcbooks.org*).

Since 1990, the National Council of Teachers of English (NCTE) has presented the Orbis Pictus Award for Outstanding Nonfiction for Children each year to an excellent information trade book. Winners, honor books, and recommended titles are available from the NCTE and on its website (*www.ncte.org*). The Association for Library Services to Children presents the Robert F. Sibert Information Book Award to the author of the most outstanding information book published in the United States during the year. Lists of these winners are available from the American Library Association (*www.ala.org*) or the Children's Book Council (*www.cbcbooks.org*).

Caldecott and Newbery Medals honor the authors and illustrators of outstanding children's books, both fiction and nonfiction, published in the United States. Lists of the winning authors and illustrators and the books for which they were honored are available from the American Library Association (*www.ala.org*) and the Children's Book Council (*www.cbcbooks.org*).

A list of Outstanding Science Trade Books for Children is published annually in the March issues of *Science and Children*. This list is created through the National Science Teachers Association (NSTA) and the Children's Book Council. It is available from the NSTA and Children's Book Council and is also available online at *www.nsta.org*. This science listing provides annotations of the books and recommended grade levels for their use.

Similarly, the National Council for the Social Studies (NCSS), in cooperation with the Children's Book Council, publishes Notable Children's Trade Books in the Field of Social Studies in the April/May issue of *Social Education*, or it can be ordered from the CBC. The list is also available online at *www.socialstudies.org*. This list includes both fiction and information books and is divided into social studies themes. It includes annotations and recommended grade levels for each book.

Although the proportion of information books listed in Teachers' Choices, the NCSS's Notable Children's Trade Books, and the NSTA's Outstanding Science Trade Books for Children has increased over the past 10 years, most of these recommended books are narrative in structure (Dreher & Kletzien, 2015). So, teachers need to examine these books carefully to assure that they are providing their students with sufficient experience with expository structures (as explained in Chapter 2).

The Horn Book, published six times a year, and *Book Links: Connecting Books, Libraries and Classrooms*, published by the American Library Association, are other sources for finding good-quality information books.

A Guide for Choosing Information Books

To help teachers evaluate information books, we have developed a guide (see Appendix 3.2) that they can use to identify particular characteristics of books and to decide which ones will be valuable in their classroom libraries and in their teaching. Using the guide can also alert teachers to particular problems that they and their students may encounter with a particular book. Once the teacher is aware of these problems, he or she can plan activities to be sure that the students are able to learn successfully from the book.

To illustrate use of the guide, we analyzed *It's Snowing* (Gibbons, 2011b) and *Saving Animals from Oil Spills* (Person, 2012) and present the results in Figures 3.2 and 3.3. Both books offer opportunities for instruction, and yet both have shortcomings that would have to be taken into account in a classroom. By analyzing the books, we discovered ways that they could be used to improve students' content knowledge as well as their knowledge of how to use information books.

Guide for Choosing Information Books

Title: _It's Snowing_   Author: _Gibbons_   Type of Book: _Expository_

(narrative, expository, mixed)

Characteristic	Notes	Possible Instruction
Content Accuracy		
Author's and illustrator's qualifications Experts in field "Insiders" (if multicultural book) Award winning	_Gail Gibbons noted author of information books._	_Do an author study, using Gibbons's many information books._
References used Consultants who are experts Print and Internet sources	_Thanks the National Weather Service of Vermont. Additional websites listed._	
Information current Copyright date recent (if important) Information up to date	_2011_	
Distinguishes between fact and theory Clear what is believed and what is known	_Yes, uses "scientists believe."_	_Point out to children._
Text and illustrations clear	_Yes_	
Stereotypes used in text or illustration	_No_	

(continued)

FIGURE 3.2. Example of a completed guide for _It's Snowing_ (Gibbons, 2011b).

Guide for Choosing Information Books *(page 2 of 3)*

Characteristic	Notes	Possible Instruction
Design		
Illustrations appropriate for content	Drawings appropriate, though on pp. 14–15 it is not clear where parts of countries illustrated would be on the map.	Use better map to show children where the specific locations illustrated are.
Illustrations well placed on the page Clear where to begin reading	Text in different typeface from captions and information about illustrations.	Show children that they need to read text, captions, and additional information.
Illustrations labeled and explained Captions clear and informative	Yes, with additional information from the text and in different type size.	Point out the different type size.
Relative sizes indicated Enlargements noted	On only two pages–not on snowflakes.	Point out to children that snowflakes are much smaller than the illustration.
Writing Style		
Lively, engaging language	Yes	
Accurate terminology used	Yes, with words explained in a "kid–friendly" way.	Use the text to develop vocabulary lessons with weather words.
Appropriate for children's level	Yes	
Generalizations and concepts given (not just a collection of facts)	Yes	
Enthusiasm for topic evident	Yes	

FIGURE 3.2. *(continued)*

(continued)

Guide for Choosing Information Books *(page 3 of 3)*

Characteristic	Notes	Possible Instruction
Organization		
Information book characteristics Pagination, table of contents, index, glossary, additional reading list	Pagination, no table of contents, index, glossary, or related reading.	Discuss with children that these features would make the book easier to use.
Headings and subheadings	Some, but not very obvious.	Point out headings to children.
Clear pattern of organization	Expository	
Text Complexity		
Quantitative (word length, sentence length, word frequency, often reported as readability level)	3rd grade; Lexile,790L; Guided Reading, O.*	Use as read-aloud.
Qualitative (purpose of text, structure, language clarity, knowledge demands)	Introductory. Clear kid-friendly language.	
Reader and Task (motivation, prior knowledge, purpose of reading, complexity of the task)	Children familiar with snow. Following directions to look at snowflakes.	Use for science lesson on snowflakes and writing about children's own activities in the snow.

FIGURE 3.2. *(continued)*

*Note. Lexile scores are based on a book's sentence length and word frequency, not the content or organization (*https://lexile.com*). Guided Reading levels (Fountas & Pinnell, 2005) are based on Genre/Form, Text Structure, Content, Themes and Ideas, Sentence Complexity, Vocabulary, Words, Illustrations, and Book and Print Features (www.fountasandpinnellleveledbooks.com).

Guide for Choosing Information Books

Title: _Saving Animals from Oil Spills_   Author: _Person_   Type of Book: _Expository_

(narrative, expository, mixed)

Characteristic	Notes	Possible Instruction
Content Accuracy		
Author's and illustrator's qualifications Experts in field "Insiders" (if multicultural book) Award winning	_Author has written many science books for children_ _NSTA Outstanding Science Tradebooks for Students K–12_	
References used Consultants who are experts Print and Internet sources	_Consultant from Louisiana Department of Wildlife and Fisheries_	_Discuss with children why this person would know about saving animals from oil spills._
Information current Copyright date recent (if important) Information up to date	_2012_	
Distinguishes between fact and theory Clear what is believed and what is known	_Yes, uses "scientists believe."_	_Discuss with children why scientists don't know for sure._
Text and illustrations clear	_Yes, photos for illustrations._	
Stereotypes used in text or illustration	_No_	

(continued)

FIGURE 3.3. Example of a completed guide for _Saving Animals from Oil Spills_ (Person, 2012).

Guide for Choosing Information Books *(page 2 of 3)*

Characteristic	Notes	Possible Instruction
Design		
Illustrations appropriate for content	Yes	
Illustrations well placed on the page Clear where to begin reading	Yes, font for text different from font used for captions and additional information.	Point out to children that the information in captions and "fact boxes" is important.
Illustrations labeled and explained Captions clear and informative	Yes	
Relative sizes indicated Enlargements noted	No	Discuss sizes of turtles, sea otters, and pelicans.
Writing Style		
Lively, engaging language	Yes	
Accurate terminology used	Yes	Useful for vocabulary lessons and using a glossary.
Appropriate for children's level	Yes, though might be upsetting for some children to see the animals.	
Generalizations and concepts given (not just a collection of facts)	Yes	
Enthusiasm for topic evident	Yes	

FIGURE 3.3. *(continued)*

(continued)

Guide for Choosing Information Books *(page 3 of 3)*

Characteristic	Notes	Possible Instruction
Organization		
Information book characteristics Pagination, table of contents, index, glossary, additional reading list	*Pagination, table of contents, glossary, bibliography, additional reading list including websites; index; additional information at end of book.*	*Could be used for a lesson in finding information in the book and beyond by using websites.*
Headings and subheadings	*Chapter headings*	
Clear pattern of organization	*Yes*	
Text Complexity		
Quantitative (word length, sentence length, word frequency, often reported as readability level)	*3rd–4th grade; Lexile, 970L; Guided Reading, O.**	
Qualitative (purpose of text, structure, language clarity, knowledge demands)	*Introductory level, clear language, with kid-friendly definitions.*	
Reader and task (motivation, prior knowledge, purpose of reading, complexity of the task)	*Some prior knowledge would be helpful, motivating topic.*	*Could be used for environmental protection discussions.*

*Note. Lexile scores are based on a book's sentence length and word frequency, not the content or organization (*https://lexile.com*). Guided Reading levels (Fountas & Pinnell, 2005) are based on Genre/Form, Text Structure, Content, Themes and Ideas, Sentence Complexity, Vocabulary, Words, Illustrations, and Book and Print Features (*www.fountasandpinnellleveledbooks.com*).

FIGURE 3.3. *(continued)*

The guide developed for *It's Snowing* (Gibbons, 2011b) summarizes this book's many valuable features for the teacher to use in instruction (see Figure 3.2). For example, as noted in the guide, the book's illustrations are clear and introduce essential vocabulary in a child-friendly way. By using the illustrations, teachers can show children both how to read diagrams in information books and help them learn the new words presented there. On the other hand, some of the captions don't indicate whether an illustration is an enlargement, which can create possible confusion for children. By using the guide to evaluate the book in advance, teachers can be aware of potential problems and can plan to explain which illustrations are enlargements.

We also developed a guide for a more challenging book, *Saving Animals from Oil Spills* (Person, 2012). Many features of this book make it a good instructional tool (see Figure 3.3). The photographs are stunning and help readers understand the text. There is a glossary for vocabulary words and a listing of both books and websites that can provide additional information. Some prior knowledge of oceans and oil spills would be helpful for students to get the full benefit of this book, so teachers would want to make sure that they provided some of this background. Different kinds of captions accompany the photographs; teachers may want to help students understand what kinds of information are included in the captions. By using the guide to think through these issues in advance, teachers will be better prepared to develop lessons that focus on a book's positive features and to avoid possible problems.

Choosing E-Books and Websites

E-Books

"Interactive eBooks certainly have the potential to transform the way students engage with texts in the classroom" (Schugar, Schugar, & Smith, 2014, p. 6). E-books should meet the same standards as print texts: accurate content, appealing design and format, engaging writing style, and good organization. But there are additional factors that should be considered when choosing e-books.

Schugar et al. (2014) found that some e-books contain interactive features that can potentially distract children from understanding the text. In their study, students sometimes ignored the written text in favor of engaging with the interactive elements. When choosing e-books, teachers should be particularly careful that interactive features support the text and are not just engaging games only tangentially related to the contents of the book.

Websites

Teachers of primary grades will usually want to direct children to appropriate websites for research rather than letting them use general search engines. Because anyone can post information on the web, it is important to choose these websites carefully, keeping in mind many of the same criteria for selection of printed texts. As teachers direct children to these websites, they can take the opportunity to talk about how they chose these particular websites. This discussion can lay a foundation for children to learn how to evaluate websites on their own. (For more information about websites for students' research, see Chapter 7.)

Just as knowing who the author is can help determine whether or not the information is accurate in an information book, knowing who has written and posted information can help the reader know whether or not the digital text is accurate. Often websites will include a link to an author's biography, giving information about his expertise. Sometimes, however, the author of the material may not be given, so readers have to depend on information about the websites themselves.

Websites that are sponsored by reputable organizations will generally have information about their mission, their directors, and their contributors on their home page or on the "about us" page. For example, if one is looking for information about cheetahs and does a Google search, one of the first websites that appears is *www.awf.org*. Connecting to this site, one learns in the "About AWF" section:

> **Our Mission: The African Wildlife Foundation, together with the people of Africa, works to ensure the wildlife and wild lands of Africa will endure forever.** The African Wildlife Foundation (AWF) is the leading international conservation organization focused solely on Africa. We believe that protecting Africa's wildlife and wild landscapes is the key to the future prosperity of Africa and its people—and for over forty-five years we have made it our work to help ensure that Africa's wild resources endure. (African Wildlife Foundation, 2010)

Other sites that are suggested in the Google search include National Geographic, Friends of the National Zoo, Defenders of Wildlife, PBS Nature, YouTube, and Honolulu Zoo (not to mention the South African Cheetahs—a soccer team—or Cheetah's, a strip club in Las Vegas). The organizations' websites are probably more reliable than YouTube videos, which can be made by an amateur and might include some erroneous information in the text (such as what to do if a cheetah chases you!).

Just as in printed texts, it is useful to think about whether the information posted on any website is biased. Consider whether the organization posting the information has a stake in the issue. For example, the website of a political party might very well have biased information about its own candidates as well as about its opponents. The manufacturer of a product would be likely to include only complimentary information about a product he or she is selling.

One of the sites that Google lists about cheetahs is an African hunting safari site. The information given there about hunting cheetahs presents a very different picture of the number of cheetahs left in the wild from the wildlife protection sites! Students can be encouraged to evaluate accuracy by thinking about potential bias and comparing information across sites.

Currentness is an important issue in digital text, just as it is in print text; however, it is often easier to check the copyright date of a print text than to find the date of a posted online text. Sometimes, however, the website will supply the latest update date, the publication date, or the date of copyright.

Although accuracy is probably the most crucial element in determining which websites to use, organization and formatting can also be important for students. Site navigation should ideally be easy, enabling students to find the information they need. Information should be presented clearly, and, just as in print texts, the illustrations should be clear and support the text.

Another caution in choosing websites for students is the complexity and reading level of the text. In a recent analysis of online science texts for children, Gallagher, Fazio, and Ciampa (2013) concluded that the readability of online texts was quite variable and not always consistent with the suggested grade level. Kamil and Lane (1998) found that, even for the sites that were purportedly for children, the reading levels were considerably higher than indicated.

Summary

There are many high-quality information books and websites available to the primary-grade teacher. It is important to choose them carefully for inclusion in classroom libraries and for reading and content area instruction. By evaluating materials for accurate content, appealing design and format, engaging style, text complexity, and good organization, teachers will raise the likelihood of engaging their students with informational texts. Even if books have some shortcomings, careful evaluation and planning can enable teachers to use them effectively.

QUESTIONS AND REFLECTIONS FOR PROFESSIONAL LEARNING COMMUNITIES

1. Discuss with your professional learning community the information books you have used with your classroom recently—either as part of reading groups or as read-alouds. What characteristics made you choose these particular books? Do most of the individuals in your group use the same criteria for choosing books? Are there particular characteristics your group needs to pay more attention to?

2. With members of your professional learning community, examine the most recent NCSS or NSTA list of recommended books and the latest Sibert Award list. How many of these books are in your classroom library or your school library? Does your school librarian use these lists in deciding which books to order? Can you tell from the titles and descriptions

of the books whether they are narrative, expository, or mixed? Which genre appears to predominate?

3. Share with your group members the websites you have successfully used with your students. Can you recommend those that are suitable for specific grade levels? What has been your greatest challenge in finding appropriate online materials for your students? How have you met this challenge? How can you support one another in finding and evaluating quality websites?

CLASSROOM ENGAGEMENT ACTIVITIES

1. Using the Guide for Choosing Information Books (in Appendix 3.2), analyze an information book that you might want to use with your class. Think about what kinds of problems the book might entail and what plans you would make to avoid them.

2. Choose a topic that is part of your curriculum and identify websites for your students to access. What did you look for in deciding whether the websites were appropriate for your purpose?

3. With your classroom in mind, analyze the complexity of two information books in terms of the three factors discussed: quantitative, qualitative, and reader and task.

APPENDIX 3.1

Websites for Information Book Lists

Organization	List	Characteristics	Website
International Literacy Association	Children's Choices Teachers' Choices	Includes information books and narrative books	www.reading.org
Children's Book Council	Children's Choices Outstanding Science Trade Books for Children Notable Children's Trade Books in the Field of Social Studies Caldecott Medal Books Newbery Medal Books Robert F. Sibert Information Book Award	General source for many different book lists	www.cbcbooks.org
National Council of Teachers of English	Orbis Pictus Award for Outstanding Nonfiction for Children	Given yearly to outstanding information book; honor books also listed with annotations	www.ncte.org
National Science Teachers Association	Outstanding Science Trade Books for Children	Provides annotations and suggested grade levels	www.nsta.org
National Council for the Social Studies	Notable Children's Trade Books in the Field of Social Studies	Provides annotations and suggested grade levels; divided into social studies themes	www.socialstudies.org
Association for Library Services to Children	Robert F. Sibert Information Book Award Caldecott Medal Books Newbery Medal Books	Award-winning books	www.ala.org

From *Teaching Informational Text in K–3 Classrooms: Best Practices to Help Children Read, Write, and Learn from Nonfiction* by Mariam Jean Dreher and Sharon Benge Kletzien. Copyright 2015 by The Guilford Press. Permission to photocopy this material is granted to purchasers of this book for personal use only (see copyright page for details). Purchasers can download and print a larger version of this material from *www.guilford.com/dreher-forms*.

54

Guide for Choosing Information Books

Title: _____ Author: _____ Type of Book: _____

(narrative, expository, mixed)

Characteristic	Notes	Possible Instruction
Content Accuracy		
Author's and illustrator's qualifications Experts in field "Insiders" (if multicultural book) Award winning		
References used Consultants who are experts Print and Internet sources		
Information current Copyright date recent (if important) Information up to date		
Distinguishes between fact and theory Clear what is believed and what is known		
Text and illustrations clear		
Stereotypes used in text or illustration		

(continued)

55

Guide for Choosing Information Books *(page 2 of 3)*

Characteristic	Notes	Possible Instruction
Design		
Illustrations appropriate for content		
Illustrations well placed on the page Clear where to begin reading		
Illustrations labeled and explained Captions clear and informative		
Relative sizes indicated Enlargements noted		
Writing Style		
Lively, engaging language		
Accurate terminology used		
Appropriate for children's level		
Generalizations and concepts given (not just a collection of facts)		
Enthusiasm for topic evident		

56

(continued)

Guide for Choosing Information Books *(page 3 of 3)*

Characteristic	Notes	Possible Instruction
Organization		
Information book characteristics Pagination, table of contents, index, glossary, additional reading list		
Headings and subheadings		
Clear pattern of organization		
Text Complexity		
Quantitative (word length, sentence length, word frequency, often reported as readability level)		
Qualitative (purpose of text, structure, language clarity, knowledge demands)		
Reader and Task (motivation, prior knowledge, purpose of reading, complexity of the task)		

CHAPTER 4

Using Information Books
for Read-Alouds

There is widespread agreement that teachers should regularly read aloud to children (IRA & NAEYC, 1998; Snow et al., 1998; Shanahan et al., 2010). Reading aloud is widely recommended because it leads to increased reading achievement, promotes independent reading, and supports struggling readers. Rosenhouse, Feitelson, Kita, and Goldstein (1997), for example, found that at-risk first graders improved in decoding, reading comprehension, and storytelling ability when their teachers interacted with students before, during, and after reading a story. We also know that read-alouds in school increase children's vocabulary (Elley, 1989) and, if teachers have read a book aloud, children are more likely to select it during free reading time than other books in a class library (Martinez et al., 1997). Further, when teachers read a book to their students, they provide scaffolding that makes the book easier to approach for struggling readers (Fielding & Roller, 1992).

No wonder Allington and Gabriel (2012) included reading aloud among the practices that teachers should provide to "every child, every day" (p. 10). Many others, including teachers, researchers, and authors, agree. For example, noted children's literature author Mem Fox (2013) has argued strongly for read-alouds:

> I am reliably informed that there are educators in positions of influence who believe that reading aloud to children is a waste of time in a literacy program. Such a belief is not only asinine, but also frightening and dangerous. Research around the world has proven that children who are read to regularly are better able to learn to read easily, happily, and quickly. (p. 4)

Why Information Books Make Good Read-Alouds

According to the CCSS, "Having students listen to informational read-alouds in the early grades helps lay the necessary foundation for students' reading and understanding of increasingly complex texts on their own in subsequent grades" (NGA & CCSSO, 2010a, p. 33). Yet the evidence indicates that most read-alouds are of fiction (Hoffman, Roser, & Battle, 1993; Jacobs, Morrison, & Swinyard, 2000; Kraemer, McCabe, & Sinatra, 2012; Yopp & Yopp, 2006). But it doesn't have to be that way. Information books can and should be added to the mix, because they offer many advantages.

As we noted in Chapter 1, information books deal with interesting topics, and interest is a very important part of the intrinsic motivation to read. Reading aloud information books inspires curiosity in children, and for some, like Jeremy (the struggling reader in Chapter 1), information books may hold the key to learning to read. With appealing topics, interesting formats, and great illustrations, information books draw children in. As one second-grade girl commented, "You know that book about whales? We learned *so* much about them. I was wondering if you could bring some other books like that I can read about countries . . . like Mexico" (Dreher & Dromsky, 2000).

Not only do young children like information book read-alouds, they also learn features from these books that do not appear in stories. For example, in a classic study, Pappas (1993) showed that kindergartners not only enjoyed information book read-alouds but also performed just as well when asked to pretend read information books as they did with storybooks. They were able to use the distinctive linguistic features or book language of each genre. Duke and Kays (1998) found that at the beginning of kindergarten children were already sensitive to differences between story and information books. But when children experienced 3 months of almost daily information book read-alouds, they evidenced even more skill with the distinctive features. Duke and Kays concluded that information book read-alouds resulted in "fast-developing knowledge of information book language" (p. 295).

Other studies throughout the primary grades, including a number by Pappas and her colleagues in urban classrooms with at-risk children, have shown similar results (Pappas & Barry, 1997; Pappas, Varelas, Barry, & O'Neill, 2000). Primary-grade children respond well to interactive reading of information books, learning their features and easily making intertextual connections among the books they read (Oyler & Barry, 1996; Pappas, Varelas, Patton, Ye, & Ortiz, 2012).

In addition, information book read-alouds offer a rich venue to support both vocabulary development and comprehension. Based on her observations in kindergarten classrooms, Wright (2013) concluded that information book read-alouds were the richest context for vocabulary development during the entire school day. In studies with first graders, Smolkin and Donovan (2001) found that read-alouds of information books resulted in many more comprehension-related responses (i.e., interpreting, telling, personal association, literary association, elaborations, predictions, wondering) than did storybook read-alouds. In one first-grade classroom, 70% of children's responses as they interacted with information books were comprehension-related, while only 30% of responses during storybook read-alouds were comprehension-related. In another classroom, the figures were 78% versus 22%, respectively, for information books versus stories. Thus, information books read-alouds promote much interaction centered around seeking meaning. As Pennsylvania third-grade teacher Adria Creswell observed, "Class discussions are always so much richer with nonfiction."

A 50/50 Balance in Read-Alouds

We recommend that teachers read aloud every day and that they aim for a 50/50 balance of fiction and informational text as they do so. Just as we argued in our discussion of the classroom library collections (see Chapter 2), we believe that if children are to become equally proficient with both fiction and informational text, they need the opportunity to experience both types (Dreher, 2000; Kletzien & Dreher, 2004). And, just as with information books in the class library, we urge teachers to make an effort to include expository books as a substantial part of their informational read-alouds. If most information book read-alouds are of expository texts, then young children will have the opportunity to learn about the features of that type of writing. This experience will help children as they read such books on their own, and it will help them use those structures in their own writing, as we discuss in detail in Chapter 8.

Teachers can take the first step toward a 50/50 balance of fiction and information books by examining their current read-aloud practices. When Dreher and Dromsky (2000) asked two second-grade teachers to keep track of their daily read-alouds, they found that one teacher's choices were 84% stories and the other's 79%. This meant that approximately 20% of these teachers' read-alouds were of informational text. That sounds like a good start. However, many of the information books they read contained narrative writing. For example, when one of the second-grade teachers examined the books she read to her class over the course of a month, three were information books—but all three were biographies featuring narrative writing.

Read-Aloud Logs

To help diversify their read-alouds, we suggest that teachers keep a log of what they read. Appendix 4.1 provides a sample log that includes not only the date, author, and title but also the *type* of book read. By including the type of book as part of the log, teachers can quickly determine the balance of fiction and information books they are reading to their students. To help teachers monitor the problem of relying too much on narrative-information books, we have included separate columns for the type of information book read.

This read-aloud log can be modified as needed. In addition to subcategories for information books, for example, teachers could include subcategories for types of fiction they wish to highlight. Whatever its final form, a read-aloud log serves as a visual record of all the books read. It can be posted in the classroom so that children can see which books their class has read, and how many. Displaying the log also makes intertextual references easier because children can consult the log to refresh their memories of titles and authors they liked.

Teachers can involve their students in filling out the read-aloud log. Rather than representing an additional burden on the teacher, recording books on a read-aloud log can be both a motivating and a learning experience for students. They can also be involved in deciding which column to check for the type of book. Doing so will help children develop their sense of the characteristics of each type of book.

Paired Read-Alouds of Fiction and Information Books

One way teachers can get started in diversifying their read-alouds is to pair the stories they read with an information title. For example, a teacher who reads the classic story *Frog and Toad Are Friends* (Lobel, 1979) might also read *Frogs* (Carney, 2011), an expository book with wonderful photos and fascinating facts. Similarly, *Little Bear* (Minarik, 2003), another classic story, could be paired with *Polar Bears* (Marsh, 2013), filled with factual information about real bears.

Although this suggestion of pairing fiction and information titles has been around for a while (e.g., Sanacore, 1991), it has taken on more urgency with the current emphasis on helping children learn to deal with expository writing. Camp (2000) put her own spin on the practice of pairing fiction and informational text, terming it "teaching with Twin Texts." Among her suggestions were to pair *The Foot Book* (Dr Seuss, 1968) with *What Neat Feet!* (Machotka, 1991) and *Cloudy with a Chance of Meatballs* (Barrett, 1978) with *Comets, Meteors, and Asteroids* (Simon, 1994). Pairings like these can help teachers feel comfortable with informational read-alouds. But, of course, it is not necessary to pair every title, particularly as informational read-alouds become second nature.

Read-Alouds from Content-Area Units

Some primary-grade teachers we know select many of their read-alouds based on their science, math, and social studies units. They report that reading aloud books related to content-area units helps them maximize their time, and also that their students enjoy the books. For example, Jen Boyk and Jess Verwys, first-grade teachers in Pennsylvania, noted that "we [the first-grade teachers] have included nonfiction to coordinate with social studies and science. We don't have time for both social studies and science, but we can use read-alouds to cover a lot of important information."

Content-area read-alouds can help expand children's knowledge. Knowledge is a powerful enabler of comprehension (Neuman, 2010), and therefore knowledge is an important issue for all children. But for children living in poverty, building knowledge is especially critical. Neuman and her colleagues have presented substantial evidence documenting a knowledge gap between children living in poverty and those who are more fortunate (e.g., Neuman, 2006; Neuman & Celano, 2012a). Neuman (2010, p. 301) has argued that, to help build students' knowledge, teachers need to provide "content-rich settings in which skills are learned through meaningful activity" rather than focusing narrowly on code-based skills. Content-area read-alouds can help to provide just such rich, meaningful settings.

Tapping content-area units for read-alouds is not only likely to boost children's knowledge, it may also contribute to motivating students. When Pressley and his colleagues studied primary-grade teachers, one characteristic they noted was that teachers who were good at motivating students frequently integrated literacy, science, math, and social studies (Pressley et al., 2003).

Books like *Dinosaur* (Lambert, 2010) from the Dorling Kindersley Eyewitness series or *Show Me Dinosaurs* (Riehecky, 2013) from Capstone's My First Picture Encyclopedias series are sure to be popular read-alouds that extend a unit on dinosaurs. Similarly, books like *Lightning* (Simon, 2006) and *Weather* (Rattini, 2013) would not only be high-interest read-alouds but also could complement an instructional unit on weather. To identify likely candidates for a particular unit, teachers can consult their media specialist as well as the many sources we discuss in Chapter 3. Also, content-area teachers' manuals and curriculum guides often include suggested titles for read-alouds.

Magazines, Newspapers, and Internet Resources

Another way to diversify read-alouds is to occasionally read newspaper or magazine articles that relate to class themes or current events. Children's magazines and newspapers, such as those listed in Appendix 2.1, offer good sources, and, as we note there, almost all these children's magazines and newspapers are available not only in their print version but also offer online resources. Similarly, many organizations provide websites for children that may offer articles or news items that teachers could use in read-alouds.

Local and national newspapers may also have articles of interest to children. For primary-grade children, these articles often appear in a kids' section. For example, recent items in the KidsPost of the *Washington Post* included an article on "What's for Breakfast Around the World?" (Bennett, 2014) as well as one describing the 50th anniversary of the Wilderness Act, with amazing photos of the beautiful places that have been preserved in the United States, thanks to this act (Siegal, 2014). Teachers can access recent KidsPost articles at *www.washington-post.com/kidspost*.

Read-Alouds Can Help Support Struggling Readers— and Everyone Else!

Throughout elementary school, children's listening comprehension is typically better than their reading comprehension (Sticht & James, 1984). This means that children can listen to read-alouds (both stories and information books) that they would not be able to read independently. This fact seems particularly important for teachers to keep in mind for struggling readers, who are often not interested in the books that they can read independently. Reading aloud information books on appealing topics that might otherwise be too difficult can help extend children's knowledge and maintain their motivation.

When teachers read aloud from books that might otherwise be a bit too difficult, they provide children with the knowledge and familiarity they need to tackle a "too hard" book on their own. Donovan, Smolkin, and Lomax (2000) documented this pattern. They found that even less proficient readers will select and read information books—even books that are theoretically too hard for them—in a classroom where the teacher does a lot of reading aloud. The support and prior knowledge gained from having heard the book, along with the students' high interest in the topic, may enable some students to read harder books. (Of course, as we noted in Chapter 2, it is also important to have lots of easy books available in the class library for struggling readers.)

The interaction around the books during a read-aloud makes a difference for *all* readers, as we elaborate in the next section. This interaction may be especially important for more difficult books, as indicated by Horowitz and Freeman's (1995) work. They investigated whether kindergarteners and second graders preferred read-alouds from an expository science book or, alternatively, a narrative-information science book. They found that whether or not the read-alouds were accompanied by pre- and postreading discussion made a significant difference. With discussion, both the kindergarteners and second graders preferred an expository science book. The second graders preferred the expository book even though they recognized that it was harder and contained more words that they did not know. As Stahl (2012) stated, children's reading level "is elastic depending on the degree of instructional support provided" (pp. 47–48). Read-alouds, discussion, and similar techniques discussed in this book can enable students to read and understand more complex text than they could otherwise manage.

Making Read-Alouds Interactive

For read-alouds to be maximally effective, teachers need make them more interactive. This suggestion differs considerably from what we have seen in certain classrooms where there is little interaction around read-alouds. Indeed, we have talked to many teachers who report they were taught to read a book all the way through with no discussion. Yet, in a study of a science read-alouds with first and second graders, Heisey and Kucan (2010) found that discussion during the read-alouds led to more learning of science concepts than discussion after the read-alouds.

Clearly, discussion during read-alouds is important; however, the nature of the discussion is also important. The discussion during interactive read-alouds differs from discussions that follow an "I–R–E" pattern in which the teacher initiates, students respond, and the teacher then evaluates (Cazden, 1986). Interactive read-alouds are less teacher-controlled, with children both initiating and responding during the reading. When children ask questions, offer suggestions, and discuss one another's interpretations, this interaction engages children in seeking meaning and further motivates them to read.

Children appear to benefit more from interactive read-alouds than from a teacher-controlled I–R–E pattern or from read-alouds with no discussion. When Copenhaver (2001) studied read-alouds featuring little or no discussion or a tightly controlled I–R–E pattern, she concluded that "all students were negatively affected by the limited opportunities to respond and the small range of ways in which to deliver their responses" (p. 151). But some children, typically struggling minority children, suffered even more than the average student under that arrangement.

In contrast, with interactive read-alouds Oyler (1996) found that in an urban high-poverty area first graders actively contributed to the discussion. The children initiated a variety of book talk, ranging from questioning for understanding to personal experiences to intertextual links. These interactive read-alouds enabled the children to contribute their own knowledge to the discussion and to become critical readers who questioned "the teacher, the text, and each other" (p. 157). Similar results have been documented in a wide range of classrooms, including an urban bilingual second-grade classroom (Pappas et al., 2012) and a diverse group of suburban third graders (Cummins & Stallmeyer-Gerard, 2011).

Discussing the same teacher that Oyler studied, Pappas and Barry (1997) noted that, in moving to interactive read-alouds, the teacher reported that "she has had to take risks to give up control, to let it flow, to let the predictions, questions, intertextual links, and other kinds of initiations emerge in ongoing reading/discussion around books" (p. 231). But doing this did not mean she was giving up her authority. As Oyler (1996) observed, the teacher "jumped in to correct misconceptions; she chose her read-alouds with careful attention to genre, language, and theme; and she played an active role in negotiating her students' initiations and understandings" (p. 158).

In short, interactive read-alouds been shown to be effective and motivating in a variety of contexts. We have focused here on informational read-alouds in K–3 classrooms. But there are numerous studies of interactive read-alouds with younger children (e.g., Lennox, 2013) as well as work with stories (e.g., Swanson et al., 2011). Interactive read-alouds have great potential. They offer children the opportunity to grapple with important concepts right on the spot—taking on a meaning-making stance that draws them into the reading and learning. Although interactive read-alouds work with both fiction and informational text, we argue that informational texts are particularly powerful because well-selected informational texts offer children interesting information, important concepts, and academic vocabulary. As McGee and Schickedanz (2007) have noted, interactive read-alouds will be richer if teachers use what they term "sophisticated text"—text that offers much to support analytical thinking. Engaging informational text does just that.

Not All Information Books Need to Be Read from Start to Finish

Just like fiction, some information books need to be read sequentially from beginning to end. This is often the case in narrative-information books. For example, the storyline format of *Pablo Neruda: Poet of the People* (Brown, 2011), discussed in Chapter 2, suggests that it should be read sequentially. Many expository books for young children are also best read from start to finish. Although *Zipping, Zapping, Zooming Bats* (Earle, 1995) does not have a storyline, it also does not have a table of contents, index, or headings that would help readers determine where they might drop into the book if they didn't want to read it in page order.

In contrast, other information books are arranged so that it matters little where a reader starts. In *National Geographic Little Kids First Big Book of Why* (Shields, 2011), each chapter is marked with a question, such as "Why do balloons float?" or "Why do eyeglasses work?" During a read-aloud, teachers and children could consult the contents page and read in whatever order strikes their fancy. There is also an index that could be used to search for a particular topic. These features allow for read-alouds to proceed in the order of children's interests.

Many books for young children now follow nontraditional designs. For example, Dorling Kindersley books, such as those in the Eye Wonder series (e.g., *Reptiles* by Simon Holland, 2013), typically have two-page spreads on a topic with large and small photographs and drawings, each accompanied by related facts. This information is arrayed across the pages in ways that do not conform to the designs children usually encounter when they are learning to read. Children can begin reading such a book on just about any page, and even after they select a page they can begin just about anywhere on it. Designs like these are popular in trade books (Moss, 2001) and are now encountered even in textbooks (Walpole, 1998/1999).

Reading aloud books with nontraditional designs lets teachers help students learn how to handle these design demands. But these books may present special challenges to teachers who themselves may not be sure how to approach them. When Donovan and Smolkin (2004) observed teachers reading aloud from an original Magic School Bus title (see Chapter 2), they found that most of them read very little from the informational part of the book while others planned out how they would incorporate both story and information elements. Becoming comfortable with nontraditional designs and planning out how to handle such designs is important, with technology allowing increasingly attractive but potentially confusing multimodal books with many visual representations. Evidence indicates that, once teachers are aware of the issue, they can be quite effective in helping children engage with and learn from these appealing texts (e.g., Coleman, Bradley, & Donovan, 2012; Pappas & Varelas, 2009).

In addition, to show children how to read these books, teachers need their students to sit closely enough to see the details. This may involve reading these books only in small groups or using big books when they are available. Another alternative is to use a document camera—a device that is similar to an overhead projector except that it can display opaque objects as well as transparencies. When hooked up to a television monitor, LCD projector, SmartBoard, or computer, a document camera enables a teacher to zoom in and out on a book's pages to help the children see exactly what is being discussed. Adria Creswell, a third-grade teacher, uses her iPad as a document camera to project the books she is reading onto the screen in her classroom.

Summary

There is strong evidence that read-alouds are valuable in increasing children's achievement and motivation. Teachers should read aloud regularly from high-quality books. While there is research and long-standing tradition to support reading fiction, there is good reason to include information books as well. Information books offer rich potential for inspiring curiosity and learning. And information book read-alouds are a great vehicle for teaching comprehension strategies and content knowledge, as well as for enhancing vocabulary knowledge, as we show in Chapters 5 and 6.

QUESTIONS AND REFLECTIONS FOR PROFESSIONAL LEARNING COMMUNITIES

1. Ask your professional learning community members to list their top 10 favorite read-aloud books. Together, examine the kinds of books on this list to determine what else you may need to add to your repertoire. If, like many teachers, your group is reading mostly stories, develop an action plan to change things. Talk with your peers, including the reading specialist and media specialist, to identify information books to try. Support one another by reporting on what worked and what difficulties you encountered.

2. Along with other group members, examine the design demands of a selection of information books. To see what kinds of features you will need to be sure that students understand, consider how the text, maps, diagrams, charts, pull-out boxes, and other multimodal visual representations are arrayed across the pages. Discuss ideas for incorporating these design features into your read-alouds.

3. Work together to create a list of paired read-alouds of fiction and information books as a resource for primary-grade teachers at your school.

CLASSROOM ENGAGEMENT ACTIVITIES

1. Think about your read-aloud practices. If you don't read aloud to your students every day, plan a time to do so. If you already engage children in daily read-alouds, examine your schedule to see if you can fit in an additional session at least occasionally. For example, look for ways to integrate read-alouds into your content instruction. Experiment with time slots that could be used more effectively. You may find that children are very motivated to settle down after recess or lunch or to remain attentive even at the end of the school day, if they know that you will be reading aloud.

2. Try using a class Read-Aloud Log (see Appendix 4.1), as discussed in this chapter. Let your students help you monitor the types of material you read aloud and suggest titles they are interested in, to fill in neglected genres.

3. Record your students' discussion when you engage them in an interactive read-aloud of a concept-rich information book on an appealing topic that they know very little about. Identify the kinds of comments and questions students come up with as they engage in seeking meaning. How do their comprehension-related responses compare to those Smolkin and Donovan (2001) observed in their research such as interpreting, telling, elaborating, predicting, wondering, and making personal or literary associations.

APPENDIX 4.1

Teacher's Read-Aloud Log

Date	Title/Author	Type of Book or Article			
		Fiction	Informational		
			Narrative-informational	Mixed	Expository

CHAPTER 5

Comprehension and Close Reading
of Informational Text

Comprehension is the goal of reading. Although comprehension has been defined differently by various theorists, most teachers would say, "I know it when I see it." According to Paris and Hamilton (2009), "Reading comprehension is only a subset of an ill-defined larger set of knowledge that reflects the communicative interactions among the intentions of the author/speaker, the content of the text/ message, the abilities and purposes of the reader/listener, and the context/situation of the interaction" (p. 32). Teachers understand that, although word recognition and fluency may be necessary to comprehension, they are not sufficient. So, teaching comprehension should be an important part of early reading instruction.

The CCSS put emphasis on comprehension from the earliest grades. The anchor standards focus on students' abilities to read closely to determine key ideas and details, to understand the author's craft and structure, and to integrate knowledge and ideas (NGA & CCSSO, 2010a). It is important to note, however, that the standards are not a curriculum, nor do they prescribe how they are to be met. "The standards leave room for teachers, curriculum directors and states to determine how the standards should be reached. Teachers are thus free to provide students with whatever tools and knowledge their professional judgment and experience identify as most helpful for meeting the goals set out in the standard" (NGA & CCSSO, 2010a, p. 4). In this chapter, we present many ideas and examples of how teachers can support their students' comprehension and help them reach the standards.

Comprehension Strategies

Comprehension depends on readers' conscious or automatic use of comprehension strategies. Teaching students strategies to help them comprehend is important— even for students who are still developing word-level proficiency (Pearson & Duke, 2002; Shanahan et al., 2010; Snow et al., 1998). Children who learn comprehension strategies during their early years will become more capable readers who are better able to cope with more complex texts.

Strategies can be effectively taught when the teacher explains directly what each strategy is, how to use it, and when it is appropriate (Duffy, 2002). Explaining the strategy can be followed by teacher modeling, guided practice for the students, and gradual release of responsibility to the students for carrying out the strategy on their own (Brown, 2008; Pearson & Duke, 2002; Shanahan et al., 2010). However, this sequence is far from being a rigid plan to follow in strategy instruction. As Duffy (2002) explained, "Success depends on thoughtfully selecting and then adapting techniques that fit the situation" (p. 38). Success requires that teachers know what the strategies are and when they are appropriate; recognize when the students are ready to learn them; and help students learn to be strategic readers.

Ideally, "teachers and students act as a literary community, using strategies to construct and evaluate interpretations of text" (El-Dinary, 2002, p. 202). Sometimes students will report using strategies that have not been taught. Encouraging students to explain what strategies they used makes them aware of these and helps other students increase their strategy repertoires. "To become strategic, [students] have to learn to take the initiative and *generate* strategies" (Johnston, Ivey, & Faulkner, 2011–2012, p. 233).

Certain reading strategies are particularly useful in reading informational text and can be developed using these texts. (See Table 5.1 for a list of strategies.) The most useful strategies for informational text are accessing prior knowledge; predicting based on titles, headings, and pictures; inferencing; questioning; visualizing; using text structure to identify major ideas; making connections; paraphrasing; and summarizing (Dymock & Nicholson, 2010; Kletzien, 1991, 1992, 2009). These strategies can be used before, during, and after reading. (Note that we use the term *strategy* for what the readers themselves do to construct meaning. In this book, we do not use the term *strategies* to refer to techniques, such as DRTA [directed reading thinking activity; Stauffer, 1975] or K-W-L [Ogle, 1986], that teachers use as part of their lessons.)

Strategies can be introduced one at a time so that students can understand specifically what the strategy is, how it can be accomplished, and when it is appropriate; but the eventual goal is to enable students to learn to "be strategic" rather than simply to know a lot of strategies. This means that students need to be able to orchestrate a group of strategies by knowing which ones are appropriate for any given task or text, knowing how to choose among them, and knowing when they

TABLE 5.1. Useful Comprehension Strategies for Informational Text

Before reading	During reading	After reading
• Accessing prior knowledge • Predicting • Questioning	• Making connections • Questioning • Visualizing • Inferencing • Using text structure to identify major ideas • Paraphrasing • Reading graphs and diagrams	• Summarizing • Making graphic representations

will be useful (Brown, Pressley, Van Meter, & Schuder, 1996; National Institute of Child Health and Human Development, 2000). Or, as Harvey and Goudvis (2013) noted, children need "a repertoire of strategic tools that allow them to delve into the text and work out their thinking to construct meaning" (p. 438).

Although this may seem like a daunting task for primary-grade readers, learning to be strategic can be supported through read-alouds as well as instructional reading groups. Young readers will thus have ample opportunity to learn to be strategic even before they are proficient at decoding. Van den Broek and Kremer (2000) made the argument that, for very beginning readers, many of the important reading comprehension strategies can be taught even before children are reading; in fact, it may be easier for them to learn these strategies in settings that do not require them to decode.

A suggested plan for strategy instruction is to introduce a text by talking to the children about the topic to access their prior knowledge. Then, if it is the first time a strategy has been introduced, provide direct instruction in what the strategy is, how it is done, when it is appropriate, and why it is useful. Next, model using the strategy with the chosen text, gradually having children join in using the strategy as they read the text. As in any reading lesson, discussion should first be about the content and the interpretations of the text; however, teachers can also discuss using the strategy and then review at the end of the lesson what the strategy was, how the children used it, when they might use it again, and how it helped them.

It is important to provide ample practice for the comprehension strategies following the initial lesson. Children need to have scaffolded lessons in which the teacher gradually releases the responsibility for using the strategy to the children. This task can be done by having children first work with the teacher, then work in pairs or small groups before being expected to carry out the strategies independently. As in most other learning tasks, some children will quickly begin to use the strategies, whereas others will need additional practice before they can use them proficiently. It is vitally important, however, to have this practice within the context of real reading for meaning so that children will learn the importance of using strategies for comprehension. Using strategies in quest of comprehension in authentic reading situations will prevent the problem of children who can perform a skill in isolation but cannot transfer it to reading situations.

Providing lots of practice in authentic contexts becomes easier as teachers realize that they can teach these strategies while working with content areas such as science and social studies. As children read these content-area texts, they should always be encouraged to use the comprehension strategies that have been introduced. In this way, they are not only getting additional practice but also having the opportunity to apply the strategies to new texts for real purposes.

Once the strategies have been introduced, taught, and practiced, children can simply be reminded to use the strategies they know. Children can even be asked which ones they would find appropriate for the text and the task *before* they read and which ones they used *after* they completed the reading. It is important to remember that strategy use is idiosyncratic; that is, what may work well for one individual may not work so well for another and what may work well for one text may not work well for a different text. It's important that children have opportunities to learn and practice multiple strategies, but they may use different ones while reading the very same text.

Before-Reading Strategies

Before reading a selection, teachers should activate students' prior knowledge, assess what prior knowledge they have, provide any additional needed information, arouse curiosity, and motivate students to want to read. Strategies most likely to be useful before reading include accessing prior knowledge, and predicting from the title, headings, and pictures. Using informational texts, teachers can introduce and model each of these strategies.

Accessing Prior Knowledge

For example, to introduce the idea of accessing prior knowledge before reading, Sarah, a second-grade teacher, chose to read *Ducks!* (Gibbons, 2001a). First, she showed the cover of the book to the children and explained to them that before they start reading about a particular subject they should think about what they already know about it. She told the students that this strategy would help them be active readers who think about what they are reading and notice whether the text confirms or contradicts what they already know. She explained to the children that doing this is always a good idea when they are reading informational text.

Then, she modeled thinking about what she already knew about ducks. She mentioned seeing some ducks at the local pond, where children were feeding them bread. She talked about the ducks' colors and the quacking sounds they made. She listed these details on chart paper in front of the group. Then she asked the children what they already knew or had heard about ducks and added these ideas to the list. She intervened when one child contradicted something another one said by putting both ideas on the chart with question marks and telling the children to look for the information while they were reading.

As Sarah and the children read *Ducks!*, she referred to the list on the chart paper. If a fact was confirmed, she invited a child to put a check mark next to it. When a fact was refuted, she corrected it. For example, one of the children said that ducks live in the ocean, which the book confirmed; however, the book also added that ducks live in lakes and streams. Sarah corrected the chart to read, "Ducks live in the ocean and in lakes and streams."

At the end of the reading, Sarah directed the students to look at the chart paper with their confirmed and corrected facts. She asked them how they could find out about the facts that were neither confirmed nor corrected. The children suggested various strategies, such as reading another book, looking at the ducks in the zoo or at the local pond, or asking an adult. She asked them how thinking about what they already knew helped them to understand and remember the information.

By supporting students' efforts to access their prior knowledge, pointing out to them how to read to confirm or disconfirm their ideas, directing their attention to other ways of seeking out information, and finally reflecting on how the strategy helped them, Sarah was able to help these students develop a comprehension strategy they can use when they are reading independently.

Predicting

Predicting in information books is different from predicting in stories. In stories, readers predict what will happen, that is, how the story will unfold, what the characters will do, and what the resolution will be. In information books, predicting is used to think about what kind of information the author has most likely included.

As a small group of third graders was introduced to *Slap, Squeak and Scatter: How Animals Communicate* (Jenkins, 2001), Mark, a third-grade teacher, demonstrated the predicting strategy. First, he read the title and showed the children the cover of the book. Then he reminded them that good readers predict what a book is about before they read it. He invited the children to predict what kinds of information would be in the book. When the children seemed stuck, Mark modeled for them how to predict from the title:

"Let's see; well, it says how animals communicate, so I would predict that the author will tell us *what* the animals might want to communicate—maybe where there is food or maybe that there is danger. I guess he will also tell us *how* animals communicate since they don't talk the way we do. Because the title is *Slap, Squeak, and Scatter*, I predict that some animals may slap something to communicate, some might squeak, and I don't know what it would mean to scatter."

At this point, the children became engaged and started talking about which animals might squeak and which ones might slap something to communicate. Mark then directed their attention to the other prediction: *What* might the animals be trying to communicate?

After a brief discussion, the students took a "picture-walk" through the book, discussing the illustrations and adding to their predictions about what would be in the book. Mark reminded them that predicting what will be in the book is a good way to be active readers and that they can always use this strategy with information books.

As the group read the book, students checked their predictions, frequently commenting on particular information that they had predicted would be presented. At the end of the lesson, Mark again reminded the students of how to go about predicting what information would likely be included in an information book. He checked their understanding by holding up *Bats: Biggest! Littlest!* (Markle, 2013a). He then encouraged the children to predict what kind of information might be included in this book. After a quick picture walk, during which time the children added to their predictions of the kinds of information they might encounter, Mark added the book to the reading corner and suggested that the students check their predictions during their independent reading time.

Clearly, children will be able to use predictions for information books only if they have had experience with them. When Cathy Yost, a second-grade teacher in Pennsylvania, reads information books with her children, she makes explicit comments about the kind of information that an author has included. When she begins a new book, she asks the children to predict what the author has included. For example, before reading *Hungry, Hungry Sharks* (Cole, 1986), she asked children what kind of information they would expect to find in the book. Children began predicting specific facts about sharks, and Cathy used the opportunity to make the statements more general. One boy suggested that they would find out that sharks eat fish. Cathy responded by saying, yes, they will probably find out what sharks eat . . . maybe fish. After she modeled this kind of response two or three times, the children began making general statements about what they would expect to read, such as "where sharks live." Cathy reminded the children that they had read other books about animals that have included similar information.

Another approach to predicting in informational text is the Text Feature Walk (Kelley & Clausen-Grace, 2010), which directs students to preview all the text features in a section of text. These features might include headings or subtitles, sidebars, pictures and captions, labeled diagrams, charts and graphs, maps, cutaways and cross-sections, and inset photos. Students are asked to identify the text features, study them, and think about how they might be related to the main idea of the selection. Again, it is important for the teacher to model predicting content, based on these features. Responsibility for the text feature walk can be gradually released to small groups of children so that they can support one another as they discuss the text features.

Each time teachers prepare to read information books with their students, they can remind them of these strategies until the children use them without being prompted.

During-Reading Strategies

During reading, children should be actively engaged in reading, monitoring their comprehension, and connecting new information with what is already known. The strategies most likely to be useful during reading include questioning, using text structure, visualizing, inferencing, making connections, paraphrasing, clarifying, and interpreting illustrations, maps, and diagrams.

Questioning

Questioning is a very powerful strategy to use with informational text, either before or during reading. When teaching students about questioning, a teacher might use a text set, a collection of information books about a particular topic. For example, Megan, a first-grade teacher, used a text set about elephants to introduce a small group of children to the idea of questioning (see Figure 5.1). First, she reminded children to think about what they already knew about elephants. After a few comments from the class, she explained to them that asking questions is a good strategy to use before and while they are reading. This strategy will help them be active readers by reading to find answers to their questions.

Megan modeled how to look at one or two of the book covers and think about questions she had about elephants. Then she wrote these questions on sticky notes and placed them on the table in front of the children. She invited the students to page through the books and think about questions they had. As the students volunteered questions, she jotted them down on sticky notes and added them to the collection on the table. After many questions had been generated, Megan led the children into categorizing them. Identified categories included what elephants eat, where elephants live, and the differences between the types of elephants. Some of the children's questions related to specific pictures in the book—such as "Why are these elephants fighting?"—and thus did not fit into the categories. These questions were put into a separate group.

Megan pointed out that information books don't have to be read from beginning to end, but instead can be used to find answers to questions. She pointed to the questions about what elephants eat and showed children the table of contents

Albee, S. (2009). *Elephants (amazing animals)*. New York: Gareth Stevens.
Bender, L. (2006). *Elephant (wild animals)*. London: Chrysalis Education.
Cowcher, H. (2011). *Desert elephants*. New York: Farrar Straus Giroux.
Dineen, J. (2009). *Elephants*. New York: Weigl.
Downer, A. (2011). *Elephant talk: The surprising science of elephant communication*. Minneapolis, MN: Twenty-First Century Books.
Head, H. (1998). *What's it like to be a baby elephant?* Ill. M. Nicholas. Brookfield, CT: Millbrook Press.
Joubert, D. (2008). *Face to face with elephants*. Washington, DC: National Geographic.
Knudson, S. (2006). *African elephants*. Minneapolis, MN: Lerner.
O'Connell, C., & Jackson, D. M. (2011). *The elephant scientist*. Boston: Houghton Mifflin Harcourt.
Sexton, C. (2011). *The African elephant*. Minneapolis, MN: Bellwether Media.
Teitelbaum, M. (2008). *Baby elephant's fun in the sun*. San Anselmo, CA: Treasure Bay.
Turnbull, S. (2013). *Elephant*. Mankato, MN: Smart Apple Media.

FIGURE 5.1. A sample text set for elephants.

from *Elephant* (Bender, 2006), in which one chapter is titled "Food." She modeled for students how to read the table of contents to find the chapter about what elephants eat and find the page where the chapter begins. (See Chapter 7 for more information about using the table of contents and index.)

As the students turned to the specific page and began reading, they found the answers to several of their questions. Each time they found an answer, Megan would stop and pause to make sure that they understood that the answer had been found. She then asked the students to put the sticky note with the question on the page that answered the question.

Megan showed the students that additional questions could be raised during the reading. She put a stack of blank sticky notes on the table for the children to use to add to their questions. She explained that they might need to read other books, magazines, or Internet pages to find additional information to answer their questions.

As these first-grade students used the text set to try to find answers to their other questions, they soon discovered that not all the books had tables of contents or indexes. Megan helped them skim the pictures and text to search for clues to locate the information.

Using Text Structure

Most children have a fairly good grasp of story structure; that is, they expect to encounter characters, a problem, and a resolution. They may learn this through direct instruction or by countless hours of watching, listening to, or reading stories. Informational text structures, on the other hand, are more varied, and many children do not have the same experience with them as with stories. Yet we know that using text structure is an important part of being a strategic reader (Kletzien, 1992; Shanahan et al., 2010) and that understanding expository text structure can help children comprehend (Richgels, McGee, Lomax, & Sheard, 1987; Roller, 1980; Williams et al., 2007, 2009). Even for primary-grade students, explicit teaching of text structures can be effective in promoting reading comprehension as well as in learning and remembering content (Williams, 2005; Williams, Hall, Lauer, Stafford, & DeSisto, 2005; Williams et al., 2009; 2014).

The most common text structures in informational writing are cause–effect, compare–contrast, sequence, description, and problem–solution (Kane, 1998; Meyer et al., 1980) (see Table 5.2). Another structure commonly used in children's information books is question–answer, as found in *How Many Ways Can You Catch a Fly?* (Jenkins & Page, 2008). Yet another often-used structure, found in books such as *Even an Octopus Needs a Home* (Kelly, 2011), is generalization followed by example.

Knowledge of one particular text structure does not mean that a reader can use a different structure to support comprehension (Williams, 2005; Williams et al., 2005), so it is important to teach each of the structures individually, providing ample exposure and practice. Usually these structures have key words that signal when they are being used, and teaching children to recognize these words is helpful (Shanahan et al., 2010) (see Table 5.2).

TABLE 5.2. Common Text Structures

Text structure	Definition	Signal words
Cause–effect	Describes causes of certain events.	*because, cause, if, so, as a result of, since, in order to*
Compare–contrast	Tells how two or more things are alike or different.	*different from, like, compared to, similar to, alike, same as, on the other hand*
Sequence	Explains something in time order.	*first, next, then, finally, last, all number words*
Problem–solution	Presents a problem and suggests solution(s).	*problem, because, cause, solution, so, so that, in order to, since*
Question–answer	Presents a question and provides answers.	*who, what, why, when, where, how*
Description	Gives characteristics.	(none)
Generalization–example	Presents a general statement and then provides examples.	*for example*

In addition to teaching children to notice key words that often accompany a particular structure, teachers can introduce graphic organizers to help them record information. Children can use a simple organizer for each structure to help them focus on the major ideas from selections and to raise their awareness of the overall structure of the text (Feldt, Feldt, & Kilburg, 2002). Appropriate graphic organizers are introduced individually as books with particular text structures are discussed. As a small-group or whole-class activity, children read a selection, identify the structure, and then fill in the appropriate organizer. In the following sections, we provide examples of these graphic organizers; these also can be used for writing summaries or for reports (see Chapter 8 for writing ideas).

Cause–Effect

Using a book such as *The Reasons for Seasons* (Gibbons, 1995) is a good way to introduce children to the cause–effect structure so common in information books. Although there is description in this book as well, the primary structure is cause–effect, with the author explaining through text and diagrams what causes each season (see Figure 5.2).

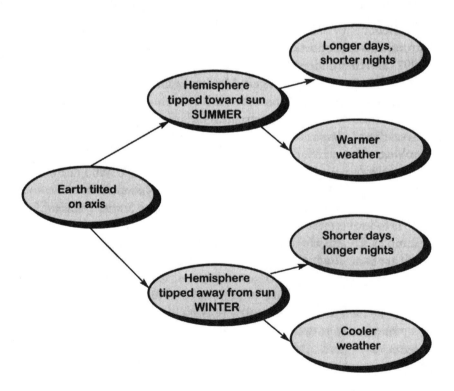

FIGURE 5.2. A sample cause–effect graphic based on *Reasons for Seasons* (Gibbons, 1995).

Compare–Contrast

Using the suggestions in the math book *If Dogs Were Dinosaurs* (Schwartz, 2005), teachers can have children compare sizes and perspectives of many familiar objects. Many compare–contrast books, such as *Wasps & Bees* (Meadows & Vial, 2003), are available about creatures that are often confused. A comparison chart or Venn diagram, both of which show similarities and differences, can be used to help children clarify their understanding of these animals' characteristics (see Figure 5.3).

Sequence

Many information books are written in sequence. Most how-to books that give directions have this structure. For example, *Kids' Fun and Healthy Cookbook* (Graimes, 2007) gives step-by-step instructions for cooking a number of different healthful dishes. In this particular book, the steps are numbered, making it easy for children to understand the idea of sequence.

Another example, *Hip-Pocket Papa* (Markle, 2010), follows the development of the hip-pocket frog's babies from the time they are eggs until they leave the protection of the father's pockets. One way that teachers could make the sequence in this book more obvious to the children would be to list the events in order or to create a timeline.

Description

The book *Dolphins* (James, 2002), written in a description structure, provides detailed information about what dolphins look like, what they eat, and where they live. A concept map could be used to help children organize this information

Wasps	Both	Bees
Thin waist	Found everywhere in the world	Thick waist
Few body hairs	Three pairs of legs	Thick coat of body hair
Most don't sting	One pair antennae	All can sting
Wasps that sting use it to kill prey and to protect themselves	Bodies have three parts	Use sting only to protect themselves
Wasps that sting can do so multiple times		Can sting only once

FIGURE 5.3. A sample compare–contrast graphic based on *A Wasp Is not a Bee* (Singer, 1995).

(see the sample concept map in Figure 5.4). Because many books are written in a descriptive structure, children should be encouraged to create concept maps showing how ideas are related. The resulting maps can also be used for writing summaries or reports (see Chapter 8).

Children can be encouraged to look for examples of these structures as they read informational text. They will find many texts with multiple structures; indeed, most authentic texts represent two or more structures (Meyer & Poon, 2001). For this reason, it is important not to insist on a single interpretation of what the text structure is; rather, encourage children to discuss which parts of the text represent different text structures. After practicing identifying these text structures, children can begin to use them in their own writing. (See Chapter 8 for ideas about writing.)

Visualization

With very young children, it is effective to use a sequence of visualization activities based on suggestions by Fredericks (1986). To help children "make pictures in their heads," he suggested starting by holding up concrete objects in class and asking children to close their eyes and "see" the object in their minds. After some practice with classroom objects, children can eventually close their eyes and see

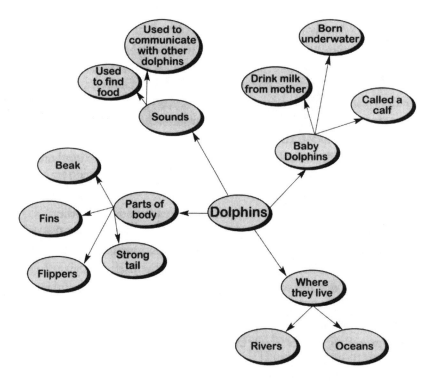

FIGURE 5.4. A sample description graphic based on *Dolphins* (James, 2002).

familiar things such as their bedroom, their mother's face, or their street. After this practice, Fredericks suggested reading aloud to the students a description of something familiar, such as a dog, and asking them to visualize it. The children can change the pictures in their minds to match the dog's color, size, posture, and activity. This progression helps young children understand what it is to make pictures in their heads. Once children understand the concept, they can visualize using simple informational texts with the illustrations covered up so that they have to use the text rather than the pictures for the visual details. A logical extension of visualization is drawing. For example, while reading the explanations and questions at the end of *If Dogs Were Dinosaurs* (Schwartz, 2005), children might draw what they have pictured as a culminating activity for that lesson.

Visualization and creating pictures can also be used to help children follow a sequence of key ideas from a text (Miller, 2013). For example, children could create a "storyboard" with a series of frames for the lessons learned by the snow leopard cubs in *Snow School* (Markle, 2013b). Each frame would represent a child's visualization of what the snow leopard cubs' lesson represented.

Inferencing

In order to make *inferences*, children connect what they already know with what they read (or hear) in the text. This means that it is difficult to make inferences about something they know nothing about. Many adults make inferences so easily and quickly that they don't realize it, so it is important for teachers to stop and think about what is actually written in the text and what "blanks" have been filled in by their previous knowledge. For example, in reading the sentence "Everyone jumped up and shouted, 'Happy birthday' when Robert, clearly astonished, came into the room," most of us would realize that this was describing a surprise birthday party for Robert. However, it is our prior knowledge of surprise birthday parties that enables us to have that understanding. If we didn't know about surprise parties, we might interpret the sentence differently.

Children can be taught to think about what they know and what they can "guess" about texts. Lessons can be developed where children are encouraged to "read beyond the text" to make inferences. For example, Cathy Yost's second graders read "As soon as they are born, the pups go their own way. It is not safe to stay near a hungry mother" from *Hungry, Hungry Sharks* (Cole, 1986, p. 24). Cathy asked the children to think about what that might mean: Why would it not be safe to stay near a hungry mother? The children quickly made the inference that mother sharks sometimes eat their babies.

Kim Gery uses a different technique to help her first graders make inferences. Before they began reading *Looking at Clouds* (Ring, 2007), she had them write down what they already knew about clouds. "Write down what is already in your brain about clouds," she instructed them. Then the children read the first few pages of the text, writing down facts that they hadn't known before their reading. During the ensuing discussion, Kim told them, "You're synthesizing the information, taking what you already knew about clouds and adding the new information. That's what we do to understand."

Making Connections

Making connections is another strategy that young children can use when reading informational text. Children can learn to make intertextual connections as well as connections with what they have experienced themselves (Oyler, 1996). Use of text sets when exploring particular topics contributes to children's ability and interest in making intertextual connections. Having a list of books that have been used as read-alouds (as suggested in Chapter 4) or a list of books that the children have read independently (as suggested in Chapter 9) will help them make these intertextual connections.

When Jess Verwys, a first-grade teacher in Pennsylvania, asked her students to share something about their books after independent reading time, she was rewarded by Dylan's reporting that "It was a good book, but I would have put a map of the farm in the book if I wrote it." When she asked him why, he responded that it would have been clearer—"like it said in that book you read to us." Earlier that morning, Jess had read *There's a Map on My Lap* (Rabe, 2002) to the class, and Dylan connected the ideas in that text with the book he had read during independent reading time.

Clarifying

Clarifying (Palincsar & Brown, 1989) is a strategy that is closely aligned with comprehension monitoring. When children realize that there is something that they don't understand, they should seek to clarify meaning. Sometimes it is a vocabulary word that they do not know; sometimes the difficulty is related to sentence construction or lack of information. It is important that children learn that reading is supposed to make sense and that if it does not, they should go back to the text and try to figure out the answer.

As her second graders read *Special Effects* (Richardson, 2006), Jenn Smith, a Pennsylvania teacher, modeled clarifying with her students. After they had read two pages of the text, she asked them, "What is bullet time photography?" One of the children read aloud the part of the text that defined it. Jenn asked, "You can read it, but can you really describe it?" The girl admitted that she couldn't. Jenn replied, "I could read all the words, but I didn't really understand it the first time I read it either. I had to go back and reread. What really helped me was the diagram on the side of the page. I looked at that, and then I reread it. Let's look at that to see if it will help you." After looking at the diagram and rereading the text, the children were able to describe what bullet time photography was. Jenn reminded them that they should always think about whether they are really understanding the text as they read and that they should try to clarify their understanding by rereading the passage if necessary.

Paraphrasing

Paraphrasing (Kletzien, 2009), or putting the content into one's own words, can be a very powerful strategy to help students monitor their comprehension and remember what they read. Paraphrasing is different from summarizing—and easier—because when creating summaries readers are expected to reduce the length of the passage. It's different also from retelling, because in retelling readers are expected to use the words of the author. To paraphrase a passage requires that a reader understand the message and "translate" it into his or her own way of expressing it. The reader cannot translate it if the passage hasn't been understood; so, it forces the reader to return to the text, reread, and use fix-up strategies to repair his or her comprehension.

To be most effective, teachers should model paraphrasing for students using short paragraphs and lots of discussion about how the teacher is translating what the text says into his or her own words. As students become more adept at paraphrasing, they can practice in pairs, again using short sections of text. Paraphrasing section by section can be used in creating summaries or in identifying the gist of a text, as in close reading.

Diane, a third-grade teacher, has her students paraphrase when they are reading challenging science texts. Using the white board, she models how she would paraphrase the first few paragraphs of a text; then, she has the students work in pairs to paraphrase the next few sentences. She asks for volunteers to share their paraphrases. If there are differences in the paraphrases, yet comprehension is evident, she congratulates the students on their ability to translate the text into their own words. She finds that this strategy is particularly important for students who seem to believe that pronouncing words correctly and reading quickly is the goal of reading.

Understanding Graphic Representations

"Although today's young students have greater exposure to graphical displays and science reading than previous generations, exposure does not ensure mastery" (McTigue & Flowers, 2011, p. 588). Informational texts are particularly rich sources of diagrams, charts, and other graphic representations, but understanding these is not necessarily intuitive for children. Visual representations are especially important in understanding science concepts, and children need instruction to understand these (Smolkin & Donovan, 2005). Often teachers ignore the accompanying diagrams or simply point to them in passing as they are conducting read-alouds (Coleman, McTigue, & Smolkin, 2011).

As children are reading information books or listening to read-alouds of these books, they can learn to understand synthetic diagrams—those that show the relationships among various parts of a drawing, such as ones for the water cycle or the life cycle of a butterfly. Arrows showing the direction of various processes appear to be particularly confusing to children, who often assume they are simply pointing to something important (McTigue & Flowers, 2011).

Children can learn about analytic diagrams—those that show what is going on inside a phenomenon that one wouldn't otherwise be able to see, such as water droplets forming inside a cloud. They can also be introduced to cross section diagrams, showing the inside of something, such as a volcano's layers. Coleman et al. (2011) found that, when children were given instruction in understanding graphic illustrations, they were able to use them in their own writing (see Figure 5.5).

Jess Verwys used the book *Reading Maps and Globes* (Bari, n.d.) to help her first-grade students learn to interpret the colors on a map or a globe. After discussing the differences between globes and maps, she directed the children to look at the map on the wall and explain the blue and green areas. The text had explained blue and green, but Jess asked what the brown represented. The children weren't sure, so Jess led them through thinking that if the forests were green and the oceans were blue, the brown areas must be land that isn't forested.

In a similar lesson, Jen Boyk asked her first graders why they might want to have a map. Some of the children said you would need a map to go somewhere,

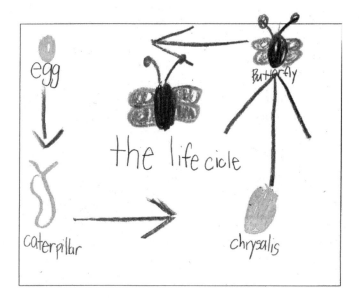

FIGURE 5.5. A first grader's diagram of the life cycle of a butterfly.

but James then said that you would use a map to drive to Africa. This response gave Jen the opening she needed to talk about the features represented on the map on the wall. She directed the children's attention to the map and asked what the various colors meant. Then she pointed out Pennsylvania's and Africa's locations. James laughed as the children decided you couldn't drive to Africa. "You could drive to the airport, though," another student reassured him.

After-Reading Strategies

After reading, students should reflect on what they have read, integrate new knowledge with what they already know, think about how the reading might be related to their own lives, and be able to apply new knowledge to new situations. Strategies most likely to be useful after reading include creating pictures or graphic representations and summarizing the material. The kind of reflection necessary to summarize either in language or in pictures helps children check their reading comprehension. Through the deep processing required to convert text into a graphic representation, children strengthen their understanding and also remember the information for a longer time.

Creating Pictures and Graphic Representations

Using pictures or graphic representations to convey understanding seems to be natural for young children. These tend to come more easily to most children than writing in complete sentences. Indeed, most children are able to draw information before they begin writing it. This natural tendency toward pictures and graphic representations can be used to help children reflect on information that they have learned from reading independently or listening to a read-aloud. These representations can include concept maps, diagrams, pictures with captions, cause–effect graphics, compare–contrast charts, or timelines. Using graphics in this way is an especially effective after-reading strategy for students whose teachers have taught them how to interpret the many kinds of graphical illustrations in informational texts.

For example, children who have read *Snakes!* (Stewart, 2009) might respond to the information by drawing pictures of the most important ideas, which might include snakes with fangs, snakes shedding their skins, or snakes swallowing their prey. Children could write captions to explain their drawings. (See Figure 5.6.)

Many teachers use concept mapping in writing instruction to help children think about what they want to write. The same kind of map can be used to help children reflect on information that they have learned from reading *Snakes!* (Stewart, 2009). In that instance, children's maps could include what snakes eat, what they look like, and which ones are venomous.

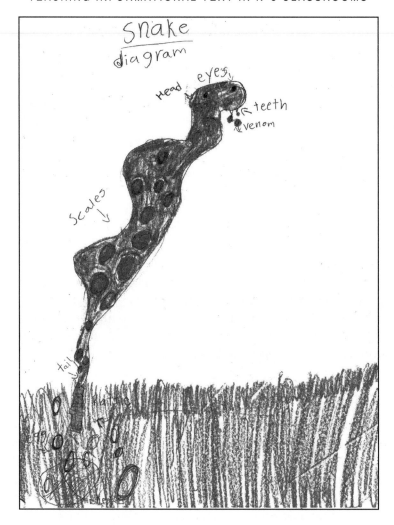

FIGURE 5.6. A first grader's labeled drawing of a snake.

A more advanced use of graphical representation might be for children who have read Schanzer's (2002) account of the Lewis and Clark expedition to create timelines of the important events of the journey or maps showing the route that Lewis and Clark took. Also, the children could draw pictures of particularly important events during the expedition and provide captions with explanatory information.

Summarizing

Summarizing, "the ability to delete irrelevant details, combine similar ideas, condense main ideas, and connect major themes into concise statements" (Block & Pressley, 2003, p. 117), is not an easy comprehension strategy. For that reason, it is better for students to begin with texts that are short and fairly easy to summarize, such as a magazine article, an Internet source, or part of a book. It is necessary to provide a lot of guidance and practice before expecting children to be able to summarize on their own.

A teacher can explain that a summary is a short way of retelling a passage in your own words. If the students have used paraphrasing as a strategy during reading, the teacher can build on that experience by asking them to combine their paraphrasing of shorter segments of the text into a whole, leaving out many of the details, thus shortening the summary. If students are not familiar with paraphrasing, the teacher can provide practice with short paragraphs in either small groups or with the whole class.

Sharon Craig, a former primary-grade teacher in Maryland, has developed a technique that teaches students to summarize. After looking at a text, she and her students generate a question or turn a subheading into a question. Together they read the first sentence, and then she asks, "Does this sentence help us answer our question?" If not, they move on to the next sentence. If it does, she says, "Show me the words or phrases we need to highlight that give us this information." Sharon tells the children to imagine that each word costs one dollar, so they have to be careful not to choose too many. They negotiate the words that should be highlighted and then reread only the highlighted part to see whether they understand the information. If they select too little information, they go back and highlight additional words. They continue in this way until they reach the end of the section, then they reread the question and do a quick read of the highlighted words and phrases to be sure they have answered the question. With first graders and early second graders, Sharon continues to guide the process. With older children, she gradually releases responsibility for the process to them, first through paired work and then through independent practice.

After the students have highlighted the information, they then construct a concept map, using the questions as categories. First, they copy the highlighted words or phrases under the appropriate categories. Next, they review the maps and check off the most important information. Then they write their summaries while referring to their maps. Through the process, students learn to paraphrase as well as summarize.

In Sharon's view "the process is very concrete, and although time-consuming, is very successful. The children not only learn how strategic readers construct and monitor meaning, but they quickly acquire the comprehension strategies for their own use" (personal communication, February 2003).

Based on the work of Brown, Campione, and Day (1981) and Kintsch and Van Dijk (1978), the key rules for summarizing are:

1. Delete unnecessary material.
2. Delete redundant material.
3. Use one word to replace a list of items.

4. Use one word to replace individual parts of an action.

5. Select a topic sentence, or create one if there isn't one.

We do not suggest teaching all these rules to primary-grade children; however, they provide a good guide for teachers in planning lessons in summarizing. Children can learn to use these rules as they work with text if they are provided with ample guidance and practice.

Repeated modeling and discussion of these strategies can encourage children to use them when reading independently. Even first graders can talk about predicting, intertextual connections, inferencing, clarifying, paraphrasing, summarizing, and making pictures in their heads, becoming metacognitively aware of these strategies when teachers and peers discuss them.

Teaching Techniques

As previously explained, the term *strategy* refers to what readers do, and *technique* refers to what teachers do. Popular teaching techniques used with informational text often embed the previously discussed comprehension strategies (Bednar & Kletzien, 1993). For example, K-W-L (Ogle, 1986) includes accessing prior knowledge (what I know), questioning (what I want to know), and summarizing (what I learned). Questioning the Author (Beck, McKeown, Sandora, & Worthy, 1996) uses clarifying, summarizing, and questioning. Reciprocal teaching (Brown & Palincsar, 1985) uses clarifying, questioning, summarizing, and predicting. When using these teaching techniques with children, it is helpful to explain the reading strategies that are being used. Few children will decide to do a full K-W-L independently but can learn the strategies that the technique is based upon. The goal is for children to learn to use the strategies independently when they are reading. Explicit explanation of and practice in connected reading are the best ways for children to become strategic readers.

Orchestrating Several Comprehension Strategies

Good readers use more than one strategy when they read; they orchestrate several strategies to construct meaning, shifting from one to another and integrating the strategies with ease. The goal is to help children learn to be strategic in their reading by being able to access a full repertoire of comprehension strategies.

Teachers can support students' ability to use strategies independently and effectively by encouraging discussions of text that focus on both content and strategy use. Students learn from one another when they are involved in active discussion of their interpretations of text and the strategies that they used to comprehend (Brown, 2008).

Becky Hatherill, a reading specialist in Pennsylvania, encourages her students to use several strategies as they read and organize information. After previewing an information book about deserts, she asked her students what questions they had. After some discussion, the group of third graders decided to answer the following question: How do plants and animals survive in the desert? Becky asked the children, "How could I organize the information so I could remember it?" One child suggested drawing a line down the middle of the page and placing plants on one side and animals on the other. Another child chimed in, "Because plants are different from animals." Becky reminded the students that they had used this type of graphic (T-chart) before to show how things were alike and different. She created the T-chart on the white board, with plants on one side and animals on the other. After the children read the first three pages of the text, they discussed the text and decided what to write in the plants column. Then Becky asked the children to draw the T-chart in their reading journals and to read the next four pages while looking for information to add to their T-charts. She reminded the children, "Remember, we read, do the thinking in our minds, and then put it in our own words before we write it down." After the children had completed the reading, they compared their T-charts and discussed the differences. When children had different ideas, Becky directed them back to the text to clarify the meaning. Toward the end of the session, Becky referred to the question written on the white board and asked, "How do plants and animals survive in the desert? Have we answered the question?" Several children nodded and then offered summaries from their T-charts. Becky and the children successfully incorporated questioning, clarifying, using graphic organizers, paraphrasing, and summarizing.

Susan Smith, a special education teacher in Pennsylvania, showed her group of learning-support students how to coordinate questioning, predicting, and making connections as they read *Rosie: A Visiting Dog's Story* (Calmenson, 2001). As Susan worked with this group, it was clear that they had had much experience with information books. She asked them to look at the pictures and tell what kind of book it is. All the children were able to identify the book as informational because of the photographs. She asked them to think about questions that they might have, based on the pictures, and she modeled for them one of her own questions. Each child contributed at least one question based on the pictures, which Susan wrote on the white board.

One boy predicted that Rosie is a therapy dog. Susan asked him to tell the group what a therapy dog is and why he thought that is what the book is about. After he shared his thoughts, Susan complimented him for making the personal connection and reminded the group to always look for connections to themselves or to other books they have read.

As the children read the book, Susan demonstrated how additional questions are generated, based on the text and pictures. One girl commented that she didn't think that dogs were allowed in hospitals, and so she wondered why there was a picture of the dog in the hospital.

Susan invited the students to provide connections between the story and their personal experiences with dogs and puppies. When the children's connections began to veer from what was needed to help understand the text, Susan skillfully reminded them that connections are useful only when they further understanding— not when they go off-topic.

This group of students was completely engaged with the text. They discussed the issues knowledgeably and were reluctant to put the books away when Susan told them to go to lunch. After checking the answered and remaining questions and with Susan's promise that they would return to the book the following day, the children left the room, still talking about *Rosie: A Visiting Dog's Story*.

Throughout the lesson, Susan and her students negotiated reading strategically, orchestrating predictions, accessing prior knowledge, making personal connections, and questioning. It is clear that these children with special learning needs were able to use these comprehension strategies effectively.

Discussion

In all the examples we cite, and in all of the excellent classrooms we have observed, active discussion of text is a prominent feature. We define discussion as open exchanges of ideas among students and teachers who are "cognitively, socially, and affectively engaged in collaboratively constructing meaning or considering alternate interpretations of texts to arrive at new understandings" (Almasi & Garas-York, 2009, p. 471). This is quite different from the teacher-directed I–R–E exchange we noted earlier, wherein the teacher asks a question, the student responds, and the teacher then evaluates (Cazden, 1986).

Discussion enables children to tell others what they already know about a subject, to share the exciting things that they have learned from reading, to practice oral language, to monitor their own understanding (they cannot explain something they have not understood), and to learn from their peers. It gives teachers a window into their students' prior knowledge, the depth of their comprehension, an opportunity to direct students back to the text if something has been misunderstood, and "teachable moments" when students are having difficulty understanding. As noted in Chapter 4, the discussion of informational text can be particularly rich (Smolkin & Donovan, 2001) when children are interested in the subject.

The discussion of text gives children the opportunity to hear a variety of interpretations and prepares them for further examination of other texts: "The exchange and exploration of ideas that occurs in discussion about text involves cognitive engagements that promote a deeper comprehension and build background knowledge and interpretive skills useful to future interactions with text" (Malloy & Gambrell, 2011, p. 261).

Kate Hartenstine, a first-grade Pennsylvania teacher, uses discussion extensively in her classroom, and her students are always eager to share. She incorporates discussion into all of her lessons, often giving students opportunities to be the "expert" on a particular topic. In a small group of four, she introduced *Trip Through Time* (Pugliano-Martin, 2009) by having students examine the cover and the title. She reminded the students that when they are reading information books they often don't have to read the book "all the way through" but, rather, can find a particular part that interests them or that answers questions that they have. The children whisper read the introduction. One child asked, "What does 'accurate' mean?" Another child suggested looking at the glossary, quickly found it, and read the definition of the word. Then Kate gave each of the children an index card with the name of a different timepiece on it. She told the children that they were detectives who needed to find out about the timepiece written on their cards, take notes in their journals, and then explain the timepiece to the other children.

The children each read their cards and turned to the table of contents in the book. They found the appropriate pages, read, took down a few words in their journals, and then waited until all were finished to share their explanations. Each child presented the information about his or her timepiece to the other children in the group. Some children asked questions, and several times they went back to the text to find the answers. They talked about the good points and the problems with the various timepieces and revisited the idea of accuracy in telling time. The discussion was animated, and the children's pride in being an "expert" about their particular timepiece was obvious. Kate's lesson incorporated content knowledge, vocabulary, the use of text features, comprehension, and oral language.

Close Reading of Informational Text

The CCSS suggest that students should "acquire the habits of reading independently and closely, which are essential to their future success" (NGA & CCSSO, 2010a, p. 10). Although "close reading" has been a staple of literature instruction for many years, it has received less attention from reading teachers, especially for the elementary grades. Most definitions of "close reading" include the concept of reading and rereading complex texts to understand both the meaning and the language used to convey that meaning. "It involves sustained probing analyses, with students reading and rereading to obtain deep and thorough understandings of texts and to grasp the ways texts shape understandings" (Hinchman & Moore, 2013, p. 443).

Many texts and purposes do not require close reading (Fisher & Frey, 2012; Shanahan, 2012). If a reader is reading a story simply for enjoyment or an expository text for a description of something, it may not be worth the kind of rereading and analysis that close reading entails. Appropriate texts should be complex, should reflect the author's point of view, should be well organized with points supported by evidence, and should reflect interesting language use and good organization.

Close reading differs from traditional reading lessons in that prereading activities are kept to a minimum; children read and reread the text on their own, searching for the author's meaning, contemplating the author's presentation, choice of organization, and language, and finally connecting the author's message with their own lives. "Close reading is an intensive analysis of a text in order to come to terms with what it says, how it says it, and what it means" (Shanahan, 2012, n.p.).

Although some have interpreted close reading procedures as not giving children any information about a text before they begin reading it, Snow (2013) made a compelling argument against "cold close reading," pointing out that starting with "engaging questions, appealing topics, and important issues" (p. 19) can motivate students and help them take on the challenge of reading complex texts. Adriana, a third-grade teacher, introducing a close reading of *Sit-In: How Four Friends Stood Up by Sitting Down* (Pinkney, 2010), began the lesson with a very short description of segregation in the South before the civil rights movement. She spent little time on this, just telling the children that before the 1960s black people and white people weren't allowed to eat in the same restaurants, sit in the same sections of movie theaters, or wait in the same areas for trains or buses. Adriana chose to introduce *Sit-In* this way because she knew that the information would surprise some of the children and would provide some context for their understanding of the book.

Following this short introduction, the children read the first few pages of the book silently. Adriana asked the children to talk to their partners about what they had read. After a few minutes of animated discussion in pairs, Adriana asked for some volunteers to explain what had happened in the text. At this point, she was simply checking for comprehension of the text, making sure that the students had understood. She repeated this sequence for the next few pages and then the final pages.

On the following day, after a brief discussion of the general meaning of the text, Adriana asked the children to go back and reread the first few pages, paying close attention to Pinkney's organization, the illustrations, and her use of words. She provided sticky notes to the students so that they could mark sections of the text that they thought were important. After several minutes, she asked them to share with their partners what sections/words they had marked and to explain why they were important. Then she invited comments to be shared with the entire class.

Several of the children remarked on the author's use of different-sized text to indicate important elements of the text. Some noticed that the author repeatedly used the phrase "a doughnut and coffee, with cream on the side" (n.p.). When one student asked why the author had used only the first names of the friends and not their last names, another responded that it made them seem "friendlier" to the reader. One child noticed the repetition, on different pages, of the words *ignore* and *refuse*. When Adriana asked the child to go back to the text and explain, she read, "Others tried to ignore them. The waitress watched and refused them" (n.p.). And then two pages later, "They *ignored* the law and *refused* to leave until they were served" (n.p.). Adriana asked the students why the author would repeat those words. After some thinking time, one child suggested it was to show that the kids could ignore and refuse just like the waitress did.

Adriana asked the students to look at the last three pages of the book. She asked them to notice carefully the language that the author used on those pages. The children read carefully, using sticky notes to mark words that they noticed. During the discussion that followed, several children pointed out Pinkney's use of food to illustrate her points. They connected the lines repeated at the beginning of the book, "a doughnut and coffee, with cream on the side," to the lines "They had taken a bite out of segregation. Now it was time to savor equality. Now they were ready for a big sip of freedom" (n.p.). Students pointed out that, even at the end, Pinkney used a recipe to summarize her points. Adriana explained to the students that Pinkney had used a metaphor linking food and recipes to the much larger idea of desegregation. Throughout the discussions, Adriana encouraged the students to search the text constantly, to go back repeatedly to the text to support what they were saying.

On the following day, after this careful look at the organization, words, and illustrations used to convey Pinkney's ideas, Adriana asked the students to go back to the text once more—this time, specifically to identify the really important ideas that Pinkney wanted to convey and to think about how those ideas might have relevance in their own lives. She asked them to use a different color of sticky note to mark the text in the places that they could connect with. On this third reading, students read the entire text through, marking some pages with the sticky notes. After paired discussion, Adriana asked the children to identify what they thought were Pinkney's major ideas. As the children offered their thoughts, Adriana listed them on the white board. She asked the students to read aloud the part of the text that described these ideas.

After listing the ideas, Adriana asked the children to explain how they were connected to their lives. Several children had marked the page with the phrase "We are all leaders." One girl's explanation was that they were all responsible for preventing bullying in the school, that each one of them had to stand up to bullies to be sure that no one was hurt. Some children marked the page with "We must meet violence with nonviolence." One boy said that they had learned that in their conflict mediation sessions earlier during the school year. Some children said the entire book related to them because "Now we don't have to have segregation."

Throughout the time that Adriana's class spent working with *Sit-In*, student discussion played a crucial part. She gave her students ample opportunity to talk in pairs, in small groups, and in the class as a whole. "Close reading and discussion go hand in hand. It is through talk that students' arguments and responses are presented, contested, and refined" (Dalton, 2013, p. 644).

Sit-In (Pinkney, 2010) is an intricately crafted complex text that is worthy of spending time to analyze its structure, use of language and illustrations, and message. The children in Adriana's class came away from the lessons with a greater understanding of the civil rights movement, the craft that the author used to present ideas, and an awareness that repeated readings of and thinking about a text can yield deeper meanings.

Reading Digital Texts

An increasing amount of reading that we do as adults is digital text, whether as a result of Internet searches, e-readers, online versions of magazines or newspapers, or online communications with friends and business associates. Recent Pew Research Center surveys have reported that in the United States 98% of adults ages 18–29 (Pew Research Center, 2013) and 95% of teens (12–17) use the Internet (Pew Research Center, 2012). As Leu (2013) pointed out, "The Internet is now this generation's defining technology for reading and learning" (n.p.). For this reason, teachers need to include more digital texts in their instruction, thereby helping children better comprehend informational text in its digital as well as more traditional print forms—even in the earliest grades. "The interactive nature of digital literacies, and the Internet in particular, is especially suited to the needs and learning styles of young children" (Forzani & Leu, 2012, p. 421). MacDonald (2013) correctly noted that "integrating online text is simply making this text a part of the range of text used in the classroom" (p. 60).

One kind of digital text that can be used in the classroom is e-books, increasingly available for tablets and e-readers. Many of these books are enhanced with interactive elements designed to supplement the actual text. Although research into children's comprehension when using these interactive books is in its infancy, there is some preliminary evidence that young students may recall more from the interactive aspects of the book than from the actual text (Schugar et al., 2014). Therefore, it is important for teachers to choose e-books carefully, making sure that the interactive elements are directly related to the text and are not just "games" that will distract the children.

Some teachers believe that, because their students are "digital natives" who "have spent their entire lives surrounded by and using computers, videogames, digital music players, video cams, cell phones, and all the other toys and tools of the digital age" (Prensky, 2001, n.p.), they do not need instruction in comprehending information presented digitally and that therefore providing it might be a waste of teachers' time. However, as Karchmer-Klein and Shinas (2012) have pointed out, "Access does not guarantee use, and use does not assure deep understanding" (p. 291). Even if a first grader is adept at swiping the screen on an iPad to play a game or watch a video, he may not know how to navigate nonlinear text, evaluate resources, synthesize, or compose messages.

MacDonald (2013) observed that, "teachers can take some comfort in knowing that much of what they currently do can be applied to helping students become effective web readers" (p. 59). Because much of what is on the Internet is informational text, many of the comprehension strategies described above can be used with these texts. Still, demands on online readers call for additional skills and strategies (Coiro & Dobler, 2007). According to Leu et al. (2011), online reading comprehension

> consists of a process of problem-based inquiry across many different online information sources, requiring several recursive reading practices: (a) reading online to identify important questions, (b) reading online to locate information, (c) reading online to critically evaluate information, (d) reading online to synthesize information, (e) and reading online to communicate information. (p. 7)

Of course, in the primary grades, competencies developed in these areas are generally in the formative stages.

Identifying Important Questions

Questioning is a natural part of learning. Children usually have many questions to which they want answers. Teachers can help their students formulate the questions so that they can find the answers online or in print text. They can also work with children to develop additional relevant questions as they find answers. In Chapter 7 we suggest ways to develop research questions and search for answers.

Locating and Evaluating Information

Locating information on the Internet involves searching for appropriate websites that would be likely to answer one's questions. Instead of asking children to explore independently to find appropriate websites, most teachers identify these ahead of time and direct children specifically to these sites. Teachers can explain to their students how they found and chose particular websites, giving them instruction in how to search and how to determine whether sites are likely to provide the needed information and whether they are trustworthy (see Chapter 3). Even though the children themselves are not searching for the sites, they can internalize the procedures to employ when they later need to search independently.

Synthesizing Information

Navigation—deciding which links to follow, keeping track of the various texts one encounters, and ignoring extraneous information—presents another challenge for Internet readers. In the primary grades, teachers can establish a foundation to help children by encouraging them to read multiple texts, both digital and print (see Chapter 7), and by aiding them in extracting and synthesizing information.

Teaching students how to interpret graphs, pictures, diagrams, and other text features can help them prepare for websites that feature these. Many sites utilize interactive diagrams and graphs. If students have already had experience with two-dimensional static graphs and diagrams, they will be more likely to understand dynamic ones.

Communicating Information

Opportunities abound to connect with parents, teachers, and other students to share projects, thoughts, interesting websites, and calendars. Students can use email, Skype, and social media to communicate with authors, experts in different fields, and other students. Many websites now exist to enable students to communicate with other classes worldwide, to share information, and to develop projects together. Teachers can protect the privacy of their students through settings on most of these sites; still, teachers need to make students aware of the possible consequences of sharing personal information online with individuals they do not know (see Chapter 8 for more information on this subject).

In the primary grades, students can learn about integrating pictures, text, and audio streams for the web. Software that enables the user to create pages utilizing various media exists and is becoming increasingly "user-friendly" (see Chapters 7 and 8). Programs such as VoiceThread, AudioBoom, and PowerPoint can support children as they incorporate sound, pictures, video, and text into presenting their ideas (see Chapter 8 for more information about multimodal composing).

Summary

Given that comprehension is the primary goal of reading, children should be taught to use reading comprehension strategies before, during, and after reading informational text. These strategies can be taught through read-alouds or in small- or large-group instruction. Teachers need to explain the strategies directly, model their use, and provide lots of guided practice. The goal is to help children become strategic readers, able to orchestrate a number of strategies to help them comprehend the texts they encounter. These strategies and additional skills are especially important when reading digital text and in developing the ability to engage with complex texts through close reading. In the chapters that follow, we provide suggestions for teaching children to use informational text for research and as models for their own writing.

QUESTIONS AND REFLECTIONS FOR PROFESSIONAL LEARNING COMMUNITIES

1. Discuss with your group members what comprehension strategies you use when you read challenging text. Were you taught these strategies, or did you develop them independently? If you were able to develop them independently, would it be helpful to children to be taught them? How do members of your professional learning community teach children to comprehend?

2. Share with your professional learning community how you read online. Is it similar to the way you read information books? Do you use additional strategies for online comprehension? Look at Leu's (2011) list of comprehension strategies that are used online that are different from reading print text. Do you use these strategies? What kinds of strategies do your students use when they are reading online?

3. Bring to your group information books that you have used in your classroom for close reading. What characteristics of these books would make them suitable for this kind of intensive instruction? What difficulties or successes have you experienced in having your students do close reading? How did you overcome the difficulties?

CLASSROOM ENGAGEMENT ACTIVITIES

1. Introduce at least one of the comprehension strategies to your class. Did it engage class members' curiosity? Were they able to use it with support? Did it improve their comprehension?

2. Ask your students to interpret the diagrams in an information book you are reading to the class. Were they able to understand the information that the author hoped to convey in the diagrams? If not, spend some time explaining the purpose and meaning of each one (note that sometimes students misinterpret the meaning of arrows).

3. Choose a complex informational text and do a close reading of it. Focus on the author's meaning, structure, word choice, and the connections with your students. Was the text sufficiently complex to warrant the close reading? Did you and your students deepen your understanding of the author's message?

CHAPTER 6

Vocabulary Development
with Informational Text

"Vocabulary development is one of the most important skills young children need to acquire to be successful in learning to read and in school" (Wasik & Iannone-Campbell, 2012, p. 322). Numerous studies have pointed out the correlation between vocabulary knowledge in the early grades and subsequent reading comprehension and academic achievement (Pearson, Hiebert, & Kamil, 2007).

The CCSS recognize the importance of vocabulary development by including the anchor standard "acquire and use accurately a range of general academic and domain specific words and phrases" (NGA & CCSSO, 2010a, p. 25) in the K–5 English language arts requirements. Additionally, the National Reading Panel suggested that vocabulary development was one of the essential components of good reading instruction (National Institute of Child Health and Human Development, 2000).

Although it is generally accepted that individuals learn many vocabulary words from reading, during the primary years much of the reading material consists of words that children already have in their listening/speaking vocabulary. Primary-grade children reading independently are not likely to come across many words that they do not know, so at this level we cannot count on students' learning new vocabulary from their reading. K–3 teachers, therefore, need to be proactive in teaching oral vocabulary through read-alouds, discussions, experiences, and direct instruction.

Unfortunately, a focus on vocabulary instruction appears to be missing in the early grades. Neuman and Dwyer (2009) reviewed preschool curricula and noted the virtual absence of vocabulary instruction. Similarly, vocabulary instruction appears to be minimal even in kindergarten and first grade. In a 2009 study, researchers found that teachers devoted an average of only 5 minutes a day to engaging children in oral language and vocabulary activities (Cunningham, Zibulsky, Stanovich, & Stanovich, 2009).

Vocabulary instruction is particularly crucial for children from less affluent homes who begin kindergarten with substantially fewer known words than children with more socioeconomic advantages (White, Graves, & Slater, 1990). Although Biemiller and Boote (2006) have pointed out that "educators' chances of successfully addressing vocabulary differences in school are greatest in the preschool and early primary years" (p. 45), actual practice hasn't heeded this call. Typically, by the end of grade 2, children starting out with average vocabularies have learned some 6,000 root word meanings, whereas those who began school with more limited vocabularies have learned only about 4,000 (Biemiller & Boote, 2006).

In discussing the importance of diminishing these vocabulary differences, Marulis and Neuman (2010) have observed, "In essence, interventions will have to accelerate—not simply improve—children's vocabulary development to narrow the achievement gap" (p. 301). However, in a 2014 study observing vocabulary instruction in a range of socioeconomic status kindergarten classrooms, Wright and Neuman found that, "not only were economically advantaged children exposed to more vocabulary words than their peers but also these additional words were likely to be the challenging words that are considered essential for vocabulary development and reading comprehension" (p. 346). They concluded that "those children who may need vocabulary instruction the most received the least in their kindergarten classrooms" (p. 348).

English language learners (ELLs) are another group for whom vocabulary instruction is crucial. While in 1990 only 1 in 20 public school students were ELLs, demographers suggest that by 2030 1 in 4 may be in this category (Goldenberg, 2008). The common myth is that young ELLs learn language quickly and pick up vocabulary readily from their surroundings, but the reality is that they learn only *conversational* language in 2–3 years, not the *academic* language that is essential for their success in school. These children typically need 6–7 years to develop proficiency in academic English (Genesee, Lindholm-Leary, Saunders, & Christian, 2006).

So, what can teachers do about these situations? Fortunately, many of the research-based suggestions for teaching vocabulary are appropriate for children who enter kindergarten with limited vocabularies (Marulis & Neuman, 2010) and for ELLs (August, Carlo, Dressler, & Snow, 2005). In the remainder of this chapter, we first address a key concern for K–3 teachers, academic vocabulary. Then we offer research-based, teacher-tested examples of vocabulary instruction designed to develop academic vocabulary for all K–3 children.

Academic Vocabulary

Vocabulary instruction in the primary grades should focus on developing academic vocabulary. Although researchers define academic vocabulary somewhat differently (Baumann & Graves, 2010), most would accept the idea that academic vocabulary represents terms that are not commonly used in conversational language but occur often in written texts, though their meanings may change according to the discipline. These words represent concepts that children will need as they progress through school. They form a foundation that subsequent instruction in the disciplines can build on (Snow & Kim, 2007). Academic vocabulary knowledge influences the development of conceptual knowledge and is closely tied to later student success (Nagy & Townsend, 2012; Neuman & Dwyer, 2011).

Academic language in early grades is different from academic language in later grades. Words that younger children are unfamiliar with may be fairly well known by the time students enter high school. Words such as *contrast* or *actual* may be considered academic vocabulary for a kindergarten student. A middle school student would be very familiar with these words but might need to learn such terms as *discrepancy* or *conflagration*.

Beck, McKeown, and Kucan (2003) conceptualized three categories of words: Tier One, familiar everyday words; Tier Two, more sophisticated words that are of use across a wide spectrum of content, similar to what others term "academic vocabulary"; and Tier Three, words that are rare or specific to particular domains. Children learn Tier One words from everyday interactions with others and with the popular media. Tier Two and Tier Three words are important for academic success but are not often found in conversation or other forms of popular oral communication. This academic vocabulary, however, is abundant in informational texts, especially in such disciplines as science and social studies.

Using Informational Texts
to Foster Academic Vocabulary

Informational texts are rich sources of general academic vocabulary, words considered necessary to understanding across a wide variety of disciplines. This general academic language may not receive much attention in vocabulary instruction in content areas where the more specific domain words (Tier Three words) are often targeted (Hiebert & Lubliner, 2008). Yet general academic language is crucial for understanding and is critically important for ELLs and less able readers.

Informational text typically has a heavier vocabulary load than literary narrative text (Pearson et al., 2007). The vocabulary that seems unfamiliar to children in informational texts exhibits several important characteristics, according to Armbruster and Nagy (1992):

1. Knowing these words is likely more crucial to getting the gist of informational texts than of narrative texts.
2. These words are likely more conceptually challenging in informational texts than in narrative texts.
3. The words in informational texts are likely more interrelated thematically than those in narrative texts.

Hiebert and Cervetti (2012) suggested that teachers should take a different approach to teaching informational texts' vocabulary than their approach to teaching narratives' vocabulary. Because vocabulary from informational texts is likely more conceptually challenging, they concluded that learning words from informational texts requires "extensive discussions, demonstrations, and experiments" (p. 341).

Neuman and Roskos (2012) have urged teachers to teach vocabulary words in related groups, because the words themselves represent "a set of emerging interconnections and concepts" (p. 65). Informational text, as just noted, is more likely to have interrelated vocabulary that is unfamiliar to students. In a recent National Geographic series for young students, Neuman presents a "vocabulary tree" at the beginning of each book. The tree organizes vocabulary in the text into categories that teachers can use for concept and vocabulary development. For example, in *Swing, Sloth* (Neuman, 2013), words are divided into the following groups: *rain forest, animals,* and *activities.* Individual pictures of a sloth, snake, butterfly, monkey, and macaw can be used to help students understand the *animals* vocabulary group. In discussion following the reading of the text, students can act out the movements that each of these animals makes to better understand the *activity* vocabulary group: *swing, slither, call, climb, flutter, lie.* Teaching these words in related groups, as used in real reading contexts, and incorporating physical activity serve to reinforce the meaning of the vocabulary words as well as to help students develop a network of concepts related to the rain forest.

Most books, however, don't have the vocabulary preselected and grouped by category. For these texts, teachers need to think through which words to focus on and how they can be grouped to help students develop concept knowledge. For example, a teacher working with the book *Catch Me If You Can! The Roadrunner* (Chukran, 2000) might identify several groups of words that would be valuable for students to learn, both for this text as well as general knowledge. He might include a group of animals: *roadrunner, scorpion, tarantula, lizard, cricket, snail, centipede.* For this group of words, he could use pictures to help students understand. Another group might relate to actions that a roadrunner takes: *flick, stab, steer, gulp, dine.* These words would require more than pictures; oral explanations, videos, and physical enactments would be helpful for students. Finally, the teacher would want to include the words *prey, predator,* and *enemy,* important terms in this text but equally important concepts for students to have as they learn about other animals. By grouping the words into categories, the teacher would be helping students build networks of understanding as they learn about roadrunners and other animals.

Vocabulary Instruction

Research into vocabulary instruction suggests that children learn words best through multiple meaningful exposures to them within contexts that support integrating meanings within a larger web of understanding. Children need to be provided child-friendly definitions of words and need to actively process words through discussion and application to their own background knowledge. Reviewing words' meanings over a period of time helps solidify children's knowledge of new vocabulary (Graves & Watts-Taffe, 2008; Wright & Neuman, 2013).

Recognizing that it is impossible to directly teach all the words that children need to learn during each school year, Graves (2006) recommended a four-part approach to vocabulary instruction: (1) provide rich and varied language experiences, (2) teach individual words, (3) teach word-learning strategies, and (4) foster word consciousness.

Provide Rich and Varied Language Experiences

Vocabulary can usefully be increased through read-alouds for young children (Santoro, Chard, Howard, & Baker, 2008) because during the early years children's listening and speaking abilities are stronger than their ability to read and write. Read-alouds can contain vocabulary and concepts that the children would be unable to read on their own (Beck & McKeown, 2007). In observing kindergarten classrooms, Wright (2013) found that "when informational texts are read aloud, they are the most generative time for vocabulary development in the entire school day" (p. 366). Simply reading texts aloud, however, does not always result in increased vocabulary gains. To be effective, teachers must engage children— including ELLs—with new words, explaining them in child-friendly ways, providing multiple exposures to the words, and creating different contexts in which the children hear and use the vocabulary (Beck & McKeown, 2007) (see Chapter 4 for more discussion of read-alouds).

During read-alouds, teachers can stop to give child-friendly definitions to words that may be unfamiliar. These explanations need not take a great deal of time, especially if the word is a concrete concept or one that the children may already be familiar with even though they do not know the vocabulary word for it. For example, in reading *A Splash of Red* (Bryant, 2013), a teacher might stop to explain "mending fences on a farm" by simply saying that Horace fixed the fences where they had been broken. Children understand the concept, though they may not have heard the word *mending* before. After reading the entire book and talking about the life and career of Horace Pippin, the teacher might revisit the word *mending*, in the process asking children what other things might be mended. This word might be added to the word wall to remind children of the word and to provide for later review.

Science is a particularly rich area in which to introduce children to new vocabulary through experiences. Even kindergarten children can experiment with materials (such as those that float versus those that sink) that will help them develop conceptual knowledge and the vocabulary necessary to explain their findings (Lauritzen, Kletzien, & Grozdanić, 2001). Observations of plant growth in a second-grade classroom can include sophisticated vocabulary, such as *photosynthesis, nutrients*, and *germination*, as children talk about their plant experiments. Content words taught through experiences help children develop a network of concepts, vocabulary, and knowledge that will give them a solid foundation for later learning related to particular disciplines (Neuman & Wright, 2014).

Teach Individual Words

In addition to providing a rich language experience in the classroom, teachers can also identify specific words to teach. Choosing which words to teach and spend valuable class time discussing is crucial because there isn't enough time in the school year to teach all the words that may be unfamiliar to the students.

One approach to deciding which words should be directly taught involves four steps:

1. Identify all the academic vocabulary words in the text that students are likely not to know.
2. Determine which ones are most important to either understanding or writing about the text.
3. Decide whether the meaning of the word can be determined from the context.
4. Think about whether the word could be used for future word study (such as useful prefixes or root words).

Chances are that there will be more words that students don't know than classroom time to teach them. Choose words, then, that are crucial for comprehension and that would be useful words for students to know in other academic settings. Preteach vocabulary terms if they are important for understanding a text, and students cannot determine their meanings from the context.

In preparing for a lesson using *Baby Sea Otter* (Tatham, 2005), Elsa looked for academic vocabulary that she believed her second graders would not know. She identified *forepaws, grooms, underlayer, waterproof, kelp, anchored, tucks, float, sea urchin, clam, slippery, plunging, webbed, raft, abalone, jetty, prey, spines, attentive*, and *nuzzling*. Knowing that she had only limited time to focus on vocabulary from this text, she decided to group the words and spend minimal time on the words that were simple concepts or that weren't critical to the children's understanding.

Elsa explained that *prey* meant animals that other animals hunted to eat. Most of the children were familiar with *pray*, so it was important for Elsa to explain that they were different words. Then she showed the children pictures of a *sea urchin*, a *clam*, and an *abalone*. She decided not to spend additional time on these words, knowing that the children would probably not use them in other situations and that the pictures provided enough meaning that the children wouldn't be confused as they were reading.

The next group of words related to the physical characteristics of the sea otter: *forepaws, underlayer, waterproof*, and *webbed*. Again, Elsa used a picture to show the children the forepaws and the webbed feet. She used the text "The mother otter blows air bubbles into her pup's brown fur, where they will be trapped between the top layer of long hair and an underlayer of very thick fur" (n.p.) while demonstrating the layers of fur.

Elsa decided that the children might very well use *waterproof* in talking not just about otters but also about everyday items; so, she spent some time talking to the children about the meaning and then asked them what kinds of things they might wear that would be waterproof. The children were able to identify boots and raincoats. Elsa added *otter, prey, webbed*, and *waterproof* to the word wall.

Sometimes an important academic vocabulary word may not even be in the text that the children are reading but is nonetheless thematically related. For example, when Adria Creswell, a third-grade Pennsylvania teacher, introduced a selection about Betsy Ross, she began by talking about the word *controversy*. She explained what it meant, and her third graders quickly understood because this was a concept that they were familiar with even though they did not know the word. The word *controversy* was not actually in the reading but was clearly key to understanding the text since it addressed the ongoing controversy about whether or not Betsy Ross actually made the first American flag by distinguishing between what was factually known and what was legend. During the discussion, Adria used the word *controversy* many times, and her students began using it as well. As a follow-up activity, Adria asked the children to weigh the known facts and the inferences that could be made and to take a stand on the controversy, supporting their position with information from the text.

Additional words that might be useful to teach directly are connectives, such as *otherwise, therefore, in addition, as a result*, and *consequently*. These "signpost" words are crucial for comprehension because they explain the relationships among ideas. They are often abstract and sometimes hard to define, and teachers often overlook their importance in vocabulary instruction.

In the early grades, most connectives should be familiar to children—that is, such words as *because, but*, or *since*. But as the complexity of the text increases, connectives are more likely to be academic words that are unfamiliar to many children. ELLs especially may have some difficulty with these terms because they are abstract and harder to explain. Integrating these words into vocabulary instruction will enable students to read with greater comprehension and write with greater precision (Crosson & Lesaux, 2013).

Cassie, a third-grade teacher, realized that her students might have trouble with connectives as they were reading *A Wasp Is Not a Bee* (Singer, 1995). Because this book contrasts animals that many people confuse, it is full of connectives that emphasize similarities and differences. Cassie wanted her students to understand how the author had used these "signpost" words. She began by writing one of the sentences on the board, "But like all reptiles, water snakes have lungs and must come up for air" (n.p.). Then she asked the students what *like* meant. As she had expected, many of the students thought it had to do with affection for reptiles. Cassie explained that one definition of *like* was that, indeed, but that in this sentence it meant "similar to" or "the same as." So the sentence meant that the water snakes were similar to other reptiles. Then Cassie put another sentence from the book on the white board—"Eels, like all fish, have gills" (n.p.)—and asked the students what the sentence meant.

After discussion, Cassie asked the students to complete the following sentence that she wrote on the white board, "Like other students in the class, I. . . . " She gave the students a few minutes to talk with one another and then complete the sentence. Next, she asked for volunteers to share their sentences. Some of these were quite humorous, but clearly the students understood the idea. Cassie ended the lesson by asking students to complete and write in their journals the following sentences: "Like other snakes, water snakes. . . . " And "Like other fish, eels have. . . . "

In the next day's lesson, Cassie reminded the students about using *like* to mean "similar to" and introduced the sentence written on the white board "Unlike toads, frogs don't have teeth." She gave the students a few minutes to talk to their partners about what the sentence meant and what the word *unlike* meant. Based on the previous day's lesson, the students were quick to realize that *unlike* meant "different from." Then Cassie referred the students to a passage in the text they had been reading the day before, *A Wasp Is Not a Bee* (Singer, 1995). The sentence read "Salamanders, unlike lizards, have four toes on their front feet and no claws at all" (n.p.). Cassie asked, "Are salamanders lizards?" After the students responded accurately to this question, she then asked, "Do lizards have four toes on their front feet?" This question was harder for the students, so Cassie modeled how she knew that lizards didn't have four toes on their front feet. Next, she asked, "Do lizards have claws?" Students were given the opportunity to talk with their partners before answering this question. Although this question was more difficult because of the negative phrase ("no claws") quoted earlier, the students were able to use Cassie's previous modeling to conclude that lizards had claws. Cassie asked the students to complete the following sentences in their journals: "Unlike insects, I. . . ." and, referring to their teacher and the classroom aide, "Ms. Smith, unlike Ms. Brown, . . ."

Vocabulary Techniques

In addition to giving child-friendly definitions for words, providing examples and nonexamples, including the words in discussions, and posting them on word walls, there are other word-learning activities that are useful in classrooms. Activities that involve physical actions, pictures, and discussion can be particularly effective. One of these is "talking drawings" (Paquette, Fello, & Jalongo, 2007). To use this technique, a teacher begins by selecting a descriptive informational text with vocabulary that she wants the students to understand, such as a description of a starfish. Before reading the text, she shares examples of diagrams of other topics labeled with appropriate terms. Many information books have these diagrams and provide good examples of them. Then the children, working individually or in pairs, create a diagram of the topic of the passage to be read. Their original diagram will likely be incomplete with few labels. After reading the text to the students, or having them read it independently, students return to their drawing, correct any misconceptions, and label the parts.

Another technique that can be used to help students remember vocabulary words that they have learned is "motor imaging" (Casale, 1985). With this technique, the teacher asks all students to come up with hand movements (seated pantomime) that would be a clue to a word's meaning after the word has been thoroughly discussed. For example, the movement for *transport* might be cupping the hands together and moving them from one side to the other. As every student in the class makes a hand movement, the teacher watches and makes a quick decision as to which movement is the most common. The class adopts that movement as the pantomime for that vocabulary word. Whenever the word is used in class for the rest of the day, students respond with the movement. Of course, students listen very closely and actively find ways to use the word so that everyone responds with the pantomime.

This technique is particularly valuable because it involves a motor response to new concepts. In related research, Glenberg and colleagues found that acting out the text with manipulatives improved children's comprehension and memory of text (Glenberg, Gutierrez, Levin, Japuntich, & Kaschak, 2004). As Paul (2014) pointed out in her review of current work in embodied cognition, "Bodily movements provide the memory with additional cues with which to represent and retrieve the knowledge learned" (p. 1).

The four-square vocabulary technique (Stahl & Kapinus, 2001) encourages children to think about examples and nonexamples of words. On a piece of paper divided into four squares, students write the word to be defined in the upper-left quadrant. Then they write or draw examples in the upper-right quadrant. In the lower-right quadrant, they write or draw nonexamples of the concept. Finally, in the lower-left quadrant, they write their own definition of the word. (See Figure 6.1.)

Another useful technique, called In the Media (McKeown et al., 2013), asks students to seek out real-world examples of the words they are learning in school in their out-of-school lives. They look for the words they are studying in books, websites, magazines, advertisements, and other media. For each word that a student finds, he fills out a "word deposit slip" giving the word, the context in which it was found, and how it was used. Students earn one point for each word slip; when they reach 10 points, they are given a reward (such as a homework pass or extra computer time). The authors noted that "finding the words out of class . . . help[s] students realize that these words are indeed important to language, not just as a part of classroom exercises" (p. 47).

Teach Word Learning Strategies

Meanings Derived from Context

As students progress through school, many of the academic words that they learn are from reading; however, of every 100 unknown words that students read, only about 15% of them are spontaneously learned under natural reading conditions

Domestic animal	dog cat goat horse cow chicken
(word)	(examples of word)
An animal that is tame and lives around people	wolf zebra coyote lion tiger hyena
(definition of word)	(nonexamples of word)

FIGURE 6.1. A sample of the four-square technique (Stahl & Kapinus, 2001) using the term *domestic animal*.

(Swanborn & de Glopper, 1999). Several factors affect the efficiency with which readers learn new words from their reading. First, the percentage of new words encountered in a text affects the ease with which readers can unlock meaning. Students need to know most of the words in the text in order to figure out the meanings of the unknown words. When unknown words are too numerous, students are unable to use the context. This is particularly problematic for ELLs, who may know many fewer words in a text than their English-only counterparts. Second, the maturity of the reader plays a part. Older students are better able to use context to figure out word meanings than younger students. Third, and most important for teachers, students who have had instruction in how to use context to figure out meanings are better able to do so.

K–3 teachers can lay a foundation for students to learn to use context to figure out meanings of unknown words. Although it's easy to say "Read the sentences around the word to see what it means," this is not a very useful directive for students who are unsure how to do this. Many of us have learned to use context without any direct instruction, and we do it so automatically that we aren't always aware of the clues that we use. Students can be taught to use these clues with instruction and modeling of the process (Baumann et al., 2002).

Definition, synonym, antonym, example, and inference are five of the most common types of context clues and as such are good candidates for instruction (see Table 6.1). For each type, the teacher should model how he or she is able to use the clues to figure out the approximate meaning of the word. One brief explanation and modeling will not be enough for students to begin to use the clues on their own; therefore, multiple think-alouds demonstrating how to use the clues should then be followed by the gradual release of responsibility to students to use the clues on their own to figure out new words. Teachers need to be alert to how these context clues are used in texts the children are reading so they can direct their attention to them.

TABLE 6.1. Useful Context Clues

Definition	Word actually defined within the sentence	A bird's *territory* is the area it lives in and which it defends against other birds.
Synonym	Word that means the same, often set off by commas	Some frogs have *toxins*, or poisons, in their skins.
Antonym	Word that contrasts with the target word	Some houses have *ornate* carving around their doors, but others have simple frames.
Example	Words that provide examples of the target word	Burning *fossil fuels* such as coal, petroleum, and natural gas adds carbon dioxide to the atmosphere.
Inference	Target word can be understood by the general meaning of the sentence.	In France, Horace and his regiment dug deep *trenches* for protection.

Sarah, a second-grade Pennsylvania teacher, knew that her students would not know the meaning of *raft* as it was used in *Baby Sea Otter* (Tatham, 2005), but she did not introduce it before the students read the text. She knew that it was defined in the text, and she wanted her students to have the experience of figuring out the meaning themselves by using the context. After the students had read the book and were discussing what they had learned about sea otters, she directed them to the page where *raft* was defined. She asked them what the word meant and how they had figured it out. Some of the students had used prior knowledge and said that a raft was a "flat thing that floats on the water." Sarah asked them to read the sentence again: "The mother and her baby spend most of their time with other female otters and pups in a group called a raft" (n.p.). Sarah pointed out that the word was actually defined in the sentence: a group of female otters and pups. Not only did Sarah use this as an opportunity to talk about how to use the context, but also she pointed out that some words have multiple meanings—in this case, both *raft* and *pups*.

Sarah's students were not unusual in not paying attention to the specific text when they encountered a word that they believed they already knew. Merisuo-Storm and Soininen (2010) found that most of the second and third graders in their study were unable to define words from context and "a great number of pupils did not pay attention to the text context and gave explanations that the words have in some other context" (p. 1628).

When third-grade teacher Caitlin encouraged her students to learn about animals of the grasslands mentioned in *Amazing Plants and Animals* (Sanchez, 2008), she used the opportunity to explain how authors sometimes indicate the meanings of words by juxtaposing antonyms. She put the sentences from this text on the white board, "The dry season is hard for herbivores, or plant-eating animals. But it is better for carnivores like lions" (p. 9). First, Caitlin asked students to figure out what the word *herbivore* means. These students had already been introduced to the idea of authors' using synonyms, often set off by commas, to define words. They were quickly able to respond that herbivores were plant-eating animals.

Caitlin then asked the students to figure out what the word *carnivore* means. Caitlin wrote *herbivores* on one side of the white board, with the definition plant-eating animals. After some paired discussion, the students guessed correctly that *carnivore* meant animals that eat meat. Caitlin probed their responses by asking how they knew the definition. Students were able to figure out that it would be different from herbivores because "it's better for them" and "the words sound alike at the end." Caitlin then wrote *carnivores* and its definition on the other side of the white board. She pointed out to the students that they used the contrast between the dry season being hard for herbivores but better for carnivores. She reminded them that the connecting word *but* often meant that an opposite would follow. The ensuing discussion among the students was to figure out why the dry season would be harder for herbivores than for carnivores. During the discussion, the words were used many times, further reinforcing these new vocabulary terms.

Teaching Students to Use Morphology to Determine Meanings

Along with context, students can be taught to use word parts to help them unlock the meaning of new words (Baumann et al., 2002; Kieffer & Lesaux, 2007). Prefixes, suffixes, and root words provide clues that students can use to figure out unknown words that they come across in their reading. Nagy and Anderson (1984) estimated that for every word known by a child who is able to apply morphology and context, an additional one to three words should be understandable. According to Dehaene (2009), mature readers quickly and unconsciously focus on the morphemes of words as they move from vision to meaning.

The earliest focus on word parts is inflectional endings used to make plurals (*-s, -es*), change tenses (*-ed*), or create comparatives and superlatives (*-er, -est*). Additionally, young children usually understand that adding *-er* will indicate a person who does something, for example, *writer, reader, climber*. Beyond these simple uses of morphemes, children can be taught to look for prefixes, suffixes, and root words that carry meaning.

Using word parts to help figure out meaning can be modeled for students and treated as a problem-solving exercise, such as, "If the word is *unreachable* and I know what *reachable* means, I can figure out that *unreachable* is not reachable." Meanings of prefixes, suffixes, and roots are best taught within a clear context. Instead of asking students to memorize a list of prefixes, suffixes, and roots, a key word can help them remember the meaning. For example, instead of requiring that students memorize *sub-* as meaning under, have them remember the word *submarine* and visualize it under the water. The meaning of *super-* (over, above) can be remembered by thinking of Superman flying over the city.

Of course, not every prefix, suffix, and root word can or should be taught, especially in the lower grades. It is important to decide which ones offer the greatest impact for study. Some of the most useful ones are the "not" prefixes, such as *un-, dis-, in-,* and *im-*. (Notice that *un-* and *dis-* do not always mean "not"; often they mean the opposite of the root that they are connected to. For example, *dismount* doesn't mean "not to mount" but, rather, to get off something that you had previously mounted. Similarly, *disconnect* doesn't mean "not to connect" but, rather, to remove the connection from something previously connected. If you "untie" a knot, it doesn't mean that you do not tie it; it means that you change it from being tied.) The prefix *in-* can also mean "into," and so this will need to be taught by using a different key word to make it clear to students. Time-related prefixes such as *pre-, mid-,* and *post-* are also useful, as are place-related prefixes such as *sub-, super-, inter-,* and *trans-*, and number-related ones such as *uni-, mono-, multi-, bi-,* and *tri-*. Other useful prefixes include *re-, ex-, co-,* and *semi-*. (See Table 6.2.)

Suffixes often help readers with the part of speech and role in the sentence of the word in question, though without instruction sophisticated knowledge of them is relatively late in developing (Nippold & Sun, 2008). Young students can learn

TABLE 6.2. Useful Prefixes, Root Words, and Suffixes

Prefixes	Root words	Suffixes
un-	*geo*	*-s*
dis-	*rupt*	*-es*
in-	*phon*	*-er*
im-	*bio*	*-est*
pre-	*meter*	*-ment*
mid-	*astro*	*-ness*
post-	*graph*	*-ly*
uni-	*port*	*-or*
mono-		*-ist*
bi-		*-able (-ible)*
tri-		*-ful*
re-		
ex-		
co-		
semi-		
micro-		
multi-		

that *-ment* and *-ness* usually indicate nouns and *-or*, *-er*, and *-ist* indicate nouns that are people. The ending *-ly* usually marks an adverb and *-able (-ible)* and *-ful* are adjective markers that carry their meaning in their spelling, "able" and "full."

ELLs can benefit from knowing the relationship between suffixes in their native language and suffixes in English. For example, in Spanish, *-mente* corresponds to the English *-ly*. Pointing this out to Spanish-speaking ELLs, especially in the context of teaching cognates, can help them learn to use morphology to increase their vocabulary knowledge (August et al., 2005; Kieffer & Lesaux, 2007).

Root words are more problematic for students because their meaning can seem a far stretch in some words. Still, some roots are regular enough that they might be helpful to students. *Geo* (earth), *rupt* (break), *phon* (sound), *port* (carry), *bio* (life), *meter* (measure), and *astro* (stars) are all candidates for teaching students about root words.

Olivia introduced the root word *port* to her third-grade classroom after talking about how the word *transport* was used in a text they had just read. She blocked the root *port* from the rest of the word as it was written on the white board. Then she asked students to think about whether they knew of any other words that had *port* in them. As the students suggested words, she wrote them on the board, creating a word matrix (see Figure 6.2) with *port* in the middle, prefixes on the left, and suffixes on the right. For the compound word *airport*, she wrote *air-* in the left column but explained that it was part of a compound word, not really a prefix.

Olivia told the children that now that they knew that *transport* meant to carry things from one place to another, they could try to figure out what the root word *port* meant. The children had identified *portable, airport, report,* and *port.*

Prefix	Root	Suffix
trans-	port	-able
re-		-er
ex-		
im-		
air- (technically not a prefix)		

FIGURE 6.2. A sample of a vocabulary matrix using the root word *port.*

Olivia added *import, export,* and *porter.* She asked the children to work in pairs to figure out the likely meaning of *port.* After several minutes of lively discussion, she invited children to share not only the meaning they had decided upon but also their process in figuring it out. Some of the children suggested that *port* probably meant "move"; others suggested "carry."

Olivia had told the children in previous lessons that sometimes root words were hard to figure out. Her students said they couldn't figure out how *report* meant carry, and they didn't understand the word *porter,* a new word for many of the students. Olivia led them through the process of thinking about other words that ended in *-er,* such as *writer, painter, thinker,* and the students realized that *porter* was someone who carried things. Olivia admitted that *report* was hard to figure out, but that it probably came from the idea that a *report* was information that was carried back.

Instruction in morphology, integrated into other literacy practices, can have positive effects on children's spelling, comprehension, and awareness of words. This benefit is especially powerful for younger or less able readers (Bowers, Kirby, & Deacon, 2010).

Use of the Dictionary and Thesaurus

Using dictionary definitions to teach vocabulary is not very effective if a teacher simply assigns a list of words and asks students to look them up and memorize the definitions. As Nagy (1988) pointed out, the dictionary definition is probably the last thing that a student needs to know about a word. We use words all the time whose meanings are somewhat fuzzy, words that we would be hard-pressed to give dictionary definitions for—yet words that we feel comfortable using in oral and written language. So, knowing a dictionary definition is not crucial for "knowing" a word.

"Dictionaries can be useful, but looking up words in a dictionary will not support students in developing their own rich mental lexicons" (Kucan, 2012, p. 361). Still, students need to learn to use dictionaries and thesauruses as part of vocabulary study. Using a dictionary to look up the meaning of a word can help students crystallize the meaning of the word and can help them distinguish the word from other similar words.

Foster Word Consciousness

"The classrooms of teachers who support the vocabulary development of their students are *energized verbal environments*—environments in which words are not only noticed and appreciated, but also savored and celebrated" (Kucan, 2012, p. 361). The classroom environment should encourage students to develop word consciousness—to think about words, to want to know about their meanings and their uses. Word consciousness invites students to be aware of the power of the words around them, how they are used, what their emotional connotations are, and how they may change in formal versus informal contexts (Graves & Watts-Taffe, 2008).

Read-alouds can introduce students to general academic language and be used to increase word consciousness. Following a read-aloud of a rich text, a teacher can point out the effective use of language, word choices, metaphors, and similes. Students will begin to note interesting uses of language as they listen. A collection of words and phrases from read-alouds and other model texts can be posted in the classroom.

Jess Verwys, a first-grade Pennsylvania teacher, encourages her students to listen for interesting words as she reads aloud each morning. Her read-alouds are often information books and are usually connected to other lessons that she has planned throughout the day. She uses the read-alouds to briefly explain some of the vocabulary that she believes her young students will be unfamiliar with. Jess knows that her vocabulary focus is effective when students begin to use the words that she has explained. When Claire reported to the class that her independent reading book was "about cherishing the earth," Jess knew that Claire had learned this word from the previous day's read-aloud. She asked her what *cherish* meant, and Claire responded, "to take good care of it and love it."

Word consciousness can also be encouraged throughout the school day by drawing students' attention to engaging words or words used in unusual ways in print, digital, or oral texts. Similar to the In the Media technique previously described (McKeown et al., 2013), students can be encouraged to find words outside of school that they find appealing to share with the class. A bulletin board with student-selected words is a good way to highlight the words that they find to be particularly interesting or useful. Students should provide a context in which the word was used along with a student-friendly definition.

Students should also have ample time to experiment with language as authors. Writing instruction can include examples of rich language use, and students can be encouraged to revise by choosing precise words and figurative language to express their ideas. Informational texts as read-alouds or shared reading can be used as writing models to help students write with effective language. (See Chapter 8 for more suggestions about writing.)

Teachers can increase word consciousness and learning by using varied vocabulary in their discussions with and directions to students. Much oral language uses only Tier One words, but teachers can make a conscious effort to include Tier Two words in their daily interactions with students. For example, a teacher can focus on words that are similar to *walk* by asking students to *march* to their desks, *amble* to their desks, or *strut* to their desks to help reinforce slightly varied meanings and to help students internalize new vocabulary.

Using Digital Resources for Vocabulary Development

Years ago, the National Reading Panel found that the use of computers in vocabulary instruction was a promising trend (National Institute of Child Health and Human Development, 2000). Since that time, the use of digital texts, access to the Internet (where informational text is prevalent), and more widespread use of technology have all increased the possibility and effectiveness of vocabulary instruction.

Multimedia vocabulary instruction, including sound, video, and dynamic interaction, may be particularly effective in helping children understand and remember vocabulary concepts. "Multimedia enhancements may provide children with more robust nonverbal information than that presented in the static pictures in storybooks and allow children to more effectively use their nonverbal processing system to support their verbal processing of the storybook content" (Silverman & Hines, 2009, p. 306). Although all children benefit from multiple exposures to words in different contexts, multimedia presentations are particularly effective for ELLs (Silverman & Hines, 2009).

Even without visual and sound enhancements, many programs and websites feature the ability to click on a word and immediately have a definition, a pronunciation, and a further example of how the word is used. Also available are word reference tools that can be used with any digital text, and it is relatively easy to bookmark dictionaries that students can access while they are reading digital text. Students can look words up with one click of the mouse. This provides immediate support and is less disruptive to comprehension than using a print dictionary.

Dalton and Grisham (2011) described using web applications that allow students to create "word clouds" based on the frequency of words encountered in a text. Using Wordle (*www.wordle.net*), students paste text into the applet and decide which layout they want, what colors are effective, and which font best matches the content. These word clouds can be used as a prereading activity to prepare students to think about what a text may be about, or they can be used by the students to show comprehension. Another website that can be used to make word clouds is WordSift (*www.wordsift.com*). In this program, clicking on a word shows a listing of the sentences from the text that include the word. This program also indicates which words are academic words.

Numerous websites have vocabulary games that provide a fun way to learn and practice vocabulary. My Vocabulary (*www.MyVocabulary.com*) offers a variety of vocabulary games and activities, as does *www.vocabulary.com*. In addition to crossword puzzles, word searches, and picture–word matches, there are activities that focus on prefixes, suffixes, and root words.

Students can also use media to demonstrate their vocabulary knowledge and share it with their classmates. Describing a multimedia glossary that students could create by using PowerPoint, Dalton and Grisham (2011) developed a template for the students to use that included "a space for the word, a short definition, an explanation for why the word is important, a graphic, an audio recording or sound, and a source" (p. 311). The students had to think deeply to show how the graphic, the sound, and the explanation of the word's importance all related to its meaning.

Technology changes quickly. As Leu (2000) pointed out, sometimes technology changes even before information about it can appear in print. Additional possibilities for vocabulary development will assuredly continue to be available.

Summary

Vocabulary development is vitally important in the K–3 classroom. "Dependence on a single vocabulary instruction method will not result in optimal learning" (National Institute of Child Health and Human Development, 2000, p. 4-4). Teachers should provide rich and varied language experiences, teach individual words (especially academic vocabulary), teach word-learning strategies, and foster word consciousness in their classrooms. This multifaceted approach will benefit ELLs as well as English-only speakers.

QUESTIONS AND REFLECTIONS FOR PROFESSIONAL LEARNING COMMUNITIES

1. Discuss with your professional learning community the most recent vocabulary word you learned. How did you learn it? Reading? Talking to friends? Hearing it on television or radio? In a professional meeting? How comfortable are you using it in oral or written language? How can you apply your experience in learning words to your classroom?

2. Define the word *marriage*. Compare your definition to those of your colleagues. Look the word up in the dictionary. Even though your definitions may vary from one another's and from the dictionary, you use the word easily and comfortably in everyday interactions.

What does this tell you about the importance of your students' knowing official diction-ary definitions? When it is important for your students to access dictionaries to find the "exact" definition?

3. As a group, decide which prefixes, suffixes, and root words are most appropriate for the grade level you are teaching. Why are these the most important ones? What experiences have you had in teaching morphology? How can you support one another as you develop lessons incorporating word parts?

CLASSROOM ENGAGEMENT ACTIVITIES

1. Create a word wall with alternative words for *nice* (or another often used word), and dis-cuss opportunities to use these more interesting exact words with your students. Do you see an increase in the use of these words in your students' oral and/or written language?

2. Try McKeown et al.'s In the Media (2013) technique with your classroom for 1 week. Does it increase your students' motivation for finding and learning new vocabulary words?

3. Try physical engagement with words you want your students to learn. Use the "motor imaging" technique, that is, have students act out word meanings. An interesting activity is to have groups of students act out word meanings (from a vocabulary list) in panto-mime (similar to charades) and have the class guess what word they are acting out.

CHAPTER 7

Using Information Books and Internet Resources for Research

As noted in Chapter 1, standards in the United States and other countries require that primary-grade children be able to read both fiction and informational text, and, moreover, current standardized tests for primary-grade children reflect these standards by including much informational text. But today's young children are expected to do more than simply read and comprehend informational material. They must be able to locate information, compare and contrast what they find in different sources, and integrate information from multiple sources in reports. Additionally, children are expected to carry out such tasks in both print and digital media.

These demands are evident in the CCSS, which follow the lead of earlier influential work such as the report of the Committee on the Prevention of Reading Difficulties in Young Children (Snow et al., 1998). Based on an intensive review of research, the Committee concluded that kindergarteners should be familiar with a broad range of text including expository books (Snow et al., 1998) and that first through third graders should be able to read grade-appropriate fiction and nonfiction. In addition, second graders should be able to read informational text "for answers to specific questions" and be able to "connect and compare information across nonfiction selections" (p. 82), and that third graders should be able to combine "information from multiple sources in writing reports" (p. 83). By the time children leave third grade, they must be "capable—independently and productively—of reading to learn" (p. 207).

The CCSS parallel these expectations, stating that students who meet the standards "demonstrate independence" (NGA & CCSSO, 2010a, p. 7). Among other characteristics, students should "become self-directed learners, effectively seeking out and using resources to assist them, including teachers, peers, and print and digital reference materials" (p. 7). Points relevant to developing independence in "seeking out and using resources" occur throughout the CCSS. For example, as part of the anchor standards for writing, students are expected to engage in "Research to Build and Present Knowledge" (p. 18). They are expected to be able to "conduct short as well as more sustained research projects" and to "gather relevant information from multiple print and digital sources, assess the credibility and accuracy of each source, and integrate the information while avoiding plagiarism" (p. 18).

Clearly, the CCSS want students to "develop the capacity to build knowledge on a subject through research projects" (p. 18). Furthermore, according to the CCSS, students who meet the standards will "use technology and digital media strategically and capably" (p. 7). Specifically, students who meet the standards are able to "tailor their searches online to acquire useful information efficiently, and they integrate what they learn using technology with what they learn offline. They are familiar with the strengths and limitations of various technological tools and mediums and can select and use those best suited to their communication goals" (p. 7).

High Expectations but Much Potential for Motivation

If students are to be capable of reading to learn, of demonstrating independence, of engaging in research projects, and of using technology strategically, then teachers must begin developing these abilities in the early grades. These expectations may appear challenging for primary-grade teachers. But teachers can take comfort in the fact that helping children achieve these outcomes can be done in ways that are highly motivating.

A wealth of research with primary-grade children shows that they can meet these expectations while enhancing their achievement and motivation. Mallett (1992) described children as young as 5 participating in class projects in which they became young "experts" as they sought information on topics of special interest to them. Guthrie et al. (2004) found that integrated reading/science projects enhanced third graders' comprehension and motivation to read. Moreover, both Mallett and Guthrie et al. noted that inquiry projects benefited not just capable readers but also struggling and reluctant readers.

More recent studies continue to confirm such findings. For example, Maloch and Horsey (2013) profiled an inquiry-focused second-grade classroom in a culturally, linguistically, and economically diverse school; Guccione (2011) focused on ELLs' experience in first-grade classrooms where teachers integrated literacy and inquiry; and Halvorsen et al. (2012) investigated the use of a project-based approach to social studies and content-area literacy in second-grade classrooms.

In all of these studies, as well as others, young children were found to be both successful and motivated.

Rather than viewing expectations solely as a challenge, therefore, teachers can consider them in light of their potential to engage children's curiosity and desire to know. In this chapter, we explore how to help young children learn to use information books and Internet resources so that they can find the information they need and want.

Teaching Children about Information Book Features

Even in kindergarten, children have long been expected to know "the parts of a book and their function" (Snow et al., 1998, p. 80). The CCSS concur. According to the Reading Standards for Informational Text, kindergarteners should be able to "identify the front cover, back cover, and title page of a book" (NGA & CCSSO, 2010a, p. 13). But, as children progress from first through third grade, they need to know and be able to use many more features of information books as well as digital sources. The CCSS call for first graders to "know and use various text features (e.g., headings, tables of contents, glossaries, electronic menus, icons) to locate key facts or information in a text" (p. 13), for second graders to "know and use various text features (e.g., captions, bold print, subheadings, glossaries, indexes, electronic menus, icons) to locate key facts or information in a text efficiently" (p. 13), and for third graders to "use text features and search tools (e.g., key words, sidebars, hyperlinks) to locate information relevant to a given topic efficiently" (p. 14).

Later in this chapter, we will discuss various Internet features. In this section, we focus on text features in books. Many features of information books are useful to children as they seek answers to their questions, including such features as the table of contents, headings and subheadings, and glossaries and indexes (see Figure 7.1). Many books also have maps, diagrams, illustrations, captions, and boldface for specialized terms. Sometimes there are brief descriptions of the contents or purpose-setting questions on the front or back covers that may help children decide whether a book is likely to contain what they are seeking. In addition, authors may include supplemental information that extends the content they have presented as well notes on sources and acknowledgments to experts, which may help children evaluate the trustworthiness of what they are reading.

To introduce children to book features, teachers can use the highly effective technique of read-alouds (see Chapter 4). For example, for a unit on penguins, Liz, a second-grade teacher in Maryland, read a selection of books about the topic. Each of these books had different search features. One book, *The Emperor's Egg* (Jenkins, 1999), provides many facts while telling the story of a male emperor penguin who hatches the egg his mate has laid. Because *The Emperor's Egg* is a

- Table of contents
- Glossary
- Index
- Headings and subheadings
- Maps
- Diagrams
- Illustrations
- Captions
- Boldface for specialized terms
- Cover information (e.g., descriptions of content or purpose-setting questions)
- Author's note
- Supplements to the main text
- Acknowledgments to experts, consultants
- Suggestions for further reading

FIGURE 7.1. Common features in information books.

narrative-information book, Liz read it from start to finish. The book provoked much interest in finding out more about penguins. As they discussed this book, the children posed questions that they wanted to answer. Liz then brought in other books about penguins that might offer answers. Sharing these books during read-alouds allowed her to explain and model search features.

One of these books, *Penguins* (Robinson, 1997), an expository information book, contained a table of contents, index, glossary, boldface type, and a list of more books to read on the subject. Liz began by having children recall the questions they had after listening to *The Emperor's Egg*. For example, several children wanted to know more about penguins' eggs and babies. Liz pointed out that there is often more than one way to find out if a book has the information they need. Using *Penguins*, she first showed them the table of contents and explained its function. Then she read the contents page, and the children noted that there were sections on eggs, babies, and growing up. They decided to start with these sections. Later, Liz showed the children how to check the index for information on some of their other questions. She was able to show her students that not all information books need to be read from start to finish. She was also able to demonstrate that, when looking for specific information, it may be necessary to read only the relevant portions of a book.

Liz also helped her students compare the search features of the various penguin books she had brought in, noting that some have many features while others have none. For example, *Penguins!* (Schrieber, 2012) has a table of contents, glossary, and lots of well-labeled photographs but no index, while *If You Were a*

Penguin (Minor, 2009) has no search features at all. The children talked about which books might best serve specific purposes. As they explored penguin books, the children went well beyond tables of contents and indexes. Among other things, they learned why certain words were highlighted in boldface. Liz pointed out the note at the bottom of the copyright page in *Penguins* (Robinson, 1997) that stated: "Some words are shown in bold, **like this**. You can find out what they mean by looking in the glossary." Together, Liz and the children located a word in bold and then checked out its meaning in the back of the book.

Read-alouds are also good vehicles for modeling conventions that will help children use search features effectively. For example, children need to know how alphabetical order works in indexes. Information on Harriet Tubman will be under T not H in the index of *Life on the Underground Railroad* (Isaacs, 2002). Children need to know the difference between index entries that read "3–6" versus "3, 6." They need to know that indexes often have a statement indicating that the numbers printed in boldface or italics have a special meaning, as in "boldface indicates illustrations" (Carney, 2011a, p. 63). And they need to know how to think of different terms if they ones they are looking for are not in the index. This may lead to talking about synonyms or a more general term that encompasses what they are looking for. For instance, if they are trying to find out what tigers eat, they may need to look up *food* or *diet*.

Helping Children Transfer What They Learn

We know from research that even older students have trouble with search skills, often because the instruction they receive involves out-of-context skill lessons that they are not able to transfer to independent learning (Dreher & Sammons, 1994). Thus, we recommend modeling the use of search features and their conventions in meaningful contexts for real purposes. Doing so helps ensure that children will actually be able to transfer the instruction to other contexts.

The case of a young student whom we observed illustrates this point. After experiencing his teacher explaining and modeling the use of tables of contents and indexes during read-alouds, this student showed that he had clearly understood that these features would allow him to make a focused search. He wanted specific information on the size and weight of whales. He found a book on whales but noted that it had no index or table of contents. He quickly proclaimed, "I'd have to read the whole thing!" and decided to try another book.

For some purposes, reading the whole book would be a good idea, but for seeking the answers to specific questions, it would not be very efficient. Therefore, it is important to teach children about search features and how to select books for different purposes so that they can make informed decisions when they seek information. When search features are modeled in meaningful contexts, children do learn their uses and value.

Helping Children Note Variations in Information Book Features

As students seek answers, they will encounter variations in information book features. In other words, not all indexes are alike, nor are other features identical. The following examples illustrate how teachers can help students be prepared for the variety of features they will encounter.

In many books, the table of contents is quite simple; *Trees* (Lessor, 2004), for example, lists three sections (What Is a Tree?, Parts of a Tree, How Does a Tree Grow?) and a glossary. Other tables of contents are much lengthier. At 24 pages, *Reptiles* (Meadows & Vial, 2002b) has the same number of pages as *Trees*, but its table of contents lists 10 sections plus a glossary and index. Some tables of contents have a more complex format. In *Love Your Hamster* (Heneghan, 2013), the table of contents is arranged in two columns, while the table of contents in *The Animal Book* (Jenkins, 2010) is spread over two pages that feature seven main sections, each with subheadings.

Indexes also vary greatly. Some are on one page in one column, as in *Clown Fish* (Sexton, 2007), while others may be on one page but in multiple columns, as in *Guinea Pig* (Rayner, 2008), which has a three-column index. Still other indexes continue beyond one page. *The Kingfisher First Animal Encyclopedia* (Reid, 2011), for example, has a multiple-page triple-column index. Other books have features that are not labeled "index" but are index-like. *Rockets and Spaceships* (Wallace, 2011), for example, has a picture word list that is a cross between a glossary and an index (e.g., the word *astronaut* is accompanied by a photograph and a page number). *Soaring Bald Eagles* (Martin-James, 2001), to cite another example, closes with a page titled Hunt and Find with entries like "an eagle **diving** on page 12."

There is also a great deal of variation in captions and labels for illustrations. Because children can learn much from illustrations in information books, they need to be aware of these differences. Captions in *A Primary Source Guide to China* (Roza, 2003) have directional triangles pointing children toward the appropriate illustrations. In many cases, information about illustrations is in the back of the book. In *Bring on the Birds* (Stockdale, 2011), each page features an illustration with a descriptive phrase; the first three pages show "Swooping birds, whooping birds, birds with puffy chests" (n.p.). At the end of the book, there is a miniature version of each illustration accompanied by a paragraph on each bird. Children searching for the appropriate illustration can determine that the illustration for "birds with puffy chests" shows a great frigatebird.

Similarly, children need to learn about differing conventions, such as arrows, that can be confusing to them. In *Penguins!* (Schrieber, 2012), some illustrations have labels with arrows that lead to the exact spot in the illustration that is being discussed, as when an arrow links "Big webbed feet for better steering" (p. 8) to the feet in a photo of an emperor penguin. But arrows are also commonly used in diagrams that show processes or sequence, such as the water cycle (e.g., Stewart, 2014). As we discussed in Chapter 5, children often misinterpret the arrows showing the direction of processes as pointing to a specific object (McTigue & Flowers, 2011).

In addition, children need to be warned that different terms may be used for the same features in information books. For example, children will often see a section labeled "Table of Contents" or simply "Contents." However, in some books, children may encounter other labels—as in *Baby Mammals* (Kalman, 2013), for example, where the contents page is labeled "What is in this book?" Glossaries are also sometimes called something else. In *Giraffes* (Riggs, 2013), the glossary is labeled "Words to Know." In *Life in a Pond* (Fowler, 1996), there is a picture glossary called "Words You Know," with words such as *lake* and *marsh* appearing under appropriate photos. Even the index is occasionally called by another name. As we just noted, *Soaring Bald Eagles* (Martin-James, 2001) features a variant on an index called "Hunt and Find."

Although at first glance all this variety may seem overwhelming for primary-grade students, children can readily adapt to these differences. They learn as teachers model how to use various types of contents pages and other features. With lots of opportunity to experience information books in read-alouds and strategy instruction across the content areas, children develop flexibility.

To encourage this flexibility, teachers can show children how to preview a book to find out what features are available. A quick look at the front and back pages will reveal much about how information can be accessed. A preview of *Polar Bears* (Orr, 2013), for example, reveals that it has features labeled "Contents," "Words to Know," "Find Out More," "Index," and "About the Author," as well as a habitat map in the back. Children can also look for notes explaining a book's features. As we mentioned, sometimes there is a note about the use of boldface type to flag glossary terms or about the conventions used in the index. Reference volumes for young children often include explanations. Just before the main text begins, *The Kingfisher First Animal Encyclopedia* (Reid, 2011) shows children examples of each type of illustration and other conventions used in the book. Similarly, the *National Geographic Little Kids First Big Book of Dinosaurs* (Hughes, 2011) opens with a section titled "How to Use This Book" that shows children all the features they will encounter for each dinosaur in the book.

Teaching Children about Internet Resources

In addition to teaching children about the information book features, primary-grade teachers need to help their students become familiar with Internet resources. As we discussed in Chapter 5, some teachers think their students have more knowledge about computers and other digital tools than they actually do because they see children interacting comfortably with games, iPads, cell phones, and similar devices (Prensky, 2001). However, studies of young children's knowledge of the Internet indicate that they have much to learn (Karchmer-Klein & Shinas, 2012). When Dodge, Husain, and Duke (2011) interviewed K–2 students, they found "limited understanding of the Internet" (p. 95). The most commonly reported use of the Internet was for playing games, while "less than one-fourth of children thought of the Internet as a place for information" (p. 93).

In this chapter, the finding that few young children see the Internet as a source of information is particularly relevant. While children may play games with ease, there is much for teachers to address when it comes to children's use of the Internet to seek information. The CCSS specially target their ability to engage in research projects and to search strategically in both print and digital sources.

As we explained in Chapter 3, in the primary grades, teachers will typically want to guide children to appropriate websites rather than having them use general search engines. Once students learn to use and critically evaluate websites, teachers can start children on the road to learning to how use search engines to identify appropriate websites themselves (see the "Using Search Engines" section on p. 125). However, we focus on how teachers can use websites they have carefully selected to help children understand the Internet as a place for information.

Modeling the Use of Internet Sources to Find Information

To guide children in using the Internet to seek information, teachers can build on their natural curiosity. For example, as children read or listen to books on an intriguing topic, they will want to know more. When Laura, a first-grade teacher, read *Cheetahs* (Marsh, 2011), her class raised questions they wanted to pursue. Using the guidelines cited in the final section of Chapter 3, Laura selected websites to use as she modeled how to find the information her students wanted. One of the students' questions related to what cheetahs eat. The book described how cheetahs stalk their prey but did not specify exactly what they eat. To address this question, Laura entered the web address for a cheetah fact sheet authored by the Smithsonian's National Zoo (*www.nationalzoo.si.edu/Animals/AfricanSavanna/ Facts/fact-cheetah.cfm*). Although this fact sheet is too difficult for most first graders to read on their own, it is readily accessible with a teacher's help. Laura guided her students to notice the subheadings, and, as they read them together, they found two subheadings on diet. The students quickly located not only what cheetahs eat in the wild but also what they eat in the zoo. Next, Laura helped students address their question about where cheetahs live. They had learned that most live in Africa, with some also in Iran, but they wanted to know where specifically in Africa and to see the cheetahs' habitat on a map. Laura entered the web address *kids.nationalgeographic.com/animals/cheetah* at the National Geographic Kids website, and immediately the children were able to view a map showing where cheetahs live. As Laura guided children through websites to answer their questions, she talked about her reasons for choosing those particular websites and the processes she had used in navigating to each website.

Selecting and Organizing Web Pages for Children to Use

A useful way to guide children to appropriate websites and to help make their use of the Internet more efficient is to select websites ahead of time and organize them into web pages. Once teachers have identified appropriate sites for children on a particular topic (see Chapter 3 for guidelines on choosing websites), they can use a web page program to organize websites in an attractive display.

Although we use the term *web page*, it should be noted that the web pages teachers create do not necessarily have to be posted on the Internet. They may be housed on a USB flash drive or similar device and used as needed. When teachers want their students to use these links, they can insert the flash drive and open that web page on a computer with Internet access.

If teachers choose to post their web pages on the Internet, then children and their parents can access them from home as well as at school. Teachers may find that their school system offers a website where they can post their web pages. Or they can use one of the many websites that provide templates and assistance to help teachers create and post web pages. A search for "free websites for teachers" yields several such sites (e.g., *www.classjump.com* and *education.weebly.com*). (See Chapter 8 for more examples of websites where teachers can post links for students to use.)

Renee Miller and Sandy Greim Connor, primary-grade teachers in Pennsylvania, used such a service to show children (and parents) which sites were good for the research projects they were doing. Renee and Sandy set up their websites with separate folders for each of the research activities that their students were working on. Children went to the website, logged into their class's account, selected the folder for the topic they were researching, and then went to any of the websites listed. For example, a folder on the solar system had links to NASA (*solarsystem. nasa.gov/planets/index.cfm*), KidsAstonomy.com (*www.kidsastronomy.com*), Astronomy for Kids (*www.frontiernet.net/~kidpower/astronomy.html*), and Zoom Astronomy (*www.enchantedlearning.com/subjects/astronomy*).

Using Search Engines: Cautions and Beginnings

As we have noted, primary-grade teachers will most likely want to guide children to appropriate websites rather than having them use general search engines. Once students learn to use websites, teachers may want to start children on the road to learning how to use search engines to identify appropriate websites themselves.

However, there is considerable research documenting the difficulties even older children and adults encounter when using general search engines (Educational Testing Service, 2006; Torres & Weber, 2011). Therefore, teachers should keep in mind some of the challenges that children will encounter with general search engines.

Torres and Weber (2011) studied thousands of sample search efforts by children from ages 6 to 18 using a commercial web search engine. This summary of a child's search efforts captures some of the difficulties searchers face:

> When a 9 years [sic] old boy submits the query hun, the search engine suggests queries such as hun school (Princeton college), hun sen (primer minister of Cambodia) and hun empire (former empire ruled by Attila). Although this user is targeting the last topic suggested by the search engine, he does not seem to notice any of the query suggestions and simply continues with his initial query. Then he clicks on the first web result which happens to be a web directory of links with adult content. Hun is also a popular term used to refer to a specific type of adult content. The user who is probably confused by the content he found decides to go back and then he clicks on the second web result, which is the Wikipedia article of the Hun empire. . . . The article is dense and its language is too advanced for the reading capabilities of this user who after few seconds aborts the search session. (pp. 393–394)

No wonder the author of *Mosquitoes Up Close* (Birch, 2005) instructs readers who want to use the Internet for more information to "have an adult help you use a search engine" (p. 30). Immediately after that advice, the author states, "Type in a keyword such as *mosquitoes* or the name of a particular mosquito" (p. 30). If a student ignores the advice to have an adult help and types *mosquitoes* into Google, he or she may well encounter, as we did, a site for insect repellent as the first search result, with the second one being Wikipedia, followed by several news items on mosquitoes, a medical website, and so forth.

Some books recommend more focused search engines, often associated with their publishing companies. These search engines offer a more limited search that may be closer to what children are seeking. For more information, *Clown Fish* (Sexton, 2007) directs children to *www.factsurfer.com*, while *Polar Bears* (Orr, 2013) suggests *www.factsfornow.scholastic.com*. Each of these search engines returns a list of possible web pages on the topic appropriate for children. But teachers will need to help students sort through the listings to find material at the appropriate reading level. Although *www.factsfornow.scholastic.com* produces a list with a key at the top to tell the reading level of each suggested website, much of what is suggested is above the primary-grade reading level in both of these search engines.

In addition to search engines recommended in books, teachers can find a variety of general search engines designed specifically for children. Examples include

KidRex (*www.kidrex.org*), KidsClick! (*www.kidsclick.org*), KidTopia (*www.kidtopia.info*), KidzSearch.com (*www.kidzsearch.com*), and Safe Search Kids (*www.safesearchkids.com*). Search engines change and new ones appear, so teachers should check what is available frequently. However, even with search engines designed for children, teachers will find that the reading level of the online materials varies greatly and may not match the suggested grade level. Moreover, children still need instruction on how to use these search engines, including how to monitor their search and evaluate what they find, as we discuss next.

Helping Children Monitor Their Hunt for Information

As teachers model searching for information, children will want to try searching too. Just as we indicated for strategy instruction (see Chapter 5), teachers should gradually release the responsibility for locating information to the children. After having opportunities to pose questions and find information with their teacher, children can work in pairs or small groups before trying individual tasks.

One way teachers can assist children as they move toward seeking answers on their own is to talk with them about what they notice about how to find information as their teachers model the search process. Studies of how people locate information for specific purposes indicate that efficient search typically involves (1) formulating a goal, (2) selecting appropriate categories of a text for inspection, (3) extracting relevant information, (4) integrating extracted information with prior knowledge, and (5) monitoring the completeness of the answer and going back for more information if necessary (Dreher, 2002). If children have observed their teacher modeling searches for information, they will have noticed many of these processes. Young children need not learn a formal model, nor do they need to learn these particular terms. But as they discuss how to find information, they will likely come up with similar concepts.

As teachers and their students talk about what is involved in searching for information, they may want to develop a list of questions to help guide the search process. These questions are likely to parallel the steps they have seen modeled and, will, of course, parallel the processes that have been identified in research. The following questions (adapted from Dreher, 1992) may emerge as children discuss searching for information.

- Before starting to look for information, children need to formulate a goal. An appropriate reminder question might be: *"What information do I need?"* As part of deciding, children need to determine what key words would help them search in an index or a search engine.
- Once children are clear on what they are looking for, they need to decide which features in the book or other resource might offer the best route to

the information. An appropriate question for this step might be: *"Does this book (or website or magazine) have search features that would help me find what I want to know?"*

- When children have located a portion of the text to inspect, they must extract relevant information. Questions to guide this process include: *"Is the information I need located here?"*; *"Does the information I have located make sense?"*

- At this point, children should also think about accuracy and timeliness with a question such as *"Is there anything in this book (or website or magazine) to help me decide whether the information is correct?"* Copyright dates and acknowledgments to experts might provide such information.

- Once children have located information they judge is relevant, they need to integrate it with prior knowledge or with other information they have already located. They might ask, *"Does this information relate to things I already know?"*

- Children also need to monitor the completeness of the answer so that they can go back for more if necessary. An appropriate question might be: *"Do I have all the information that I need to answer my question? If not, I should continue searching."*

Questions like these could be posted in the classroom to use as a guide or checklist when children are looking for information. These questions are summarized in Appendix 7.1.

Evaluating Information

When children find information, they need to evaluate what they have found. As one of the writers of the CCSS recently stated, "Whether you're dealing with the reading, writing or listening standards, there's a notion of students getting information both from print and digital sources and looking at credibility and accuracy of the sources" (Rich, 2014, p. A23). The need to teach children to evaluate what they read is not new, but it is important to underscore that addressing this issue now needs to include both books and Internet resources. When Dodge et al. (2011) interviewed K–2 students, the children knew virtually nothing about inaccurate information or other problems they might encounter on the Internet.

Part of evaluating information involves helping children decide whether what they have located makes sense, based on what they set out to find. If children are clear on what they are looking for, it will be easier for them to know if they have found it. This may sound obvious, but whether they are using a book or a website, the first information that catches a child's eye may not be the information that is needed.

For example, Dreher (1992) found that even when older students were looking for answers to questions, some simply turned to the page indicated in the index and selected the boldface terms they found there, even though the terms did not answer the question.

Problems like these can reduced when information seeking occurs in meaningful contexts for real purposes, as we have noted. In addition, classroom-developed questions like those in Appendix 7.1 will help children evaluate what they find. Children can learn to evaluate information by asking themselves such questions as "What information do I need?" and "Does the information I have located make sense?"

Another aspect of information evaluation is to decide whether the information is accurate. In Chapter 3, we discussed this issue in terms of teachers choosing appropriate books and websites for their classrooms. Teachers can help children learn to apply many of the same standards to their own searches. For example, they can guide children to notice whether authors are experts on the subjects they are writing about and, if not, whether they have consulted those who are. Teachers can also help children to take note of copyright dates in order to better assess the timeliness of the information. In addition, teachers can model their own thinking, letting children know that evaluating expertise, checking dates, and so forth are not guarantees but do provide some guidance as to the accuracy of the information. Again, questions like those presented in Appendix 7.1 will help. Children can learn to look for features that relate to accurate content by asking themselves questions such as "Is there anything in this book (or website or magazine) to help me decide if the information is correct?"

In addition, children can learn to assess accuracy by consulting more than one source. By comparing answers across books and websites, they learn about differences of opinion as well as differences in depth of coverage.

Whether considering books or websites, children can learn to evaluate them in much the same way. Just as with a book, teachers can introduce a website and model how to evaluate it. As teachers look for the date a site was last updated, the sponsoring agency, and the qualifications of the contributors, children learn what to look for. Children can gradually begin to evaluate sites on their own, working with peers and then individually.

Taking Notes and Organizing Information

Whether students are gathering information from books or Internet sources, they often need to record it for later use. They may need the information to refer to in discussions, for creating projects, or for writing (treated in Chapter 8). If students are able take notes and organize the information they find, it will be much easier for them to use the information later. In this section, we offer several examples of ways to help young children learn to take notes and organize information.

Using Sticky Notes

Just as sticky notes are good for recording and categorizing questions (see Chapter 5), they are also useful for recording and organizing the information children find. As teachers model finding information to answer questions, they can also show children how to record the information on sticky notes. Later, sticky notes can moved around so that related information is grouped together. Index cards or simple sheets of paper can serve the same purpose. These can be sorted and taped onto blackboards, tagboard, or butcher paper.

Using I-Charts

I-charts are also useful for taking notes and organizing information. I-charts are simply grids that can be formatted as needed (Hoffman, 1992). For example, after reading or listening to *Guinea Pigs* (Meister, 2014) and *Love Your Hamster* (Heneghan, 2013) for a study unit on pets, students might seek information on other pets. As they search in books and other resources, they can record what they find in an I-chart. For example, students used the I-chart shown in Figure 7.2 to list pets across the top, posing the comparison questions they wanted to answer in the left-most column and adding more pets and more questions as desired.

As children learn to gather information, they also need to learn how to credit their sources. An I-chart can easily be adapted for this purpose by adding a source column. Figure 7.3 shows a chart that would enable children to compare the information in two different sources on the same topic. The format of the source column can be determined by the teacher's specific preferences.

	Hamsters	Guinea pigs	Goldfish	Dogs	Cats	Rabbits
How to tell if they are healthy						
How to feed them						
How to keep them clean						

FIGURE 7.2. Example of an I-chart on pets.

Source	Questions		
	1. What is a rain forest?	2. Where are the world's rain forests?	3. What animals live in the rain forest?
In the Rainforest by Kate Duke HarperCollins			
A Rainforest Habitat by Molly Aloian and Bobbie Kalman Crabtree Publishing			

FIGURE 7.3. Using more than one source on rain forests.

As with other techniques, the best way to approach note taking and organizing is to start by modeling. For example, Joanna, a second-grade teacher, asked her students how cheetahs and tigers are alike and different. She posed a specific question about the two animals' hunting practices and guided the children to scan the table of contents of *Cheetahs* (Marsh, 2011). They found a section called Great Hunters. Similarly, when they previewed the table of contents of *Tigers* (Marsh, 2012), they found a section called Built for Hunting and another called Meat Eaters. Working together, Joanna and her students concluded that these would be appropriate sections to read. Joanna then read aloud those sections and modeled for the children how to take notes to answer the question. When they finished with the first question, Joanna and the students posed another question: "What are their babies like?" They then determined whether the *Cheetahs* and *Tigers* books contained relevant information. Figure 7.4 shows a partially completed example. In this example, Joanna had modeled taking notes by listing key words and phrases in note taking, as we discussed in Chapter 5 in the section on summarization. Once the children have taken notes and reflected on what they have found, they may wish to consult other sources to gather additional information if their questions haven't been fully answered.

Using Other Options

There are many other options for taking notes and organizing information. Once children understand how to use I-charts, for example, they can modify them for their own purposes. Similarly, children can use other types of graphic organizers, as described in Chapter 5, to take and organize notes. In addition, children can use software programs such as Kidspiration to takes notes in graphic form and to rearrange their notes as needed. In Chapter 8, we describe the use of Kidspiration as well as several iPad apps as part of children's writing processes.

Source	Questions		
	1. What do they hunt and how do they hunt it?	2. What are their babies like?	3. Where do they live?
Cheetahs by Laura Marsh National Geographic		Called cubs 3–5 cubs at a time Can't do anything at first and can't see By 10 days, can see and crawl Camouflaged coats	
Tigers by Laura Marsh National Geographic		Called cubs 2–3 cubs at a time Raised by mother Drink only mother's milk at first, meat at around 3 months All grown up in 2 years	

FIGURE 7.4. Sample of a partially completed I-chart on "How do cheetahs and tigers compare and contrast?"

Summary

Today's children are expected to read to learn—demonstrating independence, engaging in research projects, and using technology strategically. They need to know how to find information in books as well as on the Internet. Teachers can help children develop these skills by providing many opportunities for them to seek information in meaningful contexts for real purposes. With information books and websites, teachers can model how to use search features, how to monitor their hunt for information, how to evaluate located information, and how to take notes and organize information. Chapter 8 builds on these ideas by showing how students can write about what they have learned.

QUESTIONS AND REFLECTIONS FOR PROFESSIONAL LEARNING COMMUNITIES

1. Discuss your experiences when you were first asked to write a report that required combining information from multiple sources. How did you learn to locate and evaluate information? How did you learn to take notes and organize your thoughts? Did you have to figure out what to do on your own, or did your teachers provide instruction? If the former, what steps can you take so your students won't face a similar situation? If the latter, were there effective techniques that you can adopt for use with your students?

2. In this chapter, we discussed the high expectations set for today's children in terms of finding, evaluating, and using information. We also noted the potential for motivating young children with appropriate research tasks. What types of research tasks have you seen that motivate young children? What have you tried that has successfully tapped into the motivating potential of inquiry? What difficulties have you encountered? How might you change things to address those difficulties? How can your professional learning community members support each other's inquiry efforts?

3. Consider the finding that K–2 students reported knowing virtually nothing about inaccurate information or other problems they might encounter on the Internet. Does this finding match your observations of your students' Internet use? Brainstorm ways that your group's members might address this important issue. Perhaps you can locate the episode "Buster the Myth Maker" from the PBS children's television series *Arthur*. This episode—in which Buster believes *everything* he reads on the Internet—helps address the importance of evaluating information.

CLASSROOM ENGAGEMENT ACTIVITIES

1. Identify a set of three to five information books on a topic that is part of your grade level's curriculum. Use these books in read-alouds not only to teach the topic but also to model the use of diverse information book features.

2. Think about instances when you needed to locate a trustworthy source for a product or service on the Internet. How did you decide which website was most trustworthy? What difficulties did you encounter? What insights from your experience can help you guide students in identifying appropriate websites?

3. Starting with the examples listed in this chapter, explore Internet search engines designed for children. Try the same search terms and compare the results. Which search engines appear best for your students?

Examples of Questions
to Help Children Monitor Their Hunt for Information

What information do I need?

Does this book (or website or magazine) have search features that would help me find what I want to know?

Is the information I need located here?

Does the information I have located make sense?

Is there anything in this book (or website or magazine) to help me decide if the information is correct?

Does this information relate to things I already know?

Do I have all the information that I need to answer my question? If not, I should continue searching.

CHAPTER 8

Teaching Children
to Write Informational Text

Just as most of the reading we do as adults is informational text, most of the writing we do is also informational. Yet the National Commission on Writing in America's Schools and Colleges (2003) concluded that writing is the "neglected R." The report quoted Bureau of Labor Statistics data that indicate that "more than 90 percent of midcareer professionals recently cited the 'need to write effectively' as a skill 'of great importance' in their day-to-day work" (p. 11).

Results of the recent National Assessment of Educational Progress indicated that many students in 8th and 12th grades have difficulty with writing. Although three-fourths of the students scored at a basic or above level, fewer than one-third of the students scored proficient or above on the most recent computer-based writing assessment (National Center for Education Statistics, 2012).

In 2002, the National Assessment of Educational Progress measured children's ability to write narrative, informative, and persuasive texts in grades 4, 8, and 12 (Greenwald, Persky, Campbell, & Mazzeo, 2002). Disturbingly, 72% of 4th-grade students, 69% of 8th-grade students, and 77% of 12th-grade students did not meet the NAEP writing proficiency goals (Persky, Daane, & Jin, 2003).

The CCSS call for a focus on writing instruction. Specifically, they call for students to learn to:

1. Write arguments to support claims in an analysis of substantive topics or texts using valid reasoning and relevant and sufficient evidence.
2. Write informative/explanatory texts to examine and convey complex ideas and information clearly and accurately through the effective selection, organization, and analysis of content.
3. Write narratives to develop real or imagined experiences or events using

effective technique, well-chosen details and well-structured event sequences. (NGA & CCSSO, 2010a, p. 18)

In addition to being able to meet the CCSS standards, "We also know that writing is the primary means by which students demonstrate their knowledge in today's classrooms" (Harris, Graham, Friedlander, & Laud, 2013, p. 538). The inability to write effectively in expressing their ideas can hold children back from academic success. "Good writing is needed for college and increasingly in the workplace as well. Indeed, the impact of poor writing skills on future income and life chances is becoming more substantial" (Pimentel, 2012, n.p.).

If children are to develop into proficient writers, teachers in the early grades have to establish the foundation. Kellogg (2008) asserted that even young children can begin to develop the first stage of writing, which he described as "knowledge-telling." According to Kellogg (2008), "Learning to become an accomplished writer is parallel to becoming an expert in other complex cognitive domains. It appears to require more than two decades of maturation, instruction, and training" (p. 2). Therefore, writing instruction and support clearly must begin in the early grades.

Kristine Gannon, a kindergarten teacher in Providence, Rhode Island, believes strongly that writing instruction can begin as early as kindergarten. Her 26 students write every day. She believes that, given plenty of early practice and encouragement, these students will "not be afraid of writing" (personal communication, April 4, 2014).

Kristine begins the day with shared writing focusing on one of the students or on someone else whom all the students know. One day in April, she began by telling the students that there was a new "star" that they would write about. She began by printing "Mr." on lined paper on the easel in front of where the children were gathered on the rug. Then she asked whether the star was a girl or a boy. The students quickly said a boy, and one explained that "Mr." had to be a boy. Next, Kristine printed the capital letter *R* on the lined paper. The students guessed that it represented Richard, a student in the class. No, explained Kristine, and added an *oy* to make *Roy*. The students were excited—Mr. Roy was the gym teacher.

The students suggested writing "He is in charge of the gym." Kristine said that was a good sentence but that they should start the writing by putting his name in the first sentence. She wrote: "Mr. Roy is in charge of the gym." "We need a period at the end of my thought," she said as she modeled putting the period in place. The children suggested that next she should write "He is fun." Kristine asked, "We have a new sentence—what do I need?" The children responded, "A capital letter!" This procedure continued until Kristine had written four sentences about Mr. Roy. Then the children read the sentences chorally.

The students all went back to their desks, where they then wrote their own version of a description of Mr. Roy, complete with a drawing. As they finished, students brought their work to Kristine to check. She commented on each child's work, sometimes asking whether he or she needed a period or a capital letter, sometimes admiring the drawing, sometimes complimenting the student on the choice of words. Even with 26 students, this did not take a great deal of time. Kristine explained that she believes that these students need immediate feedback on their writing. All the finished descriptions were posted on the blackboard and shared with Mr. Roy. (See Figure 8.1.)

Informational Texts as Models

"When children are given the opportunity and encouragement, they will write texts with structures that are similar to the texts they read—stories, rhymes and informational texts" (Hiebert & Raphael, 1998, p. 149). Because reading and writing develop together, writing informational texts can be a natural outgrowth of the reading that primary teachers encourage in their classrooms. If teachers have used information books for read-alouds and in reading instruction, as suggested in previous chapters, children will be familiar with these forms. Bradley and Donovan (2010) found that using science information books as read-alouds, with discussion about the authors' decision-making processes, improved second graders' ability to write effective compositions. Bintz, Wright, and Sheffer (2010) had similarly positive results with fifth graders using information books as models for students' writing.

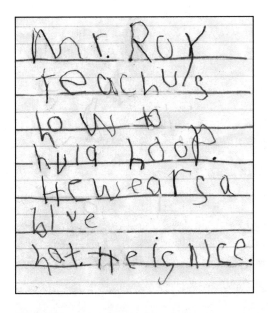

FIGURE 8.1. A kindergarten student's writing.

As Dorfman and Capelli (2009) pointed out, "Students need to immerse themselves in the reading, writing, and inquiry work of nonfiction in order to be successful with the full range of informational texts" (p. 3). Careful reading and study of model texts provide support for young writers. "Instead of needing to rely solely on the teacher for guidance, students can turn to these mentor texts for ideas and seek help when encountering writing difficulties" (Pytash & Morgan, 2014, p. 95).

Informational writing involves children in expressing their interest and knowledge about the world around them. They can write several kinds of informational texts for different purposes and for different audiences. They can write from personal knowledge and experience, and they can research topics to become experts and write about what they have learned. In fact, "Writing is a powerful means of organizing thinking, or making sense of experience" (Mallett, 1999, p. 107).

Quick Writes

One way that teachers can use informational writing is to ask children to do a "quick write" about what they have learned about a particular topic, either from a read-aloud or from reading and discussing texts. This kind of writing is informal and is used to help students clarify and organize what they have learned. It is a good place to begin asking young children to write from sources other than their own experiences.

Cathy Yost, a teacher in Pennsylvania, often uses this kind of writing with her second-grade students. She invites them to listen to a read-aloud as a whole class, to read and discuss related texts in small groups, and then to write individually what they have learned about the topic in their writing journals (see Figure 8.2). She asks students to write about what they found most interesting, and then the class shares what they have written with one another. As one child reads, the other children check their own writing to see whether they have included the same information.

Jenn Smith's second graders also write about what they have learned from their reading. While reading *Poisoned Planet* (Greeley, 2003), Jenn put information on

What have I learned about sharks.

The great white shark has a white belly. Another fact is it can eat a seal in one bite. Also it sometimes attacks people. I also learned that a great white is one of the biggest sharks.

FIGURE 8.2. A second-grade student's "quick write."

sticky notes that the children suggested contained important ideas. After categorizing the notes with the children, she put them into a graphic organizer on an iPad situated so that the four children in the group could all observe it. Jenn asked the students what the most important idea in their reading was. They all quickly responded that pollution was harmful. Then they each wrote what they had learned in their journals, with the iPad available for them to check the facts (see Figure 8.3).

Writing Assignments

More formal writing assignments are also appropriate in the primary grades. These assignments should include lots of prewriting discussions and activities and time for planning, drafting, revising, editing, and, finally, sharing with others. Children should be urged to think of the audience while writing.

Whenever children are expected to write in a particular form, they need to be provided with many examples to explore. For example, if children are asked to write procedural text, teachers can read several procedural texts with them, inviting them to notice how the authors have written the texts and having them identify

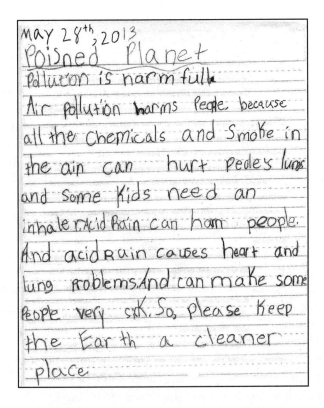

FIGURE 8.3. A second grader's journal writing.

particular characteristics of those texts. As Stead (2002) stated, "If we truly want to extend children's understanding of various nonfictional writing forms, we need to lead them to discover what it is that writers do when they write to inform . . . their readers" (p. 145).

Types of Informational Writing

Wray and Lewis (1997) identified several types of informational texts that primary-grade children can learn to write: recount, procedure, explanation, argument (persuasion), and report. Each of these has different purposes and particular characteristics (see Table 8.1). We explain how a teacher might help children learn to write each of these types of informational text.

Recounts

A recount is simply a retelling of an event or experience. This is perhaps the easiest kind of informational text that young children can write and is the type of writing that would be referred to as narrative under CCSS. Children usually have had a lot of practice in creating oral recounts because they are often called upon to describe what happened at a particular event or time. Knowing that these can be written as well as spoken is the basis for learning to write a recount.

Children are often asked to recount their experiences as shared writing with the teacher or in a writing workshop or in their daily journals. The purpose of a recount is to relate an experience to the reader. It is usually written in the past tense and in sequential order.

When talking to young children about how to write recounts, teachers can demonstrate how this is done through shared writing. One teacher modeled this through a recount of a field trip that the children had taken. She set the purpose for the recount with the statement "On Monday, our class visited the courthouse." Then she modeled writing each of the important things that the class saw or learned, in sequence. She asked for suggestions from the class as the recount developed. She used the past tense, which is typical of recounts, and concluded with the statement "We had a good time at the courthouse."

Students will need exposure to more than one example to learn the characteristics of recounts. Teachers can offer students additional shared writing recounts to examine or can provide texts written as recounts, such as memoirs, biographies, and autobiographies.

Children should be encouraged to discuss and list the characteristics of recounts, a more effective technique than simply telling them what they are. As the students identify the characteristics, the teacher can put them on a chart for the students to use later as they write their own recounts. The chart might include the following:

TABLE 8.1. Typical Characteristics of Types of Informational Writing

Recount	Report	Procedure	Explanation	Persuasion
• Past tense used	• Written using present-tense verbs indicating the timelessness of the information	• Imperative (understood to be directly addressing *you*) • *Example:* "[You] mix two cups of flour."	• Written using present-tense verbs indicating the timelessness of the information but can also use past-tense verbs	• Written using present-tense verbs indicating the timelessness of the information but can also use the past tense
• Based on personal experience	• Based on research and experience	• Based on research or experience	• Based on research or experience	• Based on research, experience, and personal opinion
• Beginning sentence to tell what it is about and to interest the reader	• Beginning sentence to tell what the report is about and to interest the reader	• Beginning sentence to tell what the procedure is	• Beginning sentence to tell what the explanation is about	• Beginning sentence that presents what the writer wants the reader to believe
• Written in the order the experience happened	• Organized according to topic • Has factual information • Often has pictures or diagrams for illustration	• Lists materials needed • Written in a step-by-step order • Often has pictures or diagrams	• Written in a step-by-step order • Often has pictures or diagrams	• Organized by arguments
• Closing sentence	• Closing sentence summarizing the report	• Closing sentence describing the outcome	• Closing sentence indicating the end of the process explained	• Closing sentence stating what the writer wants the reader to believe

- Has a beginning sentence to tell what it is about.
- Is written in the past tense.
- Includes such words as *then* and *next*.
- Tells about a real experience.
- Is written in order.
- Has a concluding sentence.

Teachers can help children plan their recounts by discussing an event, thinking about what they did, and using a concept map (see Chapter 5). Writing recounts usually is easy for children because recounts grow from personal experience, such as one second grader's recount of the class trip to a pond (see Figure 8.4).

Procedural Text

Procedural texts are explanatory in nature and follow a sequence. Examples of procedural text include directions for making something, such as a recipe, or instructions for how to do something, such as playing a game. This type of writing is included in the CCSS informative/explanatory category.

As with other types of text, children should have many examples to examine as they work with procedural text. A teacher might use a sample of a student's work that shows the elements that are usually part of a procedure. *Making Shadow Puppets* (Bryant & Heard, 2002) provides a good example of procedural text. When children examine this book, they will find that for each chapter the author lists the materials needed, a step-by-step sequence to follow, and diagrams showing what the shadow puppet will look like at each stage.

Another example of procedural text is *How to Make Salsa* (Lucero, 1996), which gives children ideas about how to write recipes. The book lists materials needed and steps to take and includes an informative glossary at the end. Children

---

My trip to the pond

Hi! My name is Bruce. One day I went to the pond with my class. My school has a pond in our environmental center. At the pond I saw a slimy slug on a big gray rock. I saw small black fish. I saw a big gray squirll as big as a rabbit chewing on a delicous nut. I saw a huge yellow bee's nest with tiny holes in it next to an oak tree. Guess what! I saw a fossil of a shell! I saw tiny black ants as small as peas crawing up a big tree trunk. It was an exciting trip to the pond! I loved it very much! I'd like to come again!

FIGURE 8.4. A second grader's recount.

might want to use the book's format, with its illustrations of ingredients, to write their own recipes. For more advanced readers, *The Sleepover Cookbook* (Warshaw, 2000) provides a different format for recipes but still includes the important ingredients and steps to follow, using photographs rather than illustrations to explain.

After examining several different models, children should be encouraged to identify and list the following characteristics of procedural texts:

- Uses directive language (i.e., *do, mix, turn, cut*, etc.).
- Lists the ingredients or implements needed.
- Offers step-by-step directions.
- Includes diagrams or pictures of the created or end product.

After having identified the components of written instructions, Kathy Simpson's second-grade students each chose an activity they felt that they knew how to do very well. In a prewriting exercise, they listed all the things needed for the described activity, and then they discussed in pairs a good beginning to catch the reader's interest. The students drafted their instructions, read them to one another, and then revised and edited them (see Figure 8.5).

Explanatory Text

Explanatory text is used to explain processes and the reasons that things happen. It is often used in describing scientific or social phenomena. It is usually written in sequential order, as is procedural text, but often uses a cause–effect structure. Explanatory text can be a combination of recounts and procedures. For example, after watching caterpillars hatch into butterflies, children might write an explanation of the life cycle of the butterfly. They would be recounting something that happened but also would be putting the steps of the event in sequential order. Recounts fit under the CCSS category of informative/explanatory text.

Swimming

I love swimming. Do you? Let me teach you how to swim. You can do it anywhere. It is fun to do and it makes you look cool! First you need a bathingsuit. Then you have to buy goggles. After that go get flippers. Now I am going to teach you how to swim. First you dive in the water. Then start your paddling. Next go faster. NOW you are swimming. Do you like swimming? I hop so.

FIGURE 8.5. A second grader's procedural text.

Children should examine and discuss a variety of explanatory texts. For example, *From Wax to Crayon* (Nelson, 2003), part of the Start to Finish series, follows the procedure used in making crayons, from melting the wax to sorting the crayons to sending them to the stores. Additional titles in this series explore cotton to T-shirt, kernel to corn, peanut to peanut butter, and tree to paper.

Another example of explanatory text is *National Geographic Little Kids First Big Book of Why* (Shields, 2011), which offers multiple explanations complete with drawings. Teachers can use this book as an example of how to include diagrams and captions in explanations.

As children examine explanatory texts, they will learn to identify the following characteristics:

- Has a beginning sentence to tell what is being explained.
- Is written using present-tense verbs, indicating the timelessness of the information.
- Includes the sequence of a process or explanations of characteristics.
- Offers diagrams or pictures.
- Concludes with an ending sentence.

It is helpful to have children begin writing explanations through shared writing with the teacher about something they have observed. For example, if the class has experimented with things that float or that sink, they could write an explanation about this phenomenon together with the teacher acting as scribe.

To further scaffold their writing, small groups or pairs of children can work to write explanations of things they have observed, such as the hatching of chicks or growth of plants. Only after children have had guided practice with this form should they be expected to write it independently.

In Jess Verwys's first-grade class, students often create explanations and diagrams to be used as a part of reports. Jess spends time with the students studying diagrams and explanations in information books. From these examples, the students work to develop their own explanations. Figure 8.6 shows one child's explanation and diagram of the life cycle of the butterfly.

Persuasive Text

Persuasive text is written to persuade or convince someone about a particular point of view. It usually makes a statement about what the writer wants the reader to believe and then provides reasons or statements that support that view.

According to the National Assessment of Educational Progress in 1998, only 18% of fourth graders were able to score at basic or above levels in writing persuasion (Greenwald et al., 2002). This seems to be the most difficult (or the most neglected) kind of informational writing in K–3 classrooms. In the CCSS, this type

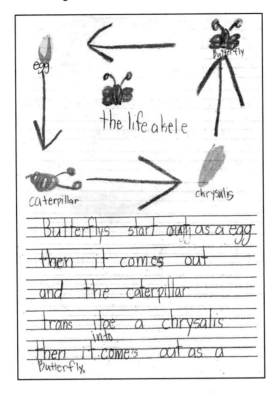

FIGURE 8.6. A first grader's explanation and diagram.

of writing is referred to as "argument" in the upper grades and "opinion" in grades K–5. "Although young children are not able to produce fully developed logical arguments, they develop a variety of methods to extend and elaborate their work by providing examples, offering reasons for their assertions, and explaining cause and effect" (NGA & CCSSO, 2010a, p. 23).

Children should examine several examples of persuasive writing before being asked to write in this particular form. Examples can include student writing from previous years or published texts. Children should be able to identify the following characteristics of persuasive text:

- Has an opening sentence with an opinion about something.
- Supports that opinion with reasons.
- Usually written in the present tense (though the past tense is not uncommon).
- Has an ending sentence restating the opinion.

To help children begin writing persuasive texts, Kathy Simpson had her second graders consider an issue for which there were different opinions in the class.

She asked the children to think about the four seasons, listing the good things they could think of about each season. After completing the list, each child chose a favorite season and wrote a short persuasive paragraph using the following format:

I think _____ is the best season.
(the opening sentence giving an opinion)

Write three reasons it is the best season.

So this is why _____ is the best season.

After children practiced persuasive writing in this structured way, they were better prepared to create their own persuasive pieces. Kathy extended the idea of persuasive writing by having her students write letters to persuade guests to visit their class. After having successfully persuaded an animal keeper at the zoo to visit and share his experiences, the children asked Kathy if they could write to other guests persuading them to visit. The persuasive letter became an important part of the classroom culture, which the children also used to try to convince their teacher to use certain classroom activities (see Figure 8.7).

Adria Creswell, a third-grade Pennsylvania teacher, often asks her students to write in their reading journals. Sometimes these are quick writes about what they have learned from reading particular texts, but sometimes Adria asks them to write persuasive entries stating their opinions and supporting them. Recently, she introduced an "academic controversy" to her students with read-alouds of books about Betsy Ross. Following a shared reading of *Betsy Ross* (Mara, 2005)—the text was read by Adria but simultaneously projected onto a screen so that the

Mrs. Simpson, I think we should really play Around the wold! We never played it in a long, long, time. Around the world is a good game because it's fun and we lean math. Around the world is also a good game because we can ether do the clocks or number model. All of us can play, that's another good reason. Am I convincing you? Well that's not even the beginning yet!

Around the world makes math less hard and it's fun too! This will help us with math asinments, triangle facts, and trades first. There are many jobs that include math for esample, a sintist he needs to know lots of math! Around the world is a fun math game, now wouldn't it be nice to play it?

FIGURE 8.7. A second grader's persuasive text.

students could see the illustrations—her students organized the information by facts, legends, and inferences. Adria explained that Betsy Ross's making the first flag was a legend, that no one knew for sure that she was the one who had actually sewn it together, but that there were facts about her life that made people believe the legend. After reading and discussing the facts and inferences, students wrote their opinions about whether the legend that Betsy Ross actually was responsible for making the first flag was true. They were reminded to include their reasons for their opinions (see Figure 8.8).

Reports

Reports are the kind of writing most often associated with informational text. The purpose of a report is to describe something—an animal, a country, a sport, a planet, or anything that a child would be interested in describing. Unlike recounts, reports are usually written in the present tense, indicating the timelessness of the information. They feature factual information and often include pictures with captions or labels and diagrams. Reports often are structured like a description, but they could also reflect other structures such as cause–effect or compare–contrast (see Table 5.2). Often children engage in research (as described in Chapter 7) in order to be able to write reports, but reports can also include personal experiences. This type of writing is referred to as informational/descriptive in the CCSS.

As with other forms of writing, children need to have experiences both reading and discussing reports. After they have had ample opportunity to examine reports and identify their characteristics, they will be ready to begin writing them.

Fortunately, there are many excellent books that fall into the category of reports. Books written about animals, people, places, or events are often written in the form of reports. Teachers who use information books as read-alouds and as part of reading instruction will have children who are familiar with the characteristics of reports.

Did Betsy Ross Make the First U.S. Flag?

I don't think Betsy Ross made the flag. One of the reasons I think she didn't make the flag because studies can test for DNA and because studies haven't shown it then she probably couldn't. I think she couldn't because there are no true facts that she actually made it. If she did make it I think she would have had more information. Those are the 3 reasons I think she didn't make the flag.

FIGURE 8.8. A third grader's opinion text.

Teachers and children can review some of these books and student samples from previous years and identify their common characteristics. Teachers can also revisit expository information books that they have used as read-alouds and encourage the children to discuss their features. For example, *Arctic Foxes and Red Foxes* (Meadows & Vial, 2002a) could be used to talk about the kind of language used, the kinds of facts that the authors present about the two types of foxes, the illustrations related to the text, the compare–contrast structure, and the headings used.

Because it was written by a first-grade class, children might be particularly interested in looking at *Penguins Are Waterbirds* (Taberski, 2002). Again, it is helpful if the children themselves generate the characteristics of reports. The teacher can list these on a chart to be posted in the room to remind children as they are doing their own writing. Some of the characteristics to be identified include the following:

- Has a beginning sentence that draws readers' interest.
- Is written using present-tense verbs, indicating the timelessness of the information.
- Includes general statements about the topic rather than specific individuals (i.e., "a fox" or "foxes" instead of "Father Fox").
- Uses factual information.
- Presents diagrams or pictures with labels and captions.
- Has a concluding sentence.

By carefully studying children's report writing, Donovan and Smolkin (2011) have identified a developmental progression that can guide teachers as they help students increase the length and complexity of their reports. Children progress from simply labeling parts of a picture they have drawn to writing one or two sentences about the picture. As they develop expertise, they write "fact lists" consisting of sentences about the topic that could be reordered without loss of meaning or cohesion and then progress to writing couplets with two or more clauses for which order is important. These may include typical text structures such as cause–effect, question–answer, statement–reason, or statement–example.

As their writing becomes more complex, children may include a collection of fact lists about two or more things where the order of the sentences is not important. From this point, they begin to use couplets referring to different subtopics and then to paragraphs where sentences could be rearranged without changing the meaning. Finally, they write in ordered paragraphs that use connecting words and whose sentences couldn't be rearranged without loss of meaning (Donovan & Smolkin, 2011).

REPORT TOPICS

Children should be given a choice when selecting report topics because they will be more successful when motivated by interest. Gambrell (2011) pointed out that children are more motivated to read when they can make choices about what they read, and the same is true for writing. Children enjoy sharing with others what they have learned about a favorite subject and usually have more prior knowledge about a subject in which they are interested. In fact, after interviewing seven children's authors about writing, Peterson (2014) found that a theme running through all the interviews was that "student writers' passions and curiosity should guide topic choice" (p. 499).

Jess Verwys's first-grade students were given their choice of topics to write about, using all that they had learned about reports. The children all included a table of contents, page numbers, diagrams, drawings, maps, and facts in their reports. The range of topics reflected the wide variety of the first graders' interests: gymnastics, cats, Pokemon, baseball, butterflies, reptiles, and Costco, among others.

RESOURCES

One of the greatest concerns that teachers have is that children may copy directly from the Internet or an encyclopedia when they are writing reports. Children often do this because the reading material that they are using is too difficult for them to understand (Mallett, 1999). It is important that children be able to read at an independent or instructional level when they are doing research for a report. This means, of course, that teachers need to have many resources written at different levels available for their classroom of young researchers.

It is important to have several sources for each possible topic that children will choose. One way to be sure to have enough resources is to limit children's choices to topics for which there are enough books. Another way to make resources go further is to have children work in groups. Teachers can work with school and public librarians to identify a collection of books, magazines, websites, and articles for children to use. (See Chapter 7 for more information about research.)

As mentioned in Chapter 5, many websites, even those created for children, feature text that is too difficult for the intended grade level (Gallagher et al., 2013; Kamil & Lane, 1998). Consequently, teacher guidance must play an important role in helping children choose sites that they can understand easily. Some teachers have voiced concern that, although well-meaning parents sometimes help their children search for information on the web, often the information found is far too difficult for the children to understand. It is a good idea at the beginning of a research project to send a letter home to parents explaining what the children are doing and alerting parents to the problems of giving children text that is too difficult. It is also useful to let children and parents know particular websites that may be useful in the research. Often schools or teachers have their own web page where they can place links to the preferred websites that can then be accessed from home (see Chapter 7).

If children use graphic organizers or I-charts (as described in Chapters 5 and 7), they will be more likely to use their own words in their reports. Children take notes on the graphic organizers or I-charts by using only key words, not complete sentences. When children begin to write their reports, the key words help them remember the information but not the exact wording of the article, book, or website. Thus, they use their own words to rephrase the information in sentences.

ORGANIZING REPORTS

Young children need structure to help them organize their research and note taking before they begin writing. When Kathy Simpson helps her second-grade students organize their research and report writing, she leads them through a discussion about the kinds of information they are interested in finding. Then she provides them with photocopied sheets for each of their questions to take notes on (see Appendix 8.1). She leaves spaces for what they already know about the topic and what they learn through their research.

Kathy teaches her students how to find information in an information book or on the Internet, how to take notes, how to create an interesting opening for their reports, how to organize their reports into paragraphs that answer the questions they plan to research, how to write a concluding sentence, and how to use their own words in their writing. She uses samples of other students' writing and models how to accomplish these goals. Kathy finds it helpful to provide the children with a checklist so they can evaluate their own work (see Appendix 8.2 for such a checklist).

Using effective instruction and modeling, Kathy works with her second-grade students to be sure that they use their own words in their writing. For example, one student researching kangaroos found the following sentence from an Internet source: "Kangaroos can live for months without water." The student, surprised at that fact, started to write it down but—remembering that she needed to use her own words instead wrote, "Kangaroos can go for a long time without drinking." Kathy's instruction and modeling had had an impact.

When the children finish their reports, they share them by reading them aloud to classmates and then take them home to their parents. Each child had become an "expert" about the topic of the research (see Figure 8.9).

When Lindsay Stout, a first-grade teacher in Pennsylvania, helps her students organize longer reports, she often refers them to previous classes' *All About . . .*

Bats of the World

My favorite animals are bats. Bats are really cool creatures! Here's some cool facts about bats I want to share with you.

Bats look like little furballs with wings. Sometimes they look like birds. Some bats are brown, black, and gray. But no bat looks the same.

Bats live all over the wolrd. But not in really cold or really hot places. Bats live in trees and caves.

Some bats eat blood. Some eat bugs + fish. Did you know this? Some bats even drink necter and pass it like bees.

Their enimies are crocodiles and snakes. They even attack each other sometimes!

Do you know what? Bats are mammals like us! Also bats can't see well. And they hibernate in the winter. Guess what?! Bats have fingers too! The biggest bat is Samoan Flying Fox and the smallest is the Bumble Bee Bat. The Samoan Flying Fox's wingspan is 6½ feet. Also the vampire bat can help people with heart problems.

Bats are amazing. I'd like to see them in the wild some day.

FIGURE 8.9. A second grader's report.

books for ideas about what to include and how to format their reports. Lindsay has different kinds of paper available to her students: lined paper; blank table of contents forms with spaces for chapter titles and page numbers; paper with boxes; paper with space at the top for drawing and lines underneath; and paper with "About the Author" centered at the top with lines below. Lindsay discusses with the students which type of paper would be the best for the part of the report they are writing. She makes certain that the students understand that sometimes different types of paper might be used for the same purpose—that is, diagrams could be put on pages with boxes, or they could be drawn in the upper space of papers with lines underneath.

Students organize their reports by deciding what chapters to include. Lindsay refers them to previous classes' books, books that have been used in read-alouds, or books that they have read. As the students work on their books, Lindsay has conferences with them individually and in groups. She reminds them that everything in a chapter has to relate to the title of the chapter. As students read individual sentences, Lindsay asks, "Does that tell about . . . ?" If the child says it doesn't tell about the title of that chapter, Lindsay asks, "What chapter might that sentence go into?" In this way, students write and revise to make sure that their reports are properly organized (see Figure 8.10).

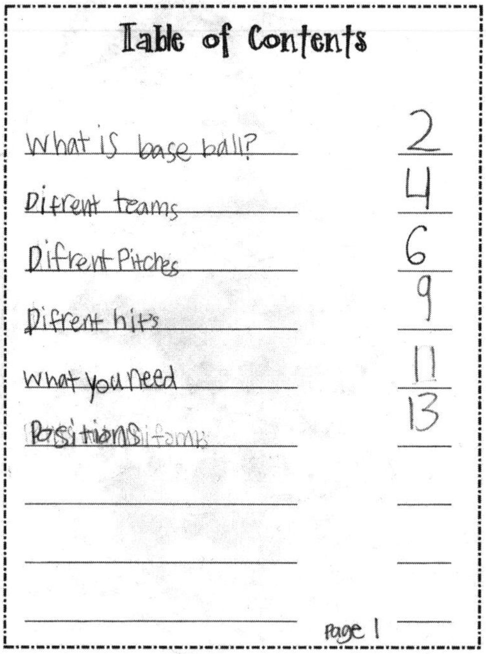

FIGURE 8.10. A first grader's table of contents for an *All About . . .* book.

DIFFERENT FORMATS

Written reports also may be done in different formats. Renee Miller, a third-grade teacher, has her students write reports using a "step book" in which the answers to each of the questions the children have posed and researched are featured in a small booklet. To construct the booklet, three pieces of construction paper are folded at different places so that, when they are joined together, each page is slightly different in size and the edges resemble steps. The children then divide their information into logical paragraphs based on the researched questions. Each paragraph is written on a separate page of the booklet and then illustrated. The last page is reserved for information about the author.

Writing Frames

A writing frame, which Kathy Simpson used for her students' first persuasive writing project, is an outline that scaffolds children's attempts to create particular forms of writing. Writing frames provide sentence starters so that children can fill in blanks and have well-developed paragraphs. Children who have difficulty with writing may benefit from the use of writing frames (Wray & Lewis, 1997).

Teachers can develop writing frames for each of the informational text structures (see Chapter 5) by using sentence starters and key words. For example, a compare–contrast frame could start with a sentence: "I read about _____ and _____." The next sentence could tell how the two are alike: " _____ and _____ both _____." Then a sentence (or two) could explain how they are different: "_____ has _____, but _____ has _____." The concluding sentence could be: "_____ and _____ are alike in some ways and different in others." When the children have finished filling out the frame, they have a paragraph written in the compare–contrast structure. (See Appendix 8.3 for a sample writing frame for procedural text.)

When introducing a teacher-prepared writing frame, it is important to model it with the class as a shared writing. For example, a teacher could use the compare–contrast frame described above after reading a chapter of *A Wasp Is Not a Bee* (Singer, 1995) filling in the blanks with the class as a whole. For the second chapter, comparing a bat and a bird, pairs of students working together could complete the frame. Once children are familiar with the procedure, they can complete the frames independently. As children become used to writing a particular genre, they will no longer need the frames.

Kristine Gannon provides her kindergarten students with examples and models as she encourages their writing. After discussion about what the children wanted to be when they grew up, the class created a book called, *I Can Do It!* Each child wrote a page and illustrated it, following the model "When I grow up, I want to be. . . . The next sentences described what the child would do in that role, and then the final sentence was "I can do it." (See Figure 8.11.)

Poetry as Informational Text

Although most of us don't think of poetry as informational text, children can use poems to write factual information. As Frye, Trathen, and Schlagal (2010)

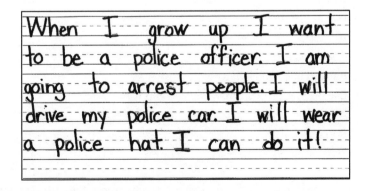

FIGURE 8.11. A kindergarten student's patterned writing.

have asserted, "Encoding information in poetic form is a thoughtful and thought-provoking way to capture and retain important information" (p. 595). The poems can be rhyming or patterned poems such as information poems, acrostic poems, or cinquains. For example, after children have studied a particular topic, they could brainstorm a list of words related to the topic and arrange them into a patterned information poem. For the topic of fall, the list of words might include *fall, autumn, falling leaves, cool, raking, school, pumpkins*, or holidays such as *Thanksgiving* or *Halloween*. For an informational poem, children put one word in the first line, two words in the second line, three words in the third line, and one word in the fourth line:

Fall
Halloween, Thanksgiving
Raking falling leaves
Autumn

To further enhance young children's creativity and enjoyment, Bromley (2000) suggested making shape books; for example, this poem could be written on pages in the shape and color of a fall leaf.

Acrostic poems, built by using the letters of the word written vertically, can encourage children to use interesting word choices as they integrate their knowledge of a topic. As with other writing instruction, teachers could begin by sharing books that feature acrostics, such as *African Acrostics* (Harley, 2009). Before asking students to create these poems on their own, it is useful to experiment with shared writing to show students. It is also useful to have interesting words related to the topic on a word wall for students to use.

After reading *Polar Bears* (Gibbons, 2001b), a teacher might demonstrate how he or she constructed an acrostic poem based on the information:

Polar bears are amazing animals.
Of all bears, they are the largest.
Live in the Arctic.
Amazing sense of smell.
Rough pads on feet keep them from slipping.
Babies called cubs.
Eat seals, walruses, small whales, and fish.
Athletic.
Run really fast.
Swim long distances.

As students become adept at these poems, teachers can encourage better word choice and more accurate description, resulting in better constructed poetry.

Cinquains, with five lines, also could be used to show information about a topic. Although many teachers use a specified number of syllables per line in writing cinquains, a simpler version is to use number of words per line. The basic structure is as follows:

- One word (or two syllables) in the first line, stating the topic.
- Two words (or four syllables) in the second line, describing the topic.
- Three words (or six syllables) in the third line, telling an action.
- Four words (or eight syllables) in the fourth line, expressing feelings.
- One word (or two syllables) in the fifth line, restating the topic.

Jen Boyk and Jess Verwys use graphic organizers to help their first-grade students write cinquains to describe a person, place, or thing. Their students enjoy the format and develop creative poems, often working in pairs (see Figure 8.12). These cinquains reflect the children's knowledge of the topics.

Poetry, whether rhyming or patterned, provides particularly creative ways of writing information. Poetry may appeal especially to children who enjoy playing with language and to those for whom longer writing assignments are a challenge.

Digital Writing

Within the CCSS, there is emphasis on becoming digitally literate. The sixth anchor standard for writing states, "Use technology, including the Internet, to produce and publish writing and to interact and collaborate with others" (NGA &

```
Caterpillar
Small, fuzzy
Chewing, moving, crawling
Incect that is fuzzy
Butterfly

Clouds
White, fluffy
Floteing, passing, changing
Cirrus, cumulus, stratus in the sky
Water vaper
```

FIGURE 8.12. Two first graders' cinquains.

CCSSO, 2010a, p. 18). Students can use digital tools to compose text, collaborate with others, and share their writing with a wider audience.

Planning and Composing Text

Bogard and McMackin (2012) described the benefits of using recordings of third-grade children's talking as they sketched illustrations of their stories using Smart-Pen. This device contains both a camera and a microphone that record everything. When children begin writing, they can replay the oral commentary that they recorded for each of their illustrations. The authors found that having the oral rehearsal of the story available increased the number of sentences the children wrote. The oral recordings helped the students remember and possibly eased the cognitive load they experienced when trying to both remember and write. The recordings also helped students as they revised their writing. They were able to go back and think more about different parts of their stories.

Interactive software programs are available to help children organize their ideas before they begin writing. Kidspiration, for example, enables young writers to create concept maps with their ideas before composing. Numerous apps have been designed to be used with iPads. Popplet, for example, can be used for concept mapping and collecting ideas, images, and notes in preparation for writing. MindMash, a free app, allows users to collect information—whether text or images—and manipulate it in a variety of ways on the screen. This app also has a drawing mode, where children can draw their own sketches on the screen. Images and text can be resized and moved. Because technology changes quickly, teachers should stay up to date with programs and apps that can help students in planning, organizing, revising, and producing written and visual texts. A useful website for this is *www.freetech4teachers.com*.

Word processing programs such as Microsoft Word are valuable resources for students as they compose and revise text. These programs are particularly important for students who have difficulty with handwriting or who need the support of spell checkers. For many students, seeing their writing in "print" is very motivating. After one student's writing was printed, he exclaimed, "It looks like a real book!"

Publishing Text

Children also can learn to use presentation software such as PowerPoint and VoiceThread to present the information that they have learned through their research. Renee Miller and Sandy Connor, third-grade teachers in Pennsylvania, have their students do research on the Internet as well as in reference books. When they have completed their research, the children use PowerPoint to present their findings to their classmates and to their parents.

Renee and Sandy find that providing children with appropriate websites is crucial in supporting their students' efforts to find information on the web. The teachers discuss with students ahead of time the questions they want to answer and provide them with note-taking sheets for writing down information. Sandy's students often use print sources for confirming or disconfirming any contradictory information found on websites.

To help the children work with PowerPoint in preparing their presentations, Renee and Sandy provide hard-copy storyboards that are set up in the same format as PowerPoint slides. The children complete the storyboards before they begin working with PowerPoint. This kind of scaffolding keeps the children from being overwhelmed with trying to figure out commands for the program and trying to find accurate information from their notes. Once children have completed their work, they share their presentations with their parents, the rest of the class, and the principal.

Writing with an audience in mind is an important part of the writing process. Teachers have always looked for ways to let students share their writing from having them read to the class from the "author's chair" to publishing class books. Technology can make sharing easier and can enable students' writing to reach a wider audience. Numerous websites—some free and some available by subscription—offer opportunities for students to post their writing (or multimedia compositions) for other students to read and respond to. Access to the websites can be controlled by the teacher so that he or she can decide whether to allow only students of the class to see the postings or allow parents and potentially a wider public to view the students' creations. The website *www.padlet.com*, for example, is a free site where teachers can build a "wall" for students to post blogs, multimedia compositions, discussions, and links. Other sites, such as *www.edmodo.com*, *www.kidblog.org*, *www.edublogs.org*, and *www.blogger.com* offer similar possibilities for teachers and their students. Teachers can set up a classroom YouTube account in which privacy is assured. Because technology changes quickly, there will doubtless be other sites available with enhanced capabilities in the future.

Collaboration with Others

One advantage of working with digital and multimedia text is that it makes it easier to collaborate. Many of the websites cited above feature ways that children can work together in writing or designing as well as responding to one another's work.

Kelly Loomis's third-grade students use Google Docs so that they can work in pairs to write, accessing the documents from the classroom, the writing center, or from home. They can respond to one another's drafts, add their own sections, review changes, and start developing the skills they will need to work in creative groups.

The Internet affords other opportunities for students to collaborate online through classroom exchanges. World Wise Schools (*www.peacecorps.gov/wws/ classroom*) helps classrooms connect with Peace Corps volunteers currently serving overseas. Sharing videos, pictures, and emails enables students to engage with volunteers and learn more about the countries where the volunteers are posted. If the volunteer is a teacher, these exchanges can include their students as well. Classroom exchange (*www.epals.com*) matches classrooms where students can work together on various projects, share information about their communities, and write and share stories. The Global Classroom Project (*theglobalclassroomproject. wordpress.com*) also connects classrooms across the globe, and the School and Classroom Program of People to People International (*www.ptpi.org/community/ SCP.aspx*) has a similar program to enable students to communicate and share. Through Educators Overseas, classrooms can connect through Skype, email, Facebook, or can take a more traditional route by becoming pen pals.

Multimodal Writing

Beyond using technology for publishing "writing," vast opportunities now exist to help children communicate their ideas through pictures, video, sounds, graphics, and animations. Using multiple means of communication provides more tools for creating meaning and supporting children with additional nonverbal cues for understanding and for ways to get their ideas across. This is of particular importance for ELLs and students for whom language acquisition seems daunting.

Even in the early grades, teachers can lay the foundations for children to begin to communicate their ideas through writing, pictures, video, sounds, and graphics. Effective instruction can help students develop these emerging skills. Dalton (2012) has suggested that from the beginning students see themselves as "designers"—not just as "writers"—as they use multimedia to express their ideas.

Kelly Loomis uses her school's curriculum requirement to do "research writing" to help her third-grade students research, design, and create multimodal reports. Although traditionally these reports have been about animals, Kelly and her class, inspired by reading aloud *The Lightning Thief* (Riordan, 2005), decided to research gods and goddesses. Each student picked a god or goddess to research, and the class brainstormed questions that they wanted to answer.

With the cooperation of the school librarian, students researched the subject by using books, websites, and apps on iPads available for classroom use. Kelly chose the websites because, as she explained, some of the websites about gods and goddesses were not appropriate for third graders! She posted links to kid-friendly websites on her web page. A few of the gods and goddesses that the children had chosen had little information available on kid-friendly sites, and so

Kelly compiled crucial information from other sites and posted these documents on her web page.

As they researched, students took notes on note cards with the question and answer on one side and the source on the other side. According to Kelly, using the cards enabled the students to see what questions they had answered and which ones required more research. The cards also helped them organize and revise as they began putting together their reports.

The students then wrote essays about their god or goddess, based on their research. Because Kelly wanted her students to be able to access their essays from the classroom, the library, the writing center, or even from home, she had them use Google Docs for writing. Once completed, the students decided how to divide their essays into smaller segments. For each of the segments, they found or created an illustration and took a picture of it using the iPad. They used VoiceThread to record their explanations of each of the illustrations, with their essays as the script. Finally, they published their completed multimodal presentations to the classroom website, where all the students and parents could enjoy them.

The students enjoyed creating the presentations and learned a lot about using the technology—pictures with the iPad, VoiceThread, and posting to the websites. One particularly pleased student reported, "I liked it because you could save and go back to finish or rerecord." Another student liked VoiceThread: "When you type it hurts your fingers! So VoiceThread was much easier, and typing takes longer and you get words spelled incorrectly. VoiceThread was quicker." One student showed his presentation to his parents and siblings at home because he could access the class's website from his home computer. When he was asked what he liked best about the project, he answered, "Creating a VoiceThread and then being able to see and hear them [the images and related audio] on the computer from home, not just on the iPad or at school." Echoing Dalton's (2012) suggestion about being designers of multimodal presentations, one student said, "You didn't have to use just one picture; you could flip through different pictures, and you could change them if they weren't right."

Dalton (2012) urged teachers not to fall into the trap of thinking that writing is always the first thing to do in creating a multimodal presentation. For many children, pictures, music, or video may be the place to start to communicate. Writing—whether explanatory text, scripts for voiceovers, or captions for pictures—may come later in the designing.

Multimodal composing is motivational for many children. It gives them different ways to communicate their ideas, thus appealing to different learners' strengths. In explaining why multimodal composing worked well for his older students, Joe Malley observed: "When kids make a video about something, they know it a lot better than if they were writing a research paper. There are a lot of decisions involved when they decide how to match up music, sound effects, audio, who to video, or what shot to take. There is a deeper embedded knowledge required. When it is more real, they are more engaged; they are more motivated, but they also try harder" (College Board, National Writing Project, & Phi Delta Kappa International, 2010, p. 6).

Summary

Reading and writing develop together. As children learn from reading different kinds of informational texts, they also learn to write, using the same forms. Children should have opportunities to explore many examples of different forms and to identify their characteristics. Children can learn to write recounts, reports, explanations, procedures, descriptions, and poetry to share information. They can also experiment with multimodal compositions to communicate their ideas. Writing helps children explore, reorganize, and consolidate their knowledge. Although we have suggested a few websites, software programs, and apps for digital writing and multimodal authoring, we encourage you, as Karchmer-Kline and Shinas (2012) stated, "to focus your efforts on your own professional development by maintaining a finger on the pulse of technological advancements" (p. 289)—for these advancements come quickly and offer many opportunities for teachers and students alike. In the concluding chapter, we suggest ways to get started with informational text in classrooms.

QUESTIONS AND REFLECTIONS FOR PROFESSIONAL LEARNING COMMUNITIES

1. Bring to your professional learning community the information books that you have used as writing models. Which category (recount, procedure, explanation, persuasion, report) predominates among these books? Discuss what information books might work as models for each of the five types. What effects on your students' writing have you seen from using these models?

2. Choose examples of teacher classroom instruction described in this chapter. Discuss the strengths and possible problems with the teacher's approach. How could you adapt this lesson for your own classes? How can you support one another in trying some of the example lessons or suggestions from this chapter?

3. Discuss what technology you find particularly valuable in helping students with their writing. Have you encouraged student collaboration using technology? What challenges did you have, and how did you address them? Have you had students design multimodal informational compositions? What worked well, and what challenges did you face? How did you meet those challenges?

CLASSROOM ENGAGEMENT ACTIVITIES

1. Share several examples with your class of one of the kinds of writing described in this chapter, and work with your students to identify the characteristics. Do the characteristics your class has identified match the characteristics listed in the chapter? If not, what additional characteristics did you notice?

2. Explore one of the websites listed in the chapter. Using that website, create a space for your students to post entries. These may be responses to a book they have read, an activity they have done, or the results of research. Compare students' writing for the website with their usual classroom writing. Were the students more motivated to write for the website? How was their writing different for the website?

3. Use poetry (any one of the kinds described in this chapter) as an activity for your students to show their understanding of an information book they have read or of research they have done. How did creating a poem change the way your students interacted with the information?

My Questions

What do I want to learn?

What do I already know?

What have I learned?

Report Checklist

☐ 1. My title tells what the report is about.

☐ 2. My first sentence tells what the report is about and has something interesting to make someone want to read it.

☐ 3. My facts are written in sentences and are in my own words.

☐ 4. I have enough facts in my report to make it interesting for someone else to read.

☐ 5. I have grouped my sentences into paragraphs that make sense.

☐ 6. I have a good ending that wraps up my report.

☐ 7. I have a picture, diagram, or chart to help make my report clear.

☐ 8. I have checked my spelling and punctuation.

☐ 9. I have had someone else read my report and give me feedback.

The part I like best is _____.

Based on ideas from Kathy Simpson.

Sample Writing Frame for Procedural Text

I am going to tell you how to make _____.

You need to have _____, _____,

_____, and _____.

First, you _____

_____

_____

Then, you _____

_____

_____

Next, you _____

_____

_____

Finally, you _____

_____

_____

Now you have _____. Enjoy it!

CHAPTER 9

Putting It All Together

Although many primary-grade children continue to be exposed overwhelmingly to stories, there are compelling reasons to change this situation. We have discussed these reasons and the evidence to support them in Chapters 1–8.

First, children need experience with informational text if they are to meet current expectations. State and national standards as well as the recommendations of professional organizations call for young children to handle informational text capably. Achievement tests for young children include considerable informational text. Additionally, most of what older children and adults read and write is informational text. For all these reasons, it makes sense to give young children the chance to learn about more than just stories in school.

Second, research supports the view that student achievement benefits from the opportunity to read and receive instruction about informational text. Children whose reading is diversified attain higher achievement levels than those who read only stories.

Third, research on motivation and preferences supports including informational text in the primary grades. Informational text offers great potential for motivating children to read. Indeed, for some children informational text is the *best* route to learning to read. Young children typically like information books and choose to read them as often as stories.

Finally, young children have shown that they can handle the demands of reading, writing, and seeking answers in informational text. Clearly, children need the opportunity to read and be instructed about both stories and informational text.

Achieving a Balance

To ensure that children experience informational text, we suggest that teachers:

- Create inviting classroom libraries with lots of informational texts, including books, magazines, and Internet resources.
- Select high-quality information books and informational text to enrich children's experience.
- Make informational text an integral part of daily read-alouds.
- Teach children comprehension strategies for informational text.
- Enhance children's vocabulary with informational text.
- Guide children in seeking and using information.
- Provide children with experience in informational writing.

These goals will be difficult to accomplish, however, unless children have adequate access to informational text. Because children need to be equally proficient in reading both stories and informational text, we suggest that primary-grade teachers aim for a 50/50 balance in using these materials. Therefore, we recommend that teachers aim for informational texts to be: 50% of the classroom library, 50% of their read-alouds, and 50% of their reading instruction.

When aiming for a 50/50 balance, teachers should keep in mind the differences in informational texts. For example, as we discussed in Chapter 2, information books are not all expository. Many information books for young children are storylike in format. These narrative-information books do not afford children the opportunity to read and learn from expository writing. In addition, many information books for young children are mixed text that include both narrative and expository writing. With these books, children may attend to the story line while skipping the expository portion. Narrative-information and mixed texts may also cause children more difficulty in telling fact from fiction than expository books. Because it is important that children experience expository writing, not just story structures, we recommend that teachers limit narrative-information and mixed texts to no more than a third of their information book selections. In other words, if 50% of the material children experience is informational text, then the majority of that should be expository.

Fortunately, there are not only good stories available for young children but also many wonderful information books. Publishers offer a wide variety of beautifully illustrated information books on a multitude of interesting subjects, and there are many good places to locate appropriate books. Because so many information books are available for young children, teachers need not settle for poor examples. Instead, it is important that teachers look for quality books that are written at an appropriate level for the children with whom they will be used. As our guide in Appendix 3.2 indicates, information books for young children should feature accurate content, good design, an engaging style, clear organization, and appropriate text complexity.

Getting Started with Informational Text

Read-Alouds

Reading aloud is probably the easiest way to begin using informational text in primary-grade classrooms. Read-alouds enable children to learn the distinctive linguistic features of information books and to expand their vocabulary and world knowledge. The interaction that occurs during information book read-alouds promotes meaning seeking and motivates children to read. Further, read-alouds can provide struggling readers with the support they need to read and comprehend a book on their own. Best of all, children like information book read-alouds.

Read-alouds are perfect vehicles for modeling comprehension strategies that work for information books, for demonstrating that information books need not always be read from start to finish, and for showing children how to find information that they want and need. From read-alouds, teachers can move to small-group and whole-class instruction.

As we have noted, we recommend that half of read-alouds be informational text. Teachers can track their progress by using a chart such as the teacher's read-aloud log in Appendix 4.1, which also makes it easy to see whether they are achieving the proper balance. Children can help teachers record the books and decide which category applies best to each book. By doing so, the children will sharpen their understanding of various genres.

Children's Independent Reading

Another easy way to get started with information books is to encourage students' independent reading. Making time to read is crucially important. We ended Chapter 2 with a quote from a student who complained that "we never use our library!" Her complaint makes clear that having lots of books in the classroom will not help if children do not get time to read them.

Teachers should provide time for children to engage in independent reading, and we recommend letting children select whatever they want to read. However, the evidence indicates that when teachers read aloud a book, the likelihood that children will select it for independent reading increases. This means that, so long as teachers include information books in their read-alouds, children will include them in what they select to read on their own.

Teachers can also influence children's independent reading by having them keep logs of what they read. Just having children keep a list of what they read during independent reading will help motivate them to read. Even a simple list—with entries for the date, title, and author—gives children a concrete record of what they have read. A list like this gives children tangible evidence of their efforts.

Going beyond a simple listing is an even more powerful inducement. Dreher (1998/1999) suggested keeping a log that lets children monitor the balance of what they are reading. A reading log that calls attention to the type of reading raises children's awareness of different genres and adds to the likelihood that children will seek them out.

There are many possibilities for creating a reading log that highlights different kinds of books. One way is to modify the Teacher's Read-Aloud Log (see Appendix 4.1) by giving it a new title, such as "My Reading Record." Children could use it to record the books they read and to check off the column for type of book, just as their teachers do for read-alouds.

Another option is to have children record the type of book they read with a color code (see Appendix 9.1). Teachers and students can decide on their own color system. For example, one third-grade class used the following system.

COLOR	TYPE OF READING
Blue	Fiction
Red	Biography
Orange	How to do it
Green	Social studies
Purple	Science
Black	Poetry
Brown	Other

The children in that class helped put colored stickers that matched these codes on the books in their class library so that the various types were easy to find. Other teachers and their students may wish to color-code broader categories, perhaps using only fiction, narrative-informational, mixed text, and expository.

Moving Forward with Informational Text

Once teachers are at ease with including informational text in read-alouds and independent reading, they can extend their efforts. As we have noted, it is important to include informational text in reading instruction and to include reading instruction in content areas. Young children also need opportunities to read and learn from informational text in magazines and newspapers, to search for information not only in books but also on the Internet, and to engage in informational writing about what they have learned.

As teachers infuse their instruction with informational text, they should keep certain principles in mind. First, stories are important too. We do not suggest eliminating them, only that informational text be given roughly equal attention.

Second, the recommendations we have made is this book should not simply be added on to what is already going on in school. Instead, practices will need to be adjusted rather than expanded. For instance, teachers can replace some of the stories used in reading instruction with informational text. Reading instruction can occur in content areas—not just during "reading." Similarly, some story writing can be replaced with informational text writing.

Third, informational text should be used in meaningful contexts. We do not recommend isolated exercises in finding information or practicing comprehension strategies. Strategies for informational text should be taught in real reading situations. The focus should be on the meaningful task at hand, not on using strategies for their own sake. When modeling, guided practice, and gradual transfer of responsibility occurs in real reading situations, children are much more likely to learn what is being taught and to develop the flexibility that will let them apply it in other contexts.

Finally, all children benefit from the opportunity to experience informational text—not just stories. The examples in this book come from children and teachers in schools across the full range of achievement levels, including schools in high-poverty areas as well as those in more fortunate areas. Whether they are struggling readers and writers or average and advanced readers and writers, children respond well and learn much from literacy experiences that include informational text.

Information books and other informational text offer rich opportunities to primary-grade children and their teachers. As second-grade teacher Jenn Smith observed, "Our kids are really excited about nonfiction." We have presented many possibilities for capitalizing on the potential of informational text for creating excitement. Creative primary-grade teachers will come up with many more.

My Reading Log

Name _____

Date	Title	Author	Type (color code)

Children's Book References

Abramson, A. S. (2013). *Kids meet the bugs*. Kennebunkport, ME: Applesauce Press.

Albee, S. (2009). *Elephants (amazing animals)*. New York: Gareth Stevens.

Aloian, M., & Kalman, B. (2007). *A rainforest habitat*. New York: Crabtree.

Bari, E. (n.d.). *Reading maps and globes*. Glenview, IL: Pearson/Scott Foresman.

Barrett, J. (1978). *Cloudy with a chance of meatballs*. Ill. R. Barrett. New York: Atheneum.

Bender, L. (2006). *Elephant (wild animals)*. London: Chrysalis Children's Books.

Birch, R. (2005). *Mosquitoes up close*. Chicago: Raintree.

Bishop, N. (2010). *Nic Bishop lizards*. New York: Scholastic.

Brown, M. (2011). *Pablo Neruda: Poet of the people*. Ill. J. Paschkis. New York: Holt.

Bryant, J. (2013). *A splash of red: The life and art of Horace Pippin*. Ill. M. Sweet. New York: Knopf.

Bryant, J., & Heard, C. (2002). *Making shadow puppets*. Tonawanda, NY: Kids Can Press.

Butterworth, C. (2011). *How did that get in my lunchbox? The story of food*. Ill. L. Gaggiotti. Somerville, MA: Candlewick Press.

Calmenson, S. (2001). *Rosie: A visiting dog's story*. Boston: Houghton Mifflin.

Carney, E. (2011a). *Everything big cats*. Washington DC: National Geographic.

Carney, E. (2011b). *Frogs*. Washington, DC: National Geographic.

Christensen, B. (2009). *Django*. New York: Roaring Book Press.

Chukran, B. A. (2000). *Catch me if you can! The roadrunner*. Bothell, WA: Wright Group.

Cohn, A. L., & Schmidt, S. (2002). *Abraham Lincoln*. Ill. D. A. Johnson. New York: Scholastic.

Cole, J. (1986). *Hungry, hungry sharks*. Ill. P. Wynne. New York: Random House.

Cole, J. (1990). *The Magic School Bus: Inside the human body*. Ill. B. Degen. New York: Scholastic.

Conrad, P. (1995). *Call me Ahnighito*. Ill. R. Egielski. New York: HarperCollins.

Cowcher, H. (2011). *Desert elephants*. New York: Farrar Straus Giroux.

Crandell, R. (2009). *Hands of the rain forest: The Emberá people of Panama*. New York: Holt.

Cullen, E. (1996). *Spiders*. New York: Mondo. (Originally published by Horowitz, 1986, Australia)

Davies, N. (2006). *Extreme animals: The toughest creatures on Earth*. Ill. N. Layton. Cambridge, MA: Candlewick.

dePaola, T. (1973). *Charlie needs a cloak*. New York: Simon & Schuster.

Dineen, J. (2009). *Elephants*. New York: Weigl.

Downer, A. (2011). *Elephant talk: The surprising science of elephant communication*. Minneapolis, MN: Twenty-First Century Books.

Dr. Seuss. (1968). *The foot book*. New York: Random House.

Duke, K. (2012). *In the rainforest*. New York: HarperCollins.

Earle, A. (1995). *Zipping, zapping, zooming bats*. Ill. H. Cole. New York: HarperCollins.

Engle, M. (2010). *Summer birds: The butterflies of Maria Merian*. Ill. J. Paschkis. New York: Holt.

Fowler, A. (1996). *Life in a pond*. New York: Children's Press.

George, J. C. (1995). *Everglades*. Ill. W. Minor. New York: HarperCollins.

Gibbons, G. (1995). *The reasons for seasons*. New York: Holiday House.

Gibbons, G. (2001a). *Ducks!* New York: Holiday House.

Gibbons, G. (2001b). *Polar bears*. New York: Holiday House.

Gibbons, G. (2010). *Alligators and crocodiles*. New York: Holiday House.

Gibbons, G. (2011a). *Gorillas*. New York: Holiday House.

Gibbons, G. (2011b). *It's snowing*. New York: Holiday House.

Glaser, L. (2002). *Our big home: An Earth poem*. Ill. E. Kleven. Minneapolis, MN: Millbrook Press.

Graimes, N. (2007). *Kids' fun and healthy cookbook*. New York: DK Children.

Greeley, A. (2003). *Poisoned planet: Pollution in our world*. New York: Power Kids Press.

Harley, A. (2009). *African acrostics*. Photo. D. Noyes. Somerville, MA: Candlewick Press.

Head, H. (1998). *What's it like to be a baby elephant?* Ill. M. Nicholas. Brookfield, CT: Millbrook Press.

Heller, R. (1983). *The reason for a flower*. New York: Scholastic.

Heneghan, J. (2013). *Love your hamster*. New York: Windmill Books.

Holland, S. (2013). *Reptiles*. New York: DK Publishing.

Hughes, C. D. (2011). *National Geographic Little Kids first big book of dinosaurs*. Washington DC: National Geographic.

Isaacs, S. S. (2002). *Life on the Underground Railroad*. Chicago: Heinemann Library.

Jackson, T. (2014). *The Magic School Bus presents: Our solar system*. Ill. C. Bracken. New York: Scholastic.

James, B. (2010). *Eight spinning planets*. Ill. R. Benfanti. New York: Scholastic.

James, S. (1991). *Dear Mr. Blueberry*. New York: Maxwell Macmillan International.

James, S. M. (2002). *Dolphins*. New York. Mondo.

Jenkins, M. (1999). *The emperor's egg*. Ill. J. Chapman. Cambridge, MA: Candlewick Press.

Jenkins, M. (2011). *Can we save the tiger?* Ill. V. White. Somerville, MA: Candlewick Press.

Jenkins, S. (2001). *Slap, squeak and scatter: How animals communicate*. Boston: Houghton Mifflin.

Jenkins, S. (2010). *The animal book: A collection of the fastest, fiercest, toughest, cleverest, shyest—and most surprising—animals on earth*. Boston: Houghton Mifflin.

Jenkins, S. (2011). *Just a second*. Boston: Houghton Mifflin Harcourt.

Jenkins, S. (2012). *The beetle book*. New York: Houghton Mifflin Harcourt.

Jenkins, S., & Page, R. (2008). *How many ways can you catch a fly?* Boston: Houghton Mifflin.

Jenkins, S., & Page, R. (2011). *Time for a bath*. Ill. B. Degen. New York: Houghton Mifflin.

Joubert, D. (2008). *Face to face with elephants*. Washington, DC: National Geographic.

Kalman, B. (2013). *Baby mammals*. New York: Crabtree.

Kelly, I. (2011). *Even an octopus needs a home*. New York: Holiday House.

Knudson, S. (2006). *African elephants*. Minneapolis: Lerner Publications.

Lambert, D. (2010). *Dinosaur*. New York: DK Publishing.

Lassieur, A. (2002). *The Hopi*. Mankato, MN: Bridgestone Books.

Lessem, D. (2010). *The ultimate dinopedia*. Ill. F. Tempesta. Washington, DC: National Geographic.

Lessor, B. (2004). *Trees*. Ill. A. Salesse. New York: Mondo.

Lobel, A. (1979). *Frog and Toad are friends*. New York: HarperCollins.

Loove, J. U. (2001). *Body numbers*. Barrington, IL: Ribgy.

Lucero, J. (1996). *How to make salsa*. Ill. F. X. Mora. New York: Mondo.

Macauley, D. (2010). *Built to last*. New York: Houghton Mifflin Harcourt.

Machotka, H. (1991). *What neat feet!* New York: Morrow Junior Books.

Mara, W. (2005). *Betsy Ross*. New York: Scholastic.

Markle, S. (2010). *Hip-pocket papa*. Ill. A. Marks. Watertown, MA: Charlesbridge.

Markle, S. (2013a). *Bats: Biggest! Littlest!* Honesdale, PA: Boyds Mills Press.

Markle, S. (2013b). *Snow school*. Ill. A. Marks. Watertown, MA: Charlesbridge.

Marsh, L. (2011). *Cheetahs*. Washington DC: National Geographic.

Marsh, L. (2012). *Tigers*. Washington DC: National Geographic.

Marsh, L. (2013). *Polar bears*. Washington, DC: National Geographic.

Marsh, L. (2014). *Manatees*. Washington, DC: National Geographic.

Martin, J. B. (2010). *The chiru of high Tibet*. Ill. L. Wingerter. New York: Houghton Mifflin.

Martin-James, K. (2001). *Soaring bald eagles*. Minneapolis, MN: Lerner Publications.

Marzollo, J. (1998). *I am a leaf*. New York: Cartwheel.

Meadows, G., & Vial, C. (2002a). *Arctic foxes and red foxes*. Carlsbad, CA: Dominie Press.

Meadows, G., & Vial, C. (2002b). *Reptiles*. Carlsbad, CA: Dominie Press.

Meadows, G., & Vial, C. (2003). *Wasps & bees*. Carlsbad, CA: Dominie Press.

Meister, C. (2014). *Guinea pigs*. Minneapolis, MN: Bullfrog Books.

Minarik, E. H. (2003). *Little Bear*. Ill. M. Sendak. New York: HarperTrophy.

Minor, F. (2009). *If you were a penguin*. Ill. W. Minor. New York: Katherine Tegen Books.

Nelson, R. (2003). *From wax to crayon*. Minneapolis, MN: Lerner Publishing Group.

Nelson, R. (2006). *Exercising*. Minneapolis, MN: Lerner Publishing Group.

Neuman, S. B. (2013). *Swing, sloth*. Washington, DC: National Geographic.

O'Connell, C., & Jackson, D. M. (2011) *The elephant scientist*. Boston: Houghton Mifflin Harcourt.

Orr, T. B. (2013). *Polar bears*. New York: Scholastic.

Person, S. (2012). *Saving animals from oil spills*. New York: Bearport.

Perez, M. (2000). *Breakfast around the world*. Bothell, WA: Wright Group.

Pfeffer, W. (2014). *Light is all around us*. Ill. P. Meisel. New York: HarperCollins.

Pinkney, A. D. (2010). *Sit-in: How four friends stood up by sitting down*. Ill. B. Pinkney. New York: Little, Brown.

Pugliano-Martin, C. (2009), *Trip through time*. Chicago: McGraw-Hill.

Rabe, T. (2002). *There's a map on my lap*. Ill. A. Ruiz. New York: Random House.

Rattini, K. B. (2013). *Weather*. Washington, DC: National Geographic.

Rayner, M. (2008). *Guinea pig*. Pleasantville, NY: Gareth Stevens.

Reid, C. (Ed.). (2011). *The Kingfisher first animal encyclopedia*. Boston: Kingfisher.

Relf, P. (1996). *The Magic School Bus wet all over: A book about the water cycle*. New York: Scholastic.

Richardson, C. (2006). *Special effects*. New York: Chelsea House.

Riehecky, J. (2013). *Show me dinosaurs: My first picture encyclopedia*. North Mankato, MN: Capstone Press.

Riggs, K. (2013). *Giraffes*. Mankato, MN: Creative Paperbacks.

Ring, S. (2007). *Looking at clouds*. New York: Newbridge.

Riordan, R. (2005). *The lightning thief*. New York: Miramax.

Robinson, C. (1997). *Penguins*. Crystal Lake, IL: Heinemann Library.

Rockwell, A. (2001). *Bugs are insects*. Ill. S. Jenkins. New York: HarperCollins.

Roza, G. (2003). *A primary source guide to China*. New York: Rosen.

Sanchez, C. (2008). *Amazing plants and animals.* Carson, CA: Lakeshore Learning.

Schanzer, R. (2002). *How we crossed the West: The adventures of Lewis and Clark.* Washington, DC: National Geographic.

Schrieber, A. (2012). *Penguins!* Washington, DC: National Geographic.

Schwartz, D. M. (2005). *If dogs were dinosaurs.* Ill. J. Warhola. New York: Scholastic.

Sexton, C. (2007). *Clown fish.* Minneapolis, MN: Bellwether Media.

Sexton, C. (2011). *The African elephant.* Minneapolis, MN: Bellwether Media.

Shields, A. (2011). *National Geographic Little Kids first big book of why.* Washington, DC: National Geographic.

Shuter, J. (2005). *Life on a Viking ship.* Chicago: Heinemann Library.

Sidman, J. (2011). Ill. B. Krommes. *Swirl by swirl: Spirals in nature.* Boston: Houghton Mifflin Harcourt.

Silverman, B. (2012). *Can you tell a frog from a toad?* Minneapolis: Lerner.

Simon, S. (1994). *Comets, meteors, and asteroids.* New York: Morrow Junior Books.

Simon, S. (2006). *Lightning.* New York: HarperCollins.

Simon, S. (2013). *Extreme oceans.* San Francisco: Chronicle Books.

Singer, M. (1995). *A wasp is not a bee.* Ill. P. O'Brien. New York: Holt.

Stanley, D., & Vennema, P. (1992). *Bard of Avon: The story of William Shakespeare.* Ill. D. Stanley. New York: Morrow Junior Books.

Stewart, M. (2009). *Snakes!* Washington, DC: National Geographic.

Stewart, M. (2013) *Deadly predators.* Washington, DC: National Geographic.

Stewart, M. (2014). *Water.* Washington, DC: National Geographic.

Stockdale, S. (2011). *Bring on the birds.* Atlanta, GA: Peachtree Publishers.

Taberski, S. (and her first-grade class). (2002). *Penguins are waterbirds.* New York: Mondo.

Tatham, B. (2005). *Baby sea otter.* Ill. J. Paley. New York: Holt.

Teitelbaum, M. (2008). *Baby elephant's fun in the sun.* San Anselmo, CA: Treasure Bay.

Turnbull, S. (2013). *Elephant.* Mankato, MN: Smart Apple Media.

Van Rynbach, I., & Shea, P. D. (2010). *The taxing case of the cows: A true story about suffrage.* Ill. E. A. McCully. New York: Houghton Mifflin Harcourt.

Wallace, K. (2011). *Rockets and spaceships.* New York: DK Publishing.

Wallner, A. (1994). *Betsy Ross.* New York: Holiday House.

Warshaw, H. (2000). *The sleepover cookbook.* Photo. J. Brown. New York: Sterling.

Wilkes, A. (2001). *A farm through time: The history of a farm from medieval times to the present day.* Ill. E. Thomas. New York: Dorling Kindersley.

Yezerski, T. F. (2011). *Meadowlands: A wetlands survival story.* New York: Farrar Straus Giroux.

References

African Wildlife Federation. Our mission. Retrieved May 22, 2010, from *www.awf.org/section/about*.

Alexander, P. A. (1997). Knowledge-seeking and self-schema: A case for the motivational dimensions of exposition. *Educational Psychologist, 32*, 83.

Allington, R., & Gabriel, R. (2012). Every child, every day. *Educational Leadership, 69*(6), 10–15.

Almasi, J. F., & Garas-York, K. (2009). Comprehension and discussion of text. In S. E. Israel & G. G. Duffy (Eds.), *Handbook of research on reading comprehension* (pp. 470–493). New York: Routledge.

American Institutes for Research. (2005). *Reading framework for the 2009 National Assessment of Educational Progress*. Washington, DC: Author.

American Library Association. (n.d.). Funding problems for school library media centers nationwide causing cutbacks in library media specialists, resources, and hours. Retrieved September 8, 2014, from *www.ala.org/Template.cfm?Section=libraryfunding&Template=/ContentManagement/HTMLDisplay.cfm&ContentID=143588&MicrositeID=0*.

Anderson, R. C., Wilson, P. T., & Fielding, L. G. (1988). Growth in reading and how children spend their time outside of school. *Reading Research Quarterly, 23*, 285–303.

Armbruster, B. B., & Nagy, W. E. (1992). Vocabulary in content area lessons. *The Reading Teacher, 45*, 550–551.

August, D., Carlo, M., Dressler, C., & Snow, C. (2005). The critical role of vocabulary development for English language learners. *Learning Disabilities Research & Practice, 20*, 50–57.

Baker, L., Dreher, M. J., & Guthrie, J. T. (Eds.). (2000). *Engaging young readers: Promoting achievement and motivation*. New York: Guilford Press.

Baker, L., & Wigfield, A. (1999). Dimensions of children's motivation for reading and their relations to reading activity and reading achievement. *Reading Research Quarterly, 34*, 452–477.

Baker, L., Dreher, M. J., Shiplet, K. A., Beall, L. C., Voelker, A., Garrett, A., et al. (2011). Children's comprehension of informational text: Reading, engaging, and learning. *International Electronic Journal of Elementary Education, 4*, 197–227.

Baumann, J. F., Edwards, E. C., Font, G., Tereshinski, C. A., Kame'enui, E. J., & Olejnik,

S. (2002). Teaching morphemic and contextual analysis to fifth-grade students. *Reading Research Quarterly, 37*, 150–176.

Baumann, J. F., & Graves, M. F. (2010). What is academic vocabulary? *Journal of Adolescent and Adult Literacy, 54*, 4–12.

Beck, I. L., & McKeown, M. G. (2007). Increasing young low-income children's oral vocabulary repertoires through rich and focused instruction. *The Elementary School Journal, 107*, 251–271.

Beck, I. L., McKeown, M. G., & Kucan, L. (2013). *Bringing words to life: Robust vocabulary instruction* (2nd ed.). New York: Guilford Press.

Beck, I. L., McKeown, M. G., Sandora, D., & Worthy, J. (1996). Questioning the author: A yearlong classroom implementation to engage students with text. *The Elementary School Journal, 96*, 385–414.

Bednar, M. R., & Kletzien, S. B. (1993). Beyond the techniques: Strategic content readers. *The Reading Instruction Journal, 36*, 4–11.

Bennett, H. (2014, August 31). What's for breakfast around the world? Retrieved from *www.washingtonpost.com/lifestyle/kidspost/whats-for-breakfast-around-the-world/2014/08/31/2d9d36a2-28df-11e4-8593-da634b334390_story.html*.

Biemiller, A., & Boote, C. (2006). An effective method for building meaning vocabulary in primary grades. *Journal of Educational Psychology, 98*, 44–62.

Bintz, W. P., Wright, P., & Sheffer, J. (2010). Using copy change with trade books to teach earth science. *The Reading Teacher, 64*, 106–119.

Block, C. C., & Pressley, M. (2003). Best practices in comprehension instruction. In L. B. Gambrell, L. M. Morrow, & M. Pressley (Eds.), *Best practices in literacy instruction* (2nd ed., pp. 111–126). New York: Guilford Press.

Bogard, J. M., & McMackin, M. C. (2012). Combining traditional and new literacies in a 21st century writing workshop. *The Reading Teacher, 65*, 313–323.

Bowers, P. N., Kirby, J. R., & Deacon, S. H. (2010). The effects of morphological instruction on literacy skills: A systematic review of the literature. *Review of Educational Research, 80*, 144–179.

Brabham, E., Boyd, P., & Edgington, W. D. (2000). Sorting it out: Students' responses to fact and fiction in informational storybooks as read-alouds for science and social studies. *Reading Research and Instruction, 39*, 265–290.

Bradley, L. G., & Donovan, C. A. (2010). Information book read-alouds as models for second-grade authors. *The Reading Teacher, 64*, 246–260.

British Columbia Department of Education. (2002). British Columbia performance standards. Retrieved April 22, 2003, from *www.bced.gov.bc.ca/perf_stands/reading.htm*.

Britt, G., & Baker, L. (1997). *Engaging parents and kindergartners in reading through a class lending library* (Instructional Resource No. 41, ED405553). Washington, DC: National Reading Research Center, U.S. Department of Education.

Bromley, K. (2000). Teaching young children to be writers. In D. S. Strickland & L. M. Morrow (Eds.), *Beginning reading and writing* (pp. 111–120). New York: Teachers College Press; Newark, DE: International Reading Association.

Brown, A. L., Campione, J. C., & Day, J. D. (1981). Learning to learn: On training students to learn from texts. *Educational Researcher, 10*, 14–21.

Brown, A. L., & Palincsar, A. S. (1985). *Reciprocal teaching of comprehension strategies: A natural history of one program for enhancing learning* (Technical Report No. 334). Urbana, IL: University of Illinois, Center for the Study of Reading.

Brown, R. (2008). The road not yet taken: A transactional strategies approach to comprehension instruction. *The Reading Teacher, 61*, 538–547.

Brown, R., Pressley, M., Van Meter, P., & Schuder, T. (1996). A quasi-experimental validation of transactional strategies instruction with low-achieving second grade readers. *Journal of Educational Psychology, 88*, 18–37.

Calkins, L. M., Montgomery, K., Santman, D., & Falk, B. (1998). *A teacher's guide to standardized reading tests*. Portsmouth, NH: Heinemann.

Camp, D. (2000). It takes two: Teaching with twin texts of fact and fiction. *The Reading Teacher, 53*, 400–408.

Campbell, J. R., Kapinus, B. A., & Beatty, A. S. (1995). *Interviewing children about their literacy experiences: Data from NAEP's Integrated Reading Performance Record (IRPR) at Grade 4*. Washington, DC: National Center for Education Statistics.

Casale, U. P. (1985). Motor imaging: A reading-vocabulary strategy, *Journal of Reading, 28*, 619–621.

Caswell, L. J., & Duke, N. K. (1998). Non-narrative as a catalyst for literacy development. *Language Arts, 75*, 108–117.

Cazden, C. B. (1986). Classroom discourse. In M. C. Wittrock (Ed.), *Handbook of research on teaching* (3rd ed., pp. 432–463). New York: Macmillan.

Celano, D., & Neuman, S. B. (2010). A matter of computer time. *Phi Delta Kappan, 92*(2), 68–71.

Cervetti, G. N., Bravo, M. A., Hiebert, E. H., Pearson, P. D., & Jaynes, C. A. (2009). Text genre and science content: Ease of reading, comprehension, and reader preference. *Reading Psychology, 30*, 487–511.

Chandler, M. A. (2015, March 10). Book imbalance. *The Washington Post*, pp. B1–B2.

Coiro, J., & Dobler, E. (2007). Exploring the online reading comprehension strategies used by sixth-grade skilled readers to search for and locate information on the Internet. *Reading Research Quarterly, 42*, 214–257.

Coleman, J. M., Bradley, L. G., & Donovan, C. (2012). Visual representations in second graders' information book compositions. *The Reading Teacher, 66*, 31–45.

Coleman, J. M., McTigue, E. M., & Smolkin, L. B. (2011). Elementary teachers' use of graphical representations in science teaching. *Journal of Science Teacher Education, 22*, 613–643.

Coles, M., & Hall, C. (2003). Gendered readings: Learning from children's reading choices. *Journal of Research in Reading, 25*, 96–108.

College Board, National Writing Project, & Phi Delta Kappa International. (2010). *Teachers are the center of education: Writing, learning and leading in the digital age*. Berkeley, CA: Author. Retrieved May 14, 2014, from *http://files.eric.ed.gov/fulltext/ED510965.pdf*.

Copenhaver, J. F. (2001). Running out of time: Rushed read-alouds in a primary classroom. *Language Arts, 79*, 148–158.

Correia, M. P. (2011). Fiction vs. informational texts: Which will kindergartners choose? *Young Children, 66*(6), 100–104.

Crosson, A. C., & Lesaux, N. K. (2013). Connectives: Fitting another piece of the vocabulary puzzle. *The Reading Teacher, 67*, 193–200.

Cummins, S., & Stallmeyer-Gerard, C. (2011). Teaching for synthesis of informational texts with read-alouds. *The Reading Teacher, 64*, 394–405.

Cunningham, A. E., Zibulsky, J., Stanovich, K. E., & Stanovich, P. J. (2009). How teachers would spend their time teaching language arts: The mismatch between self-reported and best practices. *Journal of Learning Disabilities, 42*, 418–430.

Dalton, B. (2012). Multimodal composition and the Common Core State Standards. *The Reading Teacher, 66*, 333–339.

Dalton, B. (2013). Close reading and multimodal commentary. *The Reading Teacher, 66*, 642–649.

Dalton, B., & Grisham, D. L. (2011). eVoc strategies: 10 ways to use technology to build vocabulary. *The Reading Teacher, 64*, 306–317.

Dehaene, S. (2009). *Reading in the brain*. New York: Penguin Books.

Dodge, A. M., Husain, N., & Duke, N. K. (2011). Connected kids? K–2 children's use and understanding of the Internet. *Language Arts, 89*, 86–98.

Donovan, C. A., & Smolkin, L. B. (2001). Genre and other factors influencing teachers' book selections for science instruction. *Reading Research Quarterly, 36*, 412–440.

Donovan, C. A., & Smolkin, L. B. (2004). How not to get lost on The Magic School Bus: What makes high science content read alouds? In E. W. Saul (Ed.), *Crossing borders in literacy and science instruction: Perspectives on theory and practice* (pp. 291–313). Newark, DE: International Reading Association & Arlington, VA: National Science Teachers Association.

Donovan, C. A., & Smolkin, L. B. (2011). Supporting informational writing in the elementary grades. *The Reading Teacher, 64*, 406–416.

Donovan, C. A., Smolkin, L. B., & Lomax, R. G. (2000). Beyond the independent-level text: Considering the reader–text match in first graders' self-selections during recreational reading. *Reading Psychology, 21*, 309–333.

Dorfman, L. R., & Cappelli, R. (2009). *Nonfiction mentor texts: Teaching informational writing through children's literature, K–8*. Portland, ME: Stenhouse.

Dreher, M. J. (1992). Locating information in textbooks. *Journal of Reading, 35*, 364–371.

Dreher, M. J. (1998/1999). Motivating children to read more nonfiction. *The Reading Teacher, 52*, 414–417.

Dreher, M. J. (2000). Fostering reading for learning. In L. Baker, M. J. Dreher, & J. T. Guthrie (Eds.), *Engaging young readers: Promoting achievement and motivation* (pp. 68–93). New York: Guilford Press.

Dreher, M. J. (2002). Children searching and using information text: A critical part of comprehension. In C. C. Block & M. Pressley (Eds.), *Comprehension instruction: Research-based best practices* (pp. 289–304). New York: Guilford Press.

Dreher, M. J. (2003). Motivating struggling readers by tapping the potential of information books. *Reading and Writing Quarterly: Overcoming Learning Difficulties, 19*, 25–38.

Dreher, M. J., & Dromsky, A. (2000, December). *Increasing the diversity of young children's independent reading.* Paper presented at the meeting of the National Reading Conference, Scottsdale, AZ.

Dreher, M. J., & Kletzien, S. B. (2015). Have recommended book lists changed to reflect current expectations for informational text in K–3 classrooms? *Reading Psychology.* Published online June 15, 2015. DOI 10.1080/02702711.2015.1055871.

Dreher, M. J., & Sammons, R. B. (1994). Fifth-graders' search for information in a textbook. *Journal of Reading Behavior, 26*, 301–314.

Dreher, M. J., & Voelker, A. (2004). Choosing informational books for primary-grade classrooms: The importance of balance and quality. In E. W. Saul (Ed.), *Crossing borders in literacy and science instruction: Perspectives on theory and practice* (pp. 260–276). Newark, DE: International Reading Association & Arlington, VA: National Science Teachers Association.

Duffy, G. G. (2002). The case for direct explanation of strategies. In C. C. Block & M. Pressley (Eds.), *Comprehension instruction: Research-based best practices* (pp. 28–41). New York: Guilford Press.

Duke, N. K. (2000). 3.6 minutes per day: The scarcity of informational texts in first grade. *Reading Research Quarterly, 35*, 202–224.

Duke, N., & Kays, J. (1998). "Can I say 'Once upon a time'?": Kindergarten children developing knowledge of information book language. *Early Childhood Research Quarterly, 13*, 295–318.

Dymock, S., & Nicholson, T. (2010). "High 5!": Strategies to enhance comprehension of expository text. *The Reading Teacher, 64*, 166–178.

Dyson, M. J. (2010). Review of 8 Spinning Planets. Retrieved June 10, 2013, from *www.mariannedyson.com/reviews/rev8spinning.html*.

Educational Testing Service. (2006). ICT literacy assessment: Preliminary findings. Retrieved December 15, 2006, from *www.ets.org/ictliteracy*.

El-Dinary, P. B. (2002). Challenges of implementing transactional strategies instruction for reading comprehension. In C. C. Block & M. Pressley (Eds.), *Comprehension instruction: Research-based best practices* (pp. 201–215). New York: Guilford Press.

Elley, W. B. (1989). Vocabulary acquisition from listening to stories. *Reading Research Quarterly, 24,* 174–187.

Elley, W. B. (1992). *How in the world do students read?* Hamburg, Germany: International Association for the Evaluation of Educational Achievement.

Feldt, R. C., Feldt, R. A., & Kilburg, K. (2002). Acquisition, maintenance, and transfer of a questioning strategy in second- and third-grade students to learn from science textbooks. *Reading Psychology, 23,* 181–198.

Fielding., L., & Roller, C. (1992). Making difficult books accessible and easy books acceptable. *The Reading Teacher, 45,* 678–685.

Fisher, D., & Frey, N. (2012). Close reading in elementary school. *The Reading Teacher, 66,* 179–188.

Flood, J., & Lapp, D. (1986). Types of texts: The match between what students read in basals and what they encounter in tests. *Reading Research Quarterly, 21,* 284–297.

Forzani, E., & Leu, D. J. (2012). New literacies for new learners: The need for digital technologies in primary classrooms. *The Educational Forum, 76,* 421–424.

Fountas, I., & Pinnell, G. S. (2005). *Matching texts to readers for effective teaching.* Portsmouth, NH: Heinemann.

Fox, M. (2013). What next in the read-aloud battle? Win or lose? *The Reading Teacher, 67,* 4–8.

Fractor, J. S., Woodruff, M. C., Martinez, M. G., & Teale, W. H. (1993). Let's not miss opportunities to promote voluntary reading: Classroom libraries in the elementary school. *The Reading Teacher, 46,* 476–484.

Fredericks, A. D. (1986). Mental imagery activities to improve comprehension. *The Reading Teacher, 40,* 78–81.

Freedman, R. (1992). Fact or fiction? In E. B. Freeman & D. G. Person (Eds.), *Using nonfiction trade books in the elementary classroom* (pp. 2–10). Urbana, IL: National Council of Teachers of English.

Frye, E. M., Trathen, W., & Schlagal, B. (2010). Extending acrostic poetry into content learning: A scaffolding framework. *The Reading Teacher, 63,* 591–595.

Gallagher, T. L., Fazio, X. E., & Ciampa, K. (2013, December). *Readability of science-based texts: Comparing literacy readers, trade books and on-line periodicals.* Paper presented at the Literacy Research Association Conference, Dallas, TX.

Gambrell, L. B. (2011). Seven rules of engagement. *The Reading Teacher, 65,* 172–178.

Genesee, F., Lindholm-Leary, K., Saunders, W., & Christian, D. (2006). *Educating English language learners.* New York: Cambridge University Press.

Gill, S. R. (2009). What teachers need to know about the "new" nonfiction. *The Reading Teacher, 63,* 260–267.

Glenberg, A. M., Gutierrez, T., Levin, J. R., Japuntich, S., & Kaschak, M. P. (2004). Activity and imagined activity can enhance young children's reading comprehension. *Journal of Educational Psychology, 96,* 424–436.

Goldenberg, C. (2008). Teaching English language learners. *American Educator, 32,* 8–44.

Graves, M. F. (2006). *The vocabulary book: Learning and instruction.* Newark, DE: International Reading Association.

Graves, M. F., & Watts-Taffe, S. (2008). For the love of words: Fostering word consciousness in young readers. *The Reading Teacher, 62,* 185–193.

Greenwald, E. A., Persky, H. R., Campbell, J. R., & Mazzeo, J. (2002). The nation's report card: NAEP 1998 writing report card for the nation and the states. Retrieved May 14, 2003, from *http://nces.ed.gov/nationsreportcard.*

Guccione, L. M. (2011). Integrating literacy and inquiry for English learners. *The Reading Teacher, 64,* 567–577.

Guthrie, J. T., Coddington, C. S., & Wigfield, A. (2009). Profiles of reading motivation among African American and Caucasian students. *Journal of Literacy Research, 41,* 317–353.

Guthrie, J. T., & Humenick, N. M. (2004). Motivating students to read: Evidence for classroom practices that increase motivation and achievement. In P. McCardle & V. Chhabra (Eds.), *The voice of evidence in reading research* (pp. 329–354). Baltimore: Brookes.

Guthrie, J. T., Wigfield, A., Barbosa, P., Perencevich, K. C., Taboada, A., Davis, M. H., et al. (2004). Increasing reading comprehension and engagement through concept-oriented reading instruction. *Journal of Educational Psychology, 96,* 403–423.

Halvorsen, A. L., Duke, N. K., Brugar, K. A., Block, M. K., Strachan, S. L., Berka, M. B., et al. (2012). Narrowing the achievement gap in second-grade social studies and content area literacy: The promise of a project-based approach. *Theory and Research in Social Education, 40,* 198–229.

Harris, K. R., Graham, S., Friedlander, B., & Laud, L. (2013). Bring powerful writing strategies into your classroom! *The Reading Teacher, 66,* 538–542.

Harvey, S., & Goudvis, A. (2013). Comprehension at the core. *The Reading Teacher, 66,* 432–439.

Heisey, N., & Kucan, L. (2010). Introducing science concepts to primary students through read-alouds: Interactions and multiple texts make the difference. *The Reading Teacher, 63,* 666–676.

Hiebert, E. H., & Cervetti, G. N. (2012). What differences in narrative and informational texts mean for the learning and instruction of vocabulary. In E. B. Kame'enui & J. F. Baumann (Eds.), *Vocabulary instruction: Research to practice* (2nd ed., pp. 322–344). New York: Guilford Press.

Hiebert, E. H., & Fisher, C. W. (1990). Whole language: Three themes for the future. *Educational Leadership, 47,* 62–64.

Hiebert, E. H., & Lubliner, S. (2008). The nature, learning, and instruction of general academic vocabulary. In A. E. Farstrup & S. J. Samuels (Eds.), *What research has to say about vocabulary instruction* (pp. 105–129). Newark, DE: International Reading Association.

Hiebert, E. H., & Raphael, T. E. (1998). *Early literacy instruction.* New York: Harcourt Brace.

Hinchman, K. A., & Moore, D. M. (2013). Close reading, a cautionary interpretation. *Journal of Adolescent and Adult Literacy, 56,* 441–450.

Hoffman, J. V. (1992). Critical reading/thinking across the curriculum: Using I-charts to support learning. *Language Arts, 69,* 121–127.

Hoffman, J. V., Roser, N. L., & Battle, J. (1993). Reading aloud in classrooms: From modal to a "model." *The Reading Teacher, 46,* 496–505.

Horowitz, R., & Freeman, S. H. (1995). Robots versus spaceships: The role of discussion in kindergartners' and second graders' preferences for science texts. *The Reading Teacher, 49,* 30–40.

Hynes, M. (2000). "I read for facts": Reading nonfiction in a fictional world. *Language Arts, 77,* 485–495.

International Reading Association. (1999). *Providing books and other print materials for classroom and school libraries: A position statement of the International Reading Association.* Newark, DE: Author.

International Reading Association and National Association for the Education of Young Children. (1998). Learning to read and write: Developmentally appropriate practices for young children. *The Reading Teacher, 52,* 193–216.

Jacobs, J. S., Morrison, T. G., & Swinyard, W. R. (2000). Reading aloud to students: A national probability study of classroom reading practices of elementary school teachers. *Reading Psychology, 21,* 171–193.

Jeong, J., Gaffney, J. S., & Choi, J.-O. (2010). Availability and use of informational texts in second-, third-, and fourth-grade classrooms. *Research in the Teaching of English, 44,* 435–456.

Jetton, T. (1994). Information-driven versus story-driven: What children remember when they are read informational stories. *Reading Psychology, 15,* 109–130.

Johnston, P. H., Ivey, G., & Faulkner, A. (2011–2012). Talking in class. *The Reading Teacher, 65,* 232–237.

Kamil, M. L., & Lane, D. (1998, December). *Informational text, reading instruction and demands of technology in elementary school.* Paper presented at the annual meeting of the National Reading Conference, Austin, TX.

Kane, S. (1998). The view from the discourse level: Teaching relationships and text structure. *The Reading Teacher, 52,* 182–184.

Karchmer, R. A., Mallette, M. H., & Leu, D. J., Jr. (2002). Early literacy in the digital age: Moving from a singular book literacy to the multiple literacies of networked information and communication technologies. In D. M. Barone & L. M. Morrow (Eds.), *Literacy and young children: Research-based practices* (pp. 175–194). New York: Guilford Press.

Karchmer-Klein, R., & Shinas, V. H. (2012). Guiding principles for supporting new literacies in your classroom. *The Reading Teacher, 65,* 285–293.

Kelley, M. J., & Clausen-Grace, N. (2010). Guiding students through expository text with text feature walks. *The Reading Teacher, 64,* 191–195.

Kellogg, R. T. (2008). Training writing skills: A cognitive developmental perspective. *Journal of Writing Research, 1,* 1–26.

Kieffer, M. J., & Lesaux, N. K. (2007). Breaking down words to build meaning: Morphology, vocabulary, and reading comprehension in the urban classroom. *The Reading Teacher, 61,* 134–144.

Kintsch, W., & Van Dijk, T. A. (1978). Toward a model of text comprehension and production. *Psychological Review, 85,* 363–394.

Kletzien, S. B. (1991). Strategy use by good and poor comprehenders reading expository text of differing levels. *Reading Research Quarterly, 26,* 67–86.

Kletzien, S. B. (1992). Proficient and less proficient comprehenders' strategy use for different top-level structures. *Journal of Reading Behavior, 24,* 191–215.

Kletzien, S. B. (2009). Paraphrasing: An effective comprehension strategy. *The Reading Teacher, 63,* 73–77.

Kletzien, S. B., & DeRenzi, A. (2001, December). *"I like real books": Children's genre preferences.* Paper presented at the National Reading Conference, San Antonio, TX.

Kletzien, S. B., & Dreher, M. J. (2004). *Informational text in K–3 classrooms: Helping children read and write.* Newark, DE: International Reading Association.

Kletzien, S. B., & Szabo, R. J. (1998, December). *Information text or narrative text? Children's preferences revisited.* Paper presented at the National Reading Conference, Austin, TX.

Korkeamäki, R.-L., Tiainen, O., & Dreher, M. J. (1998). Helping Finnish second-graders make sense of their reading and writing in science projects. *National Reading Conference Yearbook, 47,* 334–344.

Kraemer, L., McCabe, P., & Sinatra, R. (2012). The effects of read-alouds of expository text on first graders' listening comprehension and book choice. *Literacy Research and Instruction, 51*(2), 165–178.

Krashen, S. (2011). *Free voluntary reading.* Santa Barbara, CA: Libraries Unlimited.

Krashen, S., Lee, S., & McQuillan, J. (2012). Is the library important? Multivariate studies at the national and international level. *Journal of Language and Literacy Education, 8,* 26–36.

Kucan, L. (2012). What is most important to know about vocabulary? *The Reading Teacher, 65,* 360–366.

Lauritzen, C., Kletzien, S. B., & Grozdanić, V. (2001). Critical thinking through childhood stories and experiences. *The Thinking Classroom, 6,* 27–31.

Lennox, S. (2013). Interactive read-alouds—an avenue for enhancing children's language for thinking and understanding: A review of recent research. *Early Childhood Education Journal, 41,* 381–389.

Leu, D. J., Jr. (2000). Literacy and technology: Deictic consequences for literacy education in an information age. In M. L. Kamil, P. Mosenthal, P. D. Pearson, & R. Barr (Eds.), *Handbook of reading research* (Vol. 3, pp. 743–770). Mahwah, NJ: Erlbaum.

Leu, D. J., Jr. (2013, August 7). *The new literacies of online research and comprehension: Reading with a lens to the future as well as a lens to the past.* Paper presented at the 18th European Conference on Reading, Jönköping, Sweden.

Leu, D. J., Jr., McVerry, J. G., O'Byrne, W. I., Kiili, C., Zawilinski, L., Everett-Cacopardo, H., et al. (2011). The new literacies of online reading comprehension: Expanding the literacy and learning curriculum. *Journal of Adolescent and Adult Literacy, 55,* 5–14.

Lindsay, J. (2010). Children's access to print material and education-related outcomes: Findings from a meta-analytic review. Retrieved from *www.rif.org/us/about/literacy-issues/giving-children-access-to-print-materials-improves-reading-performance.htm.*

Littlefair, A. (1991). *Reading all types of writing.* Buckingham, UK: Open University Press.

MacDonald, E. (2013). Digital age literacy and learning. *Pennsylvania Reads, 12,* 59–60.

Mallett, M. (1992). *Making facts matter.* London: Chapman.

Mallett, M. (1999). *Young researchers: Informational reading and writing in the early and primary years.* London: Routledge.

Malloy, J. A., & Gambrell, L. B. (2011). The contribution of discussion to reading comprehension and critical thinking. In A. McGill-Franzen & R. L. Allington, (Eds.), *Handbook of Reading Disability Research* (pp. 253–262). New York: Routledge.

Maloch, B., & Bomer, R. (2013). Informational text and the Common Core Standards: What are we talking about, anyway? *Language Arts, 90,* 205–211.

Maloch, B., & Horsey, M. (2013). Living inquiry: Learning from and about informational texts in a second-grade classroom. *The Reading Teacher, 66,* 475–485.

Martinez, M. G., Roser, N. L., Worthy, J., Strecker, S., & Gough, P. (1997). Classroom libraries and children's book selections: Redefining "access" in self-selected reading. In C. K. Kinzer, K. A. Hinchman, & D. J. Leu (Eds.), *Inquiries in literacy theory and practice/Forty-sixth yearbook of the National Reading Conference* (pp. 265–272). Chicago: National Reading Conference.

Marulis, L. M., & Neuman, S. B. (2010). The effects of vocabulary intervention on young children's word learning: A meta-analysis. *Review of Educational Research, 80,* 300–335.

Mayer, D. A. (1995). How can we best use children's literature in teaching science concepts? *Science and Children, 32,* 16–19, 43.

McGee, L. M., & Schickedanz, J. A. (2007). Repeated interactive read-alouds in preschool and kindergarten. *The Reading Teacher, 60,* 742–751.

McKeown, M. G., Crosson, A. C., Artz, N. J., Sandora, C., & Beck I. L. (2013). In the media: Expanding students' experience with academic vocabulary, *The Reading Teacher, 67,* 45–63.

McTigue, E. M., & Flowers, A. C. (2011). Science visual literacy: Learners' perception and knowledge of diagrams. *The Reading Teacher, 64,* 578–589.

Merisuo-Storm, T., & Soininen, M. (2010). Primary school pupils deriving word meaning from written context. *Procedia Social and Behavioral Sciences 2,* 1625–1629.

Meyer, B. J. F., Brandt, D. M., & Bluth, G. J. (1980). Use of top-level structure in text: Key for reading comprehension of ninth-grade students. *Reading Research Quarterly, 16,* 72–103.

Meyer, B. J. F., & Poon, L. W. (2001). Effects of structure strategy training and signaling on recall of text. *Journal of Educational Psychology, 93,* 141–159.

Miller, D. (2013). I can create mental images to retell and infer major ideas. *The Reading Teacher, 66,* 360–364.

Mohr, K. A. J. (2006). Children's choices for recreational reading: A three-part investigation of selection preferences, rationales, and processes. *Journal of Literacy Research, 38*, 81–104.

Morrow, L. M. (1991). Promoting voluntary reading. In J. Flood, J. M. Jensen, D. Lapp, & J. R. Squire (Eds.), *Handbook of research on teaching the English language arts* (pp. 681–690). New York: Macmillan.

Morrow, L. M., & Tracy, D. H. (2014). Best practices in early literacy instruction: Preschool, kindergarten, and first grade. In L. B. Gambrell & L. M. Morrow (Eds.), *Best practices in literacy instruction* (5th ed., pp. 85–106). New York: Guilford Press.

Moss, B. (2008). The information text gap: The mismatch between non-narrative text types in basal readers and 2009 NAEP recommended guidelines. *Journal of Literacy Research, 40*, 201–219.

Moss, B., & Newton, E. (2002). An examination of the informational text genre in basal readers. *Reading Psychology, 23*, 1–13.

Moss, G. (2001). To work or play? Junior age non-fiction as objects of design. *Reading, 35*, 106–110.

Mullis, I. V. S., Martin, M. O., Foy, P., & Drucker, K. T. (2012). *PIRLS 2011 international results in reading.* Chestnut Hill, MA: TIMSS & PIRLS International Study Center, Boston College.

Nagy, W. E. (1988). *Teaching vocabulary to improve reading comprehension.* Newark, DE: International Reading Association.

Nagy, W. E., & Anderson, R. C. (1984). How many words are there in printed school English? *Reading Research Quarterly, 19*, 304–330.

Nagy, W. E., & Townsend, D. (2012). Words as tools: Learning academic vocabulary as language acquisition. *Reading Research Quarterly, 47*, 91–108.

National Center for Education Statistics. (2012, September). The nation's report card: Writing. Retrieved September 28, 2013, from *http://ces.ed.gov/nationsreportcard/pubs/main2011/2012470.asp.*

National Commission on Writing in America's Schools and Colleges. (2003). *The neglected "R": The need for a writing revolution.* New York: College Entrance Examination Board. Retrieved May 14, 2003, from *www.writingcommission.org.*

National Governors Association Center for Best Practices & Council of Chief State School Officers. (2010a). *Common Core State Standards for English language arts and literacy in history/social studies, science, and technical subjects.* Washington, DC: Author.

National Governors Association Center for Best Practices & Council of Chief State School Officers. (2010b). *Common Core State Standards for English language arts and literacy in history/social studies, science, and technical subjects. Appendix A: Research supporting key elements of the Standards.* Washington, DC: Author.

National Institute of Child Health and Human Development. (2000). *Report of the National Reading Panel. Teaching children to read: An evidence-based assessment of the scientific research literature on reading and its implications for reading instruction* (NIH Publication No. 00–4769). Washington, DC: U.S. Government Printing Office.

Ness, M. (2011). Teachers' use of and attitudes toward informational text in K–5 classrooms. *Reading Psychology, 32*(1), 28–53.

Neuman, S. B. (1999). Books make a difference: A study of access to literacy. *Reading Research Quarterly, 34*, 286–311.

Neuman, S. B. (2006). The knowledge gap: Implications for early education. In D. Dickinson & S. B. Neuman (Eds.), *Handbook of early literacy research* (Vol. 2, pp. 29–40). New York: Guilford Press.

Neuman, S. B. (2010). Lessons from my mother: Reflections on the National Early Literacy Panel report. *Educational Researcher, 39*, 301–304.

Neuman, S. B., & Celano, D. (2001). Access to print in low-income and middle-income communities. *Reading Research Quarterly, 36,* 8–26.

Neuman, S. B., & Celano, D. C. (2012a). *Giving our children a fighting chance: Poverty, literacy, and the development of information capital.* New York: Teachers College Press.

Neuman, S. B., & Celano, D. C. (2012b). Worlds apart: One city, two libraries, and ten years of watching inequality grow. *American Educator, 36*(3), 13–23.

Neuman, S. B., & Dwyer, J. (2009). Missing in action: Vocabulary instruction in pre-K. *The Reading Teacher, 62,* 384–392.

Neuman, S. B., & Dwyer, J. (2011). Developing vocabulary and conceptual knowledge for low-income preschoolers: A design experiment. *Journal of Literacy Research, 43,* 103–129.

Neuman, S. B., & Roskos, K. (2012) More than teachable moments. *The Reading Teacher, 66,* 63–67.

Neuman, S. B., & Wright, T. S. (2014). The magic of words: Teaching vocabulary in the early childhood classroom. *American Educator, 38,* 4–15.

Nippold, M. A., & Sun, L. (2008). Knowledge of morphologically complex words: A developmental study of older children and young adolescents. *Language, Speech, and Hearing Services in Schools, 39,* 365–373.

Ogle, D. (1986). K-W-L: A teaching model that develops active reading of expository text. *The Reading Teacher, 40,* 564–570.

O'Hara, J. D., & Dreher, M. J. (2008). *Supplementary reading instruction for struggling third- and fourth-grade readers: The effects of CORI-STAR and Guided Reading upon students' comprehension, metacognitive awareness, and motivation.* Paper presented at the International Reading Association convention, Atlanta, GA.

Oyler, C. (1996). Sharing authority: Student initiations during teacher-led read-alouds of information books. *Teaching and Teacher Education, 12,* 149–160.

Oyler, C., & Barry, A. (1996). Intertextual connections in read-alouds of information books. *Language Arts, 73,* 324–329.

Palincsar, A. S., & Brown, A. L. (1989). Instruction for self-regulated reading. In L. B. Resnick & L. E. Klopfer (Eds.), *Toward the thinking curriculum: Current cognitive research* (pp. 19–39). Alexandria, VA: Association for Supervision and Curriculum Development.

Pappas, C. C. (1991). Young children's strategies in learning the "book language" of information books. *Discourse Processes, 14,* 208–225.

Pappas, C. C. (1993). Is narrative "primary"? Some insights from kindergartners' pretend readings of stories and information books. *Journal of Reading Behavior, 25,* 97–129.

Pappas, C. C., & Barry, A. (1997). Scaffolding urban students' initiations: Transactions in reading information books in the read-aloud curriculum genre. In N. J. Karolides (Ed.), *Reader response in elementary classrooms: Quest and discovery* (pp. 215–236). Mahwah, NJ: Erlbaum.

Pappas, C. C., & Varelas, M. (2009). Multimodal books in science-literacy units: Language and visual images for meaning making. *Language Arts, 86,* 201–211.

Pappas, C. C, Varelas, M., Barry, A,, & O'Neill, A. (2000, December). *The development of science discourse genres in a primary-grade integrated science-literacy unit on states of matter: Analysis of intertextuality.* Paper presented at the National Reading Conference, Scottsdale, AZ.

Pappas, C. C., Varelas, M., Patton, S. K., Ye, L., & Ortiz, I. (2012). Dialogic strategies in read-alouds of English-language information books in a second-grade bilingual classroom. *Theory into Practice, 51,* 263–272.

Paquette, K. R., Fello, S. E., & Jalongo, M. R. (2007). The talking drawings strategy: Using primary children's illustrations and oral language to improve comprehension of expository text. *Early Childhood Education Journal, 35,* 65–73.

Paris, S. G., & Hamilton, E. E. (2009). The development of children's reading comprehension. In

S. E. Israel & G. G. Duffy, *Handbook of research on reading comprehension* (pp. 32–53). New York: Routledge.

Paul, A. M. (2014). Is the body the next breakthrough in education tech? The Hechinger Report. Retrieved July 23, 2014, from *http://hechingerreport.org/content/body-next-breakthrough-education-tech_16629/print*.

Pearson, P. D., & Duke, N. K. (2002). Comprehension instruction in the primary grades. In C. C. Block & M. Pressley (Eds.), *Comprehension instruction: Research-based best practices* (pp. 247–258). New York: Guilford Press.

Pearson, P. D., Hiebert, E. H., & Kamil, M. L. (2007). Vocabulary assessment: What we know and what we need to learn. *Reading Research Quarterly, 42*, 282–296.

Pennsylvania Department of Education. (2003). Academic standards for reading, writing, speaking and listening. Retrieved April 23, 2003, from *www.pde.state.pa.us/k12*.

Persky, H. R., Daane, M. C., & Jin, Y. (2003). *The nation's report card: Writing 2002*. U.S. Department of Education, Institute of Education Sciences, National Center for Education Statistics (NCES 2003-529). Washington, DC: U.S. Government Printing Office.

Peterson, S. S. (2005). Award-winning authors and illustrators talk about writing and teaching writing. *The Reading Teacher, 67*, 498–506.

Pew Research Center. (2013). Internet and American life project, spring tracking survey, April 17–May 19, 2013. Retrieved August 19, 2013, from *www.perinternet.org/Static-Pages/Trend*.

Pew Research Center. (2012). Internet teens and privacy management survey, July 26–September 30, 2012. Retrieved August 19, 2013, from *www.pewinternet.org/Static-Pages/Trend*.

Pimentel, S. (2012). Statement on the Nation's Report Card: Writing 2011 Grades 8 and 12. Retrieved September 3, 2014, from *www.nagb.org/newsroom/naep-releases/2011–writing/statement-pimentel.html*.

Prensky, M. (2001). Digital natives, digital immigrants. *On the Horizon, 9*, 1–6.

Pressley, M., Dolezal, S. E., Raphael, L. M., Mohan, L., Roehrig, A. D., & Bogner, K. (2003). *Motivating primary-grade students*. New York: Guilford Press.

Pytash, K. E., & Morgan, D. N. (2014). Using mentor texts to teach writing in science and social studies. *The Reading Teacher, 68*, 93–102.

Rice, D. C. (2002). Using trade books in teaching elementary science: Facts and fallacies. *The Reading Teacher, 55*, 552–565.

Rich, M. (September 24, 2014). Academic skills on web are tied to income level. *New York Times*, p. A23.

Richgels, D. J., McGee, L. M., Lomax, R. G., & Sheard, D. (1987). Awareness of four text structures: Effects on recall of expository text. *Reading Research Quarterly, 25*, 80–89.

Roller, C. M. (1990). The interaction between knowledge and structure variables in the processing of expository prose. *Reading Research Quarterly, 25*. 80–89.

Rosenhouse, J., Feitelson, D., Kita, B., & Goldstein, Z. (1997). Interactive reading aloud to Israeli first graders: Its contribution to literacy development. *Reading Research Quarterly, 32*, 168–183.

Sanacore, J. (1991). Expository and narrative text: Balancing young children's reading experiences. *Childhood Education, 67*, 211–214.

Santoro, L. E., Chard, D. J., Howard, L., & Baker, S. K. (2008). Making the very most of classroom read-alouds to promote comprehension and vocabulary. *The Reading Teacher, 61*, 396–408.

Saul, E. W., & Dieckman, D. (2005). Choosing and using information trade books. *Reading Research Quarterly, 40*, 502–513.

Schugar, J. T., Schugar, H. R., & Smith C. (2014, April). *Reading in the post-PC era: Children's comprehension of interactive ebooks*. Paper presented at the annual meeting of the American Educational Research Association, Philadelphia, PA.

Schugar, H. R., Smith, C. A., & Schugar, J. T. (2013). Teaching with interactive picture e-books in grades K–6. *The Reading Teacher, 66,* 615–624.

Shanahan, T. (2012). What is close reading? Retrieved August 7, 2013, from *www.shanahanonliteracy.com/2012/06.*

Shanahan, T., Callison, K., Carriere, C., Duke, N. K., Pearson, P. D., Schatschneider, C., et al. (2010). *Improving reading comprehension in kindergarten through 3rd grade: A practice guide* (NCEE 2010–4038). Washington, DC: National Center for Education Evaluation and Regional Assistance, Institute of Education Sciences, U.S. Department of Education. Retrieved August 4, 2013, from *www.whatworks.ed.gov/publications/practiceguides.*

Shiel, G. (2001/2002). Reforming reading instruction in Ireland and England. *The Reading Teacher, 55,* 372–374.

Siegal, A. C. (2014, September 4). Preserving the wilderness for 50 years. Retrieved from *www.washingtonpost.com/lifestyle/kidspost/2014/09/04/ad124df0-2f2e-11e4-994d-202962a9150c_story.html.*

Silverman, R., & Hines, S. (2009). The effects of multimedia-enhanced instruction on the vocabulary of English-language learners and non-English-language learners in pre-kindergarten through second grade. *Journal of Educational Psychology, 101,* 305–314.

Smith, C., Constantino, R., & Krashen, S. (1997, March/April). Differences in print environment for children in Beverly Hills, Compton and Watts. *Emergency Librarian, 24,* 8–9.

Smith, M. C., Mikulecky, L., Kibby, M. W., Dreher, M. J., & Dole, J. A. (2000). What will be the demands of literacy in the workplace in the next millennium? *Reading Research Quarterly, 35,* 378–383.

Smolkin, L. B., & Donovan, C. A. (2001). The contexts of comprehension: The information book read aloud, comprehension acquisition, and comprehension instruction in a first-grade classroom. *The Elementary School Journal, 102,* 97–122.

Smolkin, L. B., & Donovan, C. A. (2005). Looking closely at a science trade book: Gail Gibbons and multimodal literacy. *Language Arts, 83,* 52–62.

Smolkin, L. B., Donovan, C. A., & Lomax, R. G. (2000). Is narrative primary? Well, it depends. . . . *National Reading Conference Yearbook, 49,* 511–520.

Snow, C. E. (2013). Cold versus warm close reading: Building students' stamina for struggling with text. *Reading Today, 30,* 18–19.

Snow, C. E., Burns, M. S., & Griffin, P. (Eds.). (1998). *Preventing reading difficulties in young children.* Washington, DC: National Academy Press.

Snow, C. E., & Kim, Y. S. (2007). Large problem spaces: The challenge of vocabulary for English language learners. In R. K. Wagner, A. E. Muse & K. R. Tannenbaum (Eds.), *Vocabulary acquisition: Implications for reading comprehension* (pp. 123–139). New York: Guilford Press.

Stahl, K. A. D. (2012). Complex text or frustration-level text: Using shared reading to bridge the difference. *The Reading Teacher, 66,* 47–51.

Stahl, S. A., & Kapinus, B. A. (2001). *Word power: What every educator needs to know about teaching vocabulary.* Washington, DC: National Education Association.

Stauffer, R. G. (1975). *Directing the reading–thinking process.* New York: Harper & Row.

Stead, T. (2002). *Is that a fact? Teaching nonfiction writing, K–3.* Portland, ME: Stenhouse.

Sticht, T. G., & James, J. H. (1984). Listening and reading. In P. D. Pearson, R. Barr, M. L. Kamil, & P. B. Mosenthal (Eds.). *Handbook of reading research* (pp. 293–318). New York: Longman.

Sutherland, Z., Monson, D. L., & Arbuthnot, M. H. (1981). *Children and books,* 6th ed. Glenview, IL: Scott, Foresman.

Swanborn, M. S. L., & de Glopper, K. (1999). Incidental word learning while reading: A meta-analysis. *Review of Educational Research, 69,* 261–285.

Swanson, E., Vaughn, S., Wanzek, J., Petscher, Y., Heckert, J., & Cavanaugh, C. (2011).

A synthesis of read-aloud interventions on early reading outcomes among preschool through third graders at risk for reading difficulties. *Journal of Learning Disabilities, 44,* 258–275.

Taylor, B. M., Frye, B. J., & Maruyama, G. M. (1990). Time spent reading and reading growth. *American Educational Research Journal, 27,* 351–362.

Torres, S. D., & Weber, I. (2011). What and how children search on the web. In *Proceedings of the 20th ACM International Conference on Information and Knowledge Management* (pp. 393–402). New York: ACM.

Van den Broek, P., & Kremer, K. E. (2000). The mind in action: What it means to comprehend. In B. M. Taylor, M. F. Graves, & P. Van den Brock (Eds.), *Reading for meaning: Fostering comprehension in the middle grades* (pp. 1–31). New York: Teachers College Press & Newark, DE: International Reading Association.

Varelas, M., & Pappas, C. C. (2006). Intertextuality in read-alouds of integrated science-literacy units in urban primary classrooms: Opportunities for the development of thought and language. *Cognition and Instruction, 24,* 211–259.

Venezky, R. L. (1982). The origins of the present-day chasm between adult literacy needs and school literacy instruction. *Visible Language, 16,* 112–127.

Virginia Department of Education. (2003). Revised English Standards of learning curriculum framework K–grade 5 (adopted February 26, 2003). Retrieved April 23, 2003, from *www.pen.k12.va.us/vDOE/Instruction/English/ElemEnglishCF.*

Walpole, S. (1998/1999). Changing texts, changing thinking: Comprehension demands of new science textbooks. *The Reading Teacher, 52,* 358–369.

Warren, L., & Fitzgerald, J. (1997). Helping parents to read expository literature to their children: Promoting main idea and detail understanding. *Reading Research and Instruction, 36,* 342–350.

Wasik, B., & Iannone-Campbell, C. (2012). Developing vocabulary through purposeful, strategic conversations. *The Reading Teacher, 66,* 321–332.

White, S., Chen, J., & Forsyth, B. (2010). Reading-related literacy activities of American adults: Time spent, task types, and cognitive skills used. *Journal of Literacy Research, 42,* 276–307.

White, T. G., Graves, M. F., & Slater, W. H. (1990). Growth of reading vocabulary in diverse elementary schools: Decoding and word meaning. *Journal of Educational Psychology, 82,* 281–290.

Williams, J. P. (2005). Instruction in reading comprehension for primary grade students: A focus on text structure. *Journal of Special Education, 39,* 6–18.

Williams, J. P., Hall, K. M., Lauer, K. D., Stafford, K. B., & DeSisto, L. A. (2005). Expository text comprehension in the primary grade classroom. *Journal of Educational Psychology, 97,* 538–550.

Williams, J. P., Nubla-Kung, A. M., Pollini, S., Stafford, K. B., Garcia, A., & Snyder, A. E. (2007). Teaching cause–effect text structure through social studies content to at-risk second graders. *Journal of Learning Disabilities, 40,* 111–120.

Williams, J. P., Pollini, S., Nubla-Kung, A. M., Snyder, A. E., Garcia, A., Ordynans, J. G., et al. (2014). An intervention to improve comprehension of cause/effect through expository text structure instruction. *Journal of Educational Psychology, 106*(1), 1–17.

Williams, J. P. Stafford, K. B., Lauer, K. D., Hall, K. M., & Pollini, S. (2009). Embedding reading comprehension training in content-area instruction. *Journal of Educational Psychology, 101,* 1–20.

Wisconsin Department of Public Instruction. (2003). Wisconsin Reading Comprehension test. Retrieved April 23, 2003, from *www.dpi.state.wi.us/oea/wrctinfo.html#contwrct.*

Wixson, K. K., & Valencia, S. W. (2014). CCSS–ELA Suggestions and cautions for addressing text complexity. *The Reading Teacher, 67,* 430–434.

Worthy, J., Moorman, M., & Turner, M. (1999). What Johnny likes to read is hard to find in school. *Reading Research Quarterly, 34,* 12–27.

Wray, D., & Lewis, M. (1997). *Extending literacy: Children reading and writing non-fiction.* New York: Routledge.

Wray, D., & Lewis, M. (1998). An approach to factual writing. Retrieved April 23, 2003, from *www.readingonline.org.*

Wright, T. S. (2013). From potential to reality: Content-rich vocabulary and informational text. *The Reading Teacher, 67,* 359–367.

Wright, T. S., & Neuman, S. B. (2013). Vocabulary instruction in commonly used kindergarten core reading curricula. *The Elementary School Journal, 113,* 386–408.

Wright, T. S., & Neuman, S. B. (2014). Paucity and disparity in kindergarten oral vocabulary instruction. *Journal of Literacy Research, 46,* 330–357.

Yopp, R. H., & Yopp, H. K. (2006). Informational texts as read-alouds at school and home. *Journal of Literacy Research, 38,* 37–51.

Index

Note. *f* or *t* following a page number indicates a figure or a table.